ARCHIVES
OF CONJURE

GENDER, THEORY, AND RELIGION

GENDER, THEORY, AND RELIGION

AMY HOLLYWOOD, EDITOR

The Gender, Theory, and Religion series provides a forum for interdisciplinary scholarship at the intersection of the study of gender, sexuality, and religion.

ARCHIVES OF CONJURE

STORIES OF THE DEAD IN AFROLATINX CULTURES

SOLIMAR OTERO

Columbia University Press / *New York*

Columbia University Press
Publishers Since 1893
New York   Chichester, West Sussex
cup.columbia.edu

This book was made possible by financial assistance
from the RUTH LANDES MEMORIAL RESEARCH FUND,
a program of the Reed Foundation.

Library of Congress Cataloging-in-Publication Data
Names: Otero, Solimar, author.
Title: Archives of conjure : stories of the dead in Afrolatinx cultures /
    Solimar Otero.
Description: New York : Columbia University Press, [2020] | Series:
    Gender, theory, and religion | Includes bibliographical references
    and index.
Identifiers: LCCN 2019038651 (print) | LCCN 2019038652 (ebook) |
    ISBN 9780231194327 (cloth) | ISBN 9780231194334 (trade
    paperback) | ISBN 9780231550765 (ebook)
Subjects: LCSH: Spiritualism—Caribbean Area. | Afro-Caribbean
    cults. | Blacks—Caribbean Area—Religious life. | Blacks—
    Caribbean Area—Rites and ceremonies. | Spirits. | Women and
    spiritualism—Caribbean Area. | Material culture—Religious
    aspects. | Water—Religious aspects. | Caribbean Area—Religious
    life and customs.
Classification: LCC BF1242.C37 O84 2020 (print) | LCC BF1242.
    C37 (ebook) | DDC 133.909729—dc23
LC record available at https://lccn.loc.gov/2019038651
LC ebook record available at https://lccn.loc.gov/2019038652

Cover image: © Martin Tsang, *Collares de Mazo for the Deities Erinle
and Olokun.*
Cover design: Lisa Hamm

Dedicated to the spirit of José Días Casada,
dear friend and teacher, *iba e.*

&

Si la Luz redentora te llama
Y te llama con amor a la tierra
Yo quisiera ver a ese ser
Cantándole gloria al divino Manuel
Oye buen ser
Avanza y ven
Que el coro te llama
Y te dice, "ven."

—Traditional Afro-Cuban spirit mediums' song

CONTENTS

ACKNOWLEDGMENTS

There are so many people and institutions to thank for their support of this book. The genesis of the project began ten years ago and has lead me on multiple paths where I met with and exchanged stories broadly with many communities. First, I must express my immense gratitude to my spiritual and biological family in Cuba, which consists of godmothers, godfathers, spirit guides, and divinities that have accompanied and continue to guide me along the way. *Mo dupe, gracias* to Tomasa, Tony, Soñia, Susy, José (*iba e*), Tita, Riguito, Maxi, Meche, and Devit. You have made my world bigger, better, and more hopeful.

Wendy Lochner and Amy Hollywood at Columbia University Press were remarkable editors and advocates of the work the book seeks to do with gender and religion. I cannot say enough about the positive support the press and its team, especially Lowell Frye and Susan Pensak, provided me in preparing the book for the world. Another special recognition goes to Dave Prout, my long-time indexer and editor who always takes on a challenge with grace.

The Women's Studies in Religion Program at the Harvard Divinity School provided vital support for the initiation of this project. While at the WSRP, Ann Braude and Jacob Olupona were especially interested in my research. I am also deeply grateful that my experiences at HDS allowed me to connect with Aisha Beliso-De Jesús, a dear *hermana* who believed in what the spirits and I had to say about Afrolatinx religions. Aisha's brilliance has influenced my development as a person, spiritually and intellectually.

The Ruth Landes Memorial Research Fund provided me with valuable resources for conducting research for this volume. Thank you to David Latham at the fund who provided institutional guidance for my archival studies and fieldwork. This support also allowed me to collaborate with the talented Cuban photographer Héctor Delgado, whose expertise in recording rituals in an ethically beautiful manner is unsurpassed.

The Smithsonian Institution's National Anthropological Archives were instrumental in getting me the vital information on Ruth Landes for the completion of this volume. A special thank you goes out to Katherine Crowe and Daisy Njoku for their generous help at the archive. Carrie Beauchamp also provided wonderful assistance in looking at Landes's material culture collection at the Anthropology Department of the Smithsonian's Museum of Natural History.

The staff at the Cuban Heritage Collection at the University of Miami Libraries are *familia* that embraced me and this book since its inception. Their endless support of my investigation of the Lydia Cabrera Papers led to fruitful scholarly, artistic, and personal growth. Elizabeth Cerejido, Annie Sansone-Martinez, Amanda Moreno, and the amazing Gladys Gomes-Rossie generously offered their considerable knowledge and kindness to me during this project. I want to express my deep gratitude to Martin Tsang, the CHC's librarian and curator of Latin American Collections, who provided the beautiful image that dons the cover of this volume. His perpetual encouragement and wisdom gave me much strength to find new ideas while doing this work.

The process of laboring through such an interdisciplinary and transnational topic meant that I built this work on the shoulders of giants. Much appreciation to anthropologists of Afrolatinx religions, J. Lorand Matory and Kristina Wirtz, for reading, commenting, and improving my research with their thoughtful suggestions. My colleagues in the field of folklore studies also provided essential feedback that helped the project to blossom. Mintzi Martínez-Rivera, Rachel González-Martin, Guillermo de los Reyes, Cory Thorne, Sabina Magliocco, Elaine Lawless, Kim Lau, Kay Turner, Norma Cantú, Mabel Cuesta, and Katey Borland all have participated with me at the many American Folklore Society meetings where I vetted this project in one form or another. Each one gave me unique insights that helped me to see how my studies could do more for our field and for the communities I work with and am a part of. Likewise, Ana-Maurine Lara, Alex Fernández, and Maria Hamilton Abegunde, all gifted practitioner-scholars-writers, kept me grounded and listening to what the *egun*, the dead, were asking me to say in this book.

Experts in the fields of multiethnic and Caribbean literature in the United States and Europe also listened graciously and promoted the transnational nature of my analysis of texts in this volume. John W. Lowe, William Boelhower, Hanétha Vété-Congolo, and Dorothea Fischer-Hornung all gave stimulating suggestions for interpreting the narratives I encountered in my research. Their critical readings allowed me to see the connections between written, oral, and embodied modes of storytelling.

Colleagues from the fields of Latinx theatre and performance studies welcomed this research with open arms. I offer special thanks to Lillian Manzor, Teresa Marrero, and Jorge Huerta for their encouragement and words of inspiration for my studies with Cuban spiritual performances. The HowlRound Theatre Commons was a fruitful space where people openly accepted and engaged with my scholarship. A warm mention must be made of playwright Femi Euba and historian Toyin Falola, two elder statesmen of Yoruba cultural studies who actively engaged with my diasporic subjects and ideas.

Louisiana State University's College of Humanities and Social Sciences, through Dean Gaines Foster, provided sabbatical support and other resources for the volume. My colleagues and friends in the Department of English and the Program in Comparative Literature shared their expertise to improve this book's accessibility to literary studies. I am grateful to Benjy Kahan, Katie Henninger, Elsie Michie, Sharon Weltman, Elena Castro, Chris Barrett, Angeletta Gourdine, Pallavi Rastogi, and Adelaide Russo for their input. Carolyn Ware, my fellow folklorist at LSU, helped me greatly by talking about fieldwork and writing with me. Helen Regis and Joyce Jackson, two gifted anthropologists who connect local cultures in Louisiana and Africa, also shared valuable perspectives on transcultural studies. Dear mentors Frank De Caro and Rosan Jordan gave me many hours of stories and lovingly guided me through the years of development of this project. Finally, my fantastic friends and colleagues, historian Cat Jacquet and gender studies scholar Liam Lair, provided me with unconditional kindness and confidence that helped me find the gumption to finish the book.

My new colleagues at Indiana University were also instrumental to this book's completion. I am especially grateful to David McDonald, chair of the Department of Folklore and Ethnomusicology, for his enthusiasm for the volume. Ray Cashman, Pravina Shukla, Henry Glassie, and John McDowell also shared constructive commentary on the work. Historian and

Latinx scholar John Nieto-Phillips was exceptionally positive and instrumental in generating support for my research at Indiana University. The American Folklore Society, particularly the previous director Tim Lloyd and the current director Jessica Turner, always welcomed and provided a forum for conversations that helped improve this book.

In no universe would I have been able to complete *Archives of Conjure* without the love, intelligence, and exceptional patience of my partner, Eric Mayer-García. He allowed me to see aspects of the study that profoundly impacted its meaning for me. A magnificent scholar of Latinx performance studies in his own right, Eric was by my side every step of the way during this research. My family, Rai Otero, Raymond Otero, Blanca and Roberto Alvarez, Luis García, and Soñia and Richard Mayer sincerely listened and gave me the strength to continue researching through sorrow, with joy.

INTRODUCTION

Archives of Conjure

It is a humid October morning in Mantilla.[1] I am sitting with my godmother, Tomasa, next to her *prenda*, an Afro-Cuban entity that is housed in a cauldron. She is communicating with "El Señor," as he is known in our house, with the *chamalongos*, discs of dried coconut. Our conversation turns to spirit guides and how they make themselves known in dreams. Tomasa shares that

> todos los muertos me han dado sus nombres en sueños. La primera vez que yo lo vi, al Señor, asomado a la ventana, me dio un susto que, me desperté, y me levanté como un bolillo. Ya después, la segunda ves que se me presentó, ya mas o menos—¿me entiende?—poco a poco me fui adaptando. Pero no es fácil. Al principio, y si les tiene miedo, imagínate tu.[2]

> all of the dead have given me their names in dreams. The first time that I saw him, El Señor, standing by the window, it frightened me so that, I woke up, and I got up like a *bolillo*. And later, the second time that he revealed himself to me, now more or less—you understand me?—little by little I became adapted to it. But, it isn't easy. At first, if you are scared of them, you can only imagine.

Tomasa, as a Yaya Nquisi, an elder priestess of the Afro-Cuban Palo tradition,[3] is well versed in talking to the dead (see figure 0.1, Tomasa). Tomasa's spirit guide, El Señor, acts like a father figure, a protector who functions as a resource for her and the spiritual community she serves. The revelation of the dead's names in dreams is significant. Naming is an especially powerful tool in conjuring reality and presence—thus the revelation by El Señor signals a transference of power, kinship, and the solidification of a mutual bond. It is understood that embarking on a journey of proclaimed kinship with the dead is not easy, will challenge accepted standards of perception and reality, and take time. Her description of the process of dreaming the dead recalls Jamaican poet laureate Lorna Goodison's own poetic summoning of her deceased mother:

> I dream that I am washing
> my mother's body in the night sea
> and that she sings slow
> and that she still breathes.[4]

These personal experience narratives, through conversation and through poetry, illustrate the residual transcripts that record the dead through archives of conjure.[5]

This book, *Archives of Conjure*, takes to heart both Tomasa's and Goodison's suggestions of dreaming the dead. In this study, the dead, ancestors, and deities are actors in multiple forms of kin and world-making. Alongside these entities, the spiritual ecologies of the Afrolatinx communities being explored here demand ontological reframings of the connections between humans, nonhumans, and the environment. In reaching for an ethically engaged world from the perspective of Afrolatinx religions, a "material semiotics" emerges that situates kinship beyond

FIGURE 0.1 Tomasa Spengler Suárez, *misa espiritual*, Havana, Cuba, May 2013. Photo by Héctor Delgado. Author's private collection.

human-centered experiences of place, time, and materiality (Haraway 2016:4).

To be specific, this work is about how Afrolatinx nonmaterial or occasionally material beings, like *egun* (the dead) and *orichas* (deities), become active agents in the world through rituals, archives, and the creation of material culture. Sites like the ocean, rivers, altars, libraries, and living rooms in Havana create the contexts for understanding where these multiple engagements are activated. Residual transcriptions are links to how copresences interact, influence, and guide human actors like scholars, artists, and practitioners. Residual transcriptions, as vernacular notations made in rituals and found in archives, create the routes to the collaborative spiritual-scholarly-activist work that are archives of conjure. This work is *not* about official discourses found in religious institutional control of social behaviors and the construction of subjectivity. Though I address histories of patriarchy, racism, colonialism, and homophobia in Afrolatinx folk religious cultures, I am most interested in revealing the creative strategies presented by nonmaterial agents in providing affective interventions in these legacies of violence.

I use the term *Afrolatinx* to describe the racial, cultural, and gendered fluidity present in transnational expressions of vernacular religious practices like Espiritismo, Palo, and Santería in order to place into historical context the vernacular narrations of stories told by the dead.[6] I do not intend to use the term anachronistically to categorize past subjects and/or experiences. Rather, I include such subjects and experiences in the present ritual history-making practices of the communities I am collaborating with in this study. Afrolatinx vernacular traditions of narration and ritual kinships reveal a range of connections with the dead whose residual forms are located in the archives, rituals, and material culture that house and activate them. Examining these practices of spirit and materiality as an archive of conjure, I argue, transmits the complexity of inhabiting multiple forms of being in terms of race, sexuality, and place. The residual transcripts and practices explored also point to different ways of looking for evidence or describing experience that both constitute and vex historiographic and ethnographic modes of investigating Afrolatinx religious expression and communities. Archives of conjure pay particular attention to how divinities and spirit guides interact with and guide the kinds of work that scholars, practitioners, authors, and artists produce. This book explores how Afrolatinx dead narrate temporality, cartography, and race into being through embodied practices like dreaming, stitching, washing, scribbling, beading, singing, dancing, and writing. In doing so, one can observe the nature of the *active presence* of entities as collaborators, muses, and coauthors in the creation of scholarship and the enactment of theory in Afrolatinx religiosity.

I choose the everyday expressions of devotion found in Afrolatinx religions as my main lenses for exploring the active presence of spirits in this study because of the unorthodox nature of quotidian personal practices and their openness to religious admixture. Throughout this study, I go back to the popular practice of *misas espirituales*, Cuban séances, as sites of religious remembering and spiritual futurity.[7] Contemporary Espiritismo originated in nineteenth-century France and became popular in Latin America and the Caribbean through the writings of Allan Kardec, né Hippolyte Léon Denizard Rivail.[8] The spiritual collaborators that emerge in the following pages, like the spirit guides Ta José and La Gitana,[9] come from my own specific points of contact, Havana, Cuba, between 2008 and 2019. However, the questions I pose about materiality and spirituality are situated in a myriad of temporalities and geographical locations explored in the archive, ritual, and literature.

The importance of non-Cartesian epistemological and ontological modes of existence are highlighted through the ritual work, storytelling practices, and ethnographic writing of Afrolatinx spiritual practitioners.[10] Cuban Espiritismo, Puerto Rican Santería, Brazilian Candomblé, and Caribbean literature provide modes of exploring questions of shared subjectivity, authorship, and creativity in this work. Based on over ten years of fieldwork and archival research with Afrolatinx spiritual communities in Cuba, the Caribbean, and the U.S., this study puts into conversation Espiritismo's philosophies of the transmigration of the soul with Édouard Glissant's concept of "transphysique de la Relation" (1981) and Fernando Ortiz's notion of "transculturación" (1963 [1940]).[11] Here, vernacular religious work with Caribbean experiences of society and history reframes the way in which the dead narrate material culture.

Archives of conjure reconfigure theoretical models of cultural and religious mixing as a re-rendering. One that shows how ritual is poetry and poetry is ritual, in the sense of the healing work Goodison's words perform. Sympathetic and contagious magic works with metonymy,[12] as poetry and language do, in ways that create an immense potential for conceptual and embodied transformation. Archives of conjure are poetic in that work produced through "residual transcriptions" are conjured metonymically through living bodies, written pages, and material culture. The poetic transformations inspired by residual transcriptions show the resonances shared between the embodied experiences of spiritual mediumship and transphysical poetics (Glissant 1992:142). In doing so, I affirm a nonuniversalist set of experiences that are rendered through a diversity of being, place, and time.

In defining the term *archives of conjure*, I want to stress that I am talking about a set of spiritual, scholarly, and artistic practices based on an awareness of the dead as active agents that work through imaginative principles. As Tomasa and Goodison relate in dreaming their dead, archives of conjure operate as a process of creative resuscitation. One that witnesses and further marks clues to vernacular expressions of the past that include unofficial sources like ritual performances, talismans, and gossip (Taylor 2003; Callaci 2017). Conjure in this sense is to make manifest a desired reality through *trabajo*, work.[13] Magical work here is a collaborative project invoking the energies of multiple tangible and intangible resources that include humans, spiritual forces, and natural elements. As Zora Neale Hurston explains in *Mules and Men*,

> Belief in magic is older than writing. So nobody knows how it started. The way we tell it, hoodoo started way back there before everything. Six days of magic spells and mighty words and the world with its elements above and below was made. And now, God is leaning back taking a seventh day rest. When the eighth day comes around, He'll start to making new again. Man wasn't made until around half-past five on the sixth day, so he can't know how anything was done.
>
> (1990 [1935]:183–84)

Hurston places magic as a principle spawning existence: words, the earth, human beings. The call to action from this principle is conjure. Conjure creates by incorporating, subverting, and rerendering the energy available at the moment. Hurston mirrors magic by recreating aspects of biblical and African folklore into her own rendition of the beginning of things. In her account, humans are left out of the loop in terms of really knowing what magic can do and has done. God is the ultimate conjure man who understands that magic is a regenerative and perpetual process of creation to be reworked and reactivated constantly. I understand Hurston's account of magic as a declaration of conjure that serves as an enmeshed space of existence. One that includes ecologies, elements, and forces beyond human domination and comprehension. The magic that created the world here very much feels like the magic that brings together material semiotics and maternal songs of the sea. They both point to the importance of mystery in exerting the promise of inspiration to act and to become. In this book, Afrolatinx spiritualities are the modality that conjures scholarship, art, and ritual. These inspired acts of engagement with unseen but felt forces trace important past and future trajectories. Conjured archives therefore operate within networks of reception and reinvention that can be hidden in plain sight, undetectable to the uninitiated observer.[14] For example, beaded jewelry, colors, and hairstyles of Afrolatinx practitioners may or may not signal relationships to historically specific deities, places, and narratives. The creation of coded, alternate public spheres based on the fluidity of vernacular, "street" archival practices is a vital practice for groups suffering from institutional repression (Cvetkovich 2003; Scott 1990). Likewise, ancestors, women, and lesbian, gay, bisexual, trans, queer+ (LGBTQ+) practitioners of Afrolatinx religions enact archives of conjure to navigate the violence of their experiences of religious intolerance, white supremacy, patriarchy, and homophobia.[15] Conjuring as an archival practice becomes a vibrant mode of restructuring past resistance into an activated guide for future resilience. Conjure creates its own cover because you have to understand its logic to see it. An archive of conjure becomes accessible in ways that weaponize its contents, as with other material artifacts created by and for the dead, because they are made with the idea of vivification and healing in mind.[16] This healing is often accessed through the generational trauma of slavery and sexual violence that the dead in this book will relate in their stories. Thus archives of conjure necessitate a kind of hidden transcript that ensures safe spaces for work with them to be efficacious and sustainable.[17]

African-inspired religions place divination, in its multiple manifestations, at the crux of creating bridges between worlds and temporalities (Bascom 1991 [1969]; Fernández 2017).[18] The fields of folklore, anthropology, and ethnomusicology have paid attention to many aspects of Afrolatinx religious cultures, including language, music, ritual, narrative, and material culture.[19] This book adopts an interdisciplinary approach to vernacular religious life that borrows greatly from Elaine Lawless's concept of "reciprocal ethnography," an approach that has taken "ethnographic studies into a new and more multi-layered, polyphonic dimension of dialogue and exchange" as an "emergent dialogue in field research that is then carried into the scholarly writing" (1991:36, 2000:199). Lawless's concerns grow out of a feminist engagement with her collaborators as subjects that speak back in ways that sometimes clashes with her own worldview and choices of representation. Working with female Christian pastors, she had to negotiate authority over the meaning of social performances and narratives shared with multiple subjects. I would like to take these initial ideas of reciprocal ethnography into consideration, with conjuring the dead as a method for creating the polyvocal subjectivity Lawless suggests. What does it mean if we take Afrolatinx dialogic practices with the dead, like spirit mediumship, divination, and sacred art-making, as the central components to creating ethnographic reciprocity? Considering that spiritual entities speak through writing as residual transcriptions from rituals and the archive, I would argue that they are voicing their own kinds of dialogic discourses and methods. In this regard, the work presented in this volume is theorized from the vernacular ethnographies and historiographies that conjure produces.

My interest in the dead comes from a multifaceted relationship to my Cuban and Puerto Rican cultural roots. As a child born in Southern California to a bilingual father and a Spanish-speaking mother, my Caribbean home life contrasted sharply with school and public life. Even in terms of *latinidad*, our spoken Spanish, foods eaten, and spiritual practices were sharply infused with an African inflection that differed from our mostly Mexican and Central American friends and neighbors. I remember my mother putting out flowers and a *vaso de agua*, a glass of fresh clean water, every July in commemoration of my grandfather's death. She spoke to him then and often, telling me about dreams where she would visit with her father in a chosen spot by a waterfall. These connections to the dead were not considered mysterious or exotic. They just were. However, I was told not to speak about them, especially at catechism or with outsiders. People would not understand and/or consider our practices *brujería*, witchcraft.

In writing this book, I faced the same dilemma in terms of trying to explain deeply held beliefs that create ways of being in the world not readily understood by outsiders. As an interdisciplinary folklore scholar, I understood that, for some, "mastery" over certain subjects required the dissection, analysis, and classification of cultures and texts. I consider this kind of approach to scholarship to be especially violent, yielding only a projection of what the researcher has had engrained as colonial practices of enforcing intellectual authority. Instead, I have opted for an approach of engagement where I am sharing authorial intent with practitioners, collaborators, and the dead. I do scholarship by putting theory and practice into critical conversation with different kinds of representations and performances. However, I believe that I have learned my propensity for bricolage from Afrolatinx and Caribbean practitioners of spirituality, philosophy, and the arts. In the spirit of reciprocal ethnography, I take interlocutors like the spirits and orichas that make up my religious, familial, and scholarly community seriously.

Folklorists researching lived vernacular religion have paved the way for the turn I am taking in this work. Sabina Magliocco's *Witching Culture: Folklore and Neo-Paganism in America* (2004) creates a template for talking about ritual as a kind of historical research. Her writing allows for multiple entry points into the web of neo-pagan religiosity. She includes deeply personal and thoroughly researched components of how conjure and ethnography mirror each other in affect and effect. She writes, "Because creativity and artistry involve evocation and transformation, these acts become equivalent to magic. Thus, the writing of ethnography becomes a magical act, no less than the creation of a ritual, the making of a spell, or the manufacture of a sacred object: the ethnographer is by definition a magician" (17–18). I agree with Magliocco in that ethnography is a kind of conjure. It creates worlds and experiences through the imagination and senses in ways that can transport and transform consciousness.

From an Afrolatinx and antiracist perspective, there is also the inherent responsibility of ethically engaging in the powerful work of ethnography that can potentially do harm.[20] Both Magliocco and I work with communities whose religious practices have been demonized by Abrahamic religions, and whose members that are women and LGBTQ+ were especially targeted for torture, abuse, and extinction.[21] Thus, the act of conjuring archives as an ethnographic ritual practice is an act of empowerment, resistance, and sustenance. It is also certainly not a set of practices reserved for solely folklorists or anthropologists. By thinking of ethnography as magic and magic as ethnography, the conjuring of culture becomes an act of reclaiming terrains that create imperfect ancestors with questions of appropriation, authenticity, and access that are important to consider (Otero 2018b:5, 12–13; Magliocco 2004:209, 215–16). Both

Magliocco and I write about the important and precarious work performed by cultural borrowing in the practice of vernacular religions that embrace conjure. Here I am inclined to embrace an Afrolatinx *espiritista*'s (spirit medium's) penchant for staying with the messy and tense racial, religious, and cultural comingling found in rituals and in her community. Archives of conjure offer more than alternative sources for creating history and remembering; they suggest new ways of traversing temporality that are connected to Black, Latinx, and LGBTQ+ projects of futurity that rely on rethinking the agents of history through enacted practice (Lara 2017; Muñoz 2009; Johnson and Rivera-Servera 2016). For Afrolatinx religious remembering, practices of inhabitation are central to understanding how materiality operates in a fluid ontological universe that operates on intention. The supple relationship between form and its animation, whether it be in the flesh or in art, can be revealed through the study of narratives of ephemerality and the materially sacred (Hufford 1995; Glassie and Shukla 2018). The ritual and writing analyzed in this volume traverses multiple routes of getting to and from the dead through scholarship, art, and the imagination. Taking a cue from work that both relies on and questions the interaction between spiritual agents, historians, and ethnographers,[22] this study also invites literary and archival cohabitation as processes of conjure that negotiate who is speaking through whom.

I experienced my own literary and archival cohabitation with Cuban ethnologist Lydia Cabrera's archive of conjure. A defiant border-crosser in terms of sexuality, scholarship, and religious expression, Cabrera wrote incessantly about water entities. Her book *Yemayá y Ochún* (1980) significantly shapes understandings of the two divinities through sexuality and the homoerotic feminine. I interrogated Cabrera's notes, letters, and scribblings in her archive at Cuban Heritage Collection for this book.[23] What I found shows a daughter of Yemayá whose ties to the ocean make her an ambivalent sojourner who never felt entirely at home in one place (Otero 2013, 2015; Cuesta 2015).[24] Her kinship with like-minded authors and scholar-artists, for example, Reinaldo Arenas and Pierre Verger, comes through the sea as a site of contemplation and acceptance within the experience of being a Caribbean sexile (sexual exile).[25] Mobility but also statelessness is fueled for Cabrera by societal structures that govern notions of gendered and sexual respectability in both Cuba and the United States. I find that she fights back by writing an ironic and gossipy reframing of oral tradition, ritual history, and mythology fueled by Yemayá and Ochún. Her work importantly creates routes to feminist and LGBTQ+ narrative histories of Santería.

Cabrera always lived, loved, and made friendships in the name of Yemayá.[26] Her writing uses secrecy, coding, and layering to show how gender-fluid manifestations of the orichas subvert patriarchy and homophobia in both Catholic and Yoruba-inspired power structures. Consider the following snapshot and narrative about Ochún and Oya from her archive:

Ochún era la dueña del cementerio primeramente. Pero lloraba cada vez que veía venir a sus hijos, sufría mucho por esto y cambió su puesto con Ollá. Que se entendiera ella con los Ikú. El ebbó de Ochún no va al cementerio va al río.[27]

Ochún was the first owner of the cemetery. But she cried every time she saw her children arrive, she suffered much because of this and she changed her post with Ollá [sic]. Let her be the one who deals with the Ikú [the dead]. Ochún's *ebbó* doesn't go to the cemetery, it goes to the river.

> Ochún era la dueña del cementerio primeramente. Pero
> lloraba cada vez que veía venir a sus hijos, sufría mu-
> cho por ésto y cambió su puesto con Ollá. Que se enten-
> diera ella con los Ikú.
> El ebbó de Ochún no va al cementerio va al río.

FIGURE O.2 Lydia Cabrera's Notes on Ochún and Oya. Photo by the author. Courtesy of the Cuban Heritage Collection, University of Miami Libraries, Coral Gables, Florida.

This story from Cabrera's papers is retold in *Yemayá y Ochún* (1980:70). In that version, Ochún cannot bear to see her former lovers arrive at the cemetery gates and consequently changes roles with Oya. The close positioning of Ochún with the dead is a significant element to understanding this deity's backstory. Most often associated with luxury, love, and fresh water, Ochún's other elements are sometimes overlooked in the popular imagination. Her proximity to the dead is an element most widely explored in her avatar as Ibú Kole, the queen of the witches and the savior of humankind in the form of a vulture. Ochún's sensitivity aside, she can master work with the dead because of her role as the seventeenth foundational oricha described in the divination verse, the *oshe-tura*.[28] Thus, the note from Cabrera's papers serves as a fluid residual transcript that can be revised and revisited to extend the meanings of stories, symbols, and agency in transnational oricha traditions and belief. For me, it is the portability and the vernacular nature of Cabrera's notations that makes them essential residual transcripts that suggestively point to ongoing links beneath the surface. The dead in this book repeatedly relay sacred histories as mysteries. This is especially true of the trickster-ancestor-storyteller of Lydia Cabrera.

Residual transcriptions, like Cabrera's story, work in archives of conjure to produce methodological questions with regard to how we think about the connections between ephemerality, temporality, and material culture. Like the dead in a *misa*, scholars as ancestors leave clues in the archive on paper and through artifacts. My own search revealed that beading and sewing are referenced and reproduced in papers, objects, and drawings left behind by Lydia Cabrera and Ruth Landes in their archives. These testaments created by scholarly ancestors speak to the importance of materially traced spiritual cartographies. Patterns, colors, and stitches in beads, dolls, and cloth are vital elements to understanding the roads of transformation that residual transcripts can take in becoming archives of conjure. The literal handiwork of beading or writing left behind by the dead is brought back to life through the restitching or rescribbling of the living. Thus the transgenerational shared labor that occurs in archives of conjure reveals how an element of cyclical flow is central to navigating the very objects found in these repositories.

This last point brings me back to Goodison's poem "My Mother's Sea Chanty," referenced earlier. In the stanza quoted, Goodison dreams her mother's body into the sea, where she is sung back to life and breath. As stated, the vivification of Goodison's mother through poetry is a kind of conjure. Her words are necessary for building worlds, for creating the spell that puts us in the water with both of them. The connection between her washing her mother's body in the sea and the regeneration of Black women's knowledge of traditions of conjure through touch and witnessing is evident in the dreaming of the poem. There is a potentiality for transformation when we pay attention to dreams, spells, and poetry. Goodison further evokes,

I see my sweet mother
a plump mermaid in my dreams

and I wash her white hair with
ambergris and foaming seaweed
. . .
I hear my dark mother
speaking sea-speak with pilot fish,
showing them how to direct barks
that bear away our grief.

(215)

There is a logic to water-work and worlds, one that operates
in an amorphous collectivity that sparks the human imagination
and begs connections to life forms and ecologies larger and different from our own. In Haitian Vodou and Cuban Santería, the
ocean is a site where the dead reside and do important work on
behalf of the living. Deep-sea deities like Agwe and Olókùn pre-
side over the mysteries that the dead encounter upon reaching
their watery realms.[29] In the stanzas, Goodison's sweet and dark
mother becomes a plump mermaid who speaks the languages of
fish in the depths of the ocean to create a space where the grief
of the world is taken in and transformed. It is important to note
how her "sea-speak," like Hurston's "mighty words" of magic, has
the power to set new realities into motion. These utterances allow
for active remembering and healing.

The cyclical nature of aquatic currents is at the heart of this
book's organization. The deities Yemayá, Ochún, Erinle, guardian spirits, and mermaids are important guides to encountering
how residual transcripts become archives of conjure in the following chapters. Each chapter operates as a séance that invites
water entities and scholarly ancestors to the table for conversation and work. The flow of topics in each chapter has attending
dead, deities, and scholarly ancestors at the center of their connections. In this manner, I am inspired by both Todd Ramón

Ochoa's notion of *kalunga*, the ambient dead in Cuban Palo, and Maya Deren's understanding of the dead's residual home as the sea in Haitian Vodou (Ochoa 2010a:33–35; Deren 1983:338). That is, the dead that are at the center of each of the book's chapters also create a larger pattern, a web of connections similar to Haraway's material semiotics referred to earlier. These patterns illustrate the interplay between spiritual microcosms and macrocosms, especially through Afrolatinx scholarship, art, and ritual work. Ancestors, writers, and mediums are thus brought together in this book to represent a cycle of inspiration, invention, and authorship that feeds off and into each other. I see the residual artifacts of this interconnection as resembling the variegated sediment drawn together in an undertow.

Undertow as metaphor creates a space for recognizing the significant role that women and LGBTQ+ communities have played in Afrolatinx religious histories and experiences. Like undertows and countercurrents, their stories and spiritual lives flow vitally away and against *machista*, homophobic, and colonial interpretations of practices. Often unnoticeable to the naked eye and working beneath the surface, the contributions of women and LGBTQ+ practitioners of Afrolatinx religions are often recorded in the residual transcriptions of the dead because of the nourishment they each provide to one another. In this volume, the religious histories revealed by the dead, scholars, and orichas assert the centrality of groups and individuals often marginalized by patriarchal-nationalist iterations of African diaspora religious traditions.[30] The flow of the undertow in this book invites readers to consider how unseen yet felt collaborations create patterns of spiritual discovery for Afrolatinx authorship, activism, and creative expression.

In chapter 1, "Residual Transcriptions," I explore how anthropologists Ruth Landes, J. Lorand Matory, spirit ancestor Ta

José, and Oxúm create a tapestry of paper and beads that tell a story of cyclical regeneration.[31] Here the dead tell stories, give advice, propose future rituals, and request that certain materials be produced on their behalf. These mandates are communicated with/through mediums' bodies and are transcribed on site, copied, and then passed around after a seánce. My idea of residual transcriptions has at its base this vernacular practice of transcribing the words and wishes of the dead in rituals and relates it back to the ethnographic practice of making transcripts. Through my own transcriptions of research at Cuban misas, alongside the transcribed observations of Matory's work with Brazilian deities and priests, and anthropologist Ruth Landes's transcriptions of rituals in Brazil done with Oxúm, I suggest that residual transcriptions are clues that serve as testaments to related experiential bonds. I also argue that these residual transcriptions are both visible yet hidden in Afrolatinx religions.

In the chapter, Oxúm's river currents lead us to the concept of imperfect ancestors in relation to unfinished stories and undisclosed relationships found in archives of conjure.[32] Ruth Landes's career as an early anthropologist of race, gender, and religion was touched by Oxúm's presence in her life, especially while she worked in 1930s Brazil. Her lifelong interest in women and ritual created a testimonial writing style ahead of its time, and she suffered considerably in her career for these bold choices (Cole 2003). The deep connection between Landes and Oxúm becomes clear in the study of the residual transcripts she herself created in her fieldnotes, poetry, and notations of spiritual awakening through Candomblé practices.[33] Her notes on personal involvement and affective entanglements with deities and priests create a narrative of religious development that includes conjure and divination. These rituals make her spiritual kin as an ancestor in the archive. The mediation of her Jewishness and whiteness by practitioners highlights how Afrolatinx religions like Candomblé and Santería navigate race and national origin in ways that highlight tensions and contradictions.[34]

Beading and sewing are referenced and reproduced through Landes, Oxúm, and spirit mediums as artistic testaments to spiritual cartographies. By evaluating a conjured archive that is coproduced by the dead, I conclude that we need to rethink ethnographic methodologies and frameworks in folklore and anthropology. By conjured, here, I mean paying attention to the invention of sites, agents, and affects in conducting research. Reframing ethnographic methods and notations based on vernacular transcription practices also requires asking what kinds of work are notations taken from ritual contexts created to do. More than invoking an "ethnographic present," such transcriptions on site and in the archive urge the construction of a magical futurity. One where the transformative properties of conjure are collaboratively harnessed through practices like sewing and beading for the continued elaboration of transnational Afrolatinx histories and communities.

The following chapter, "Crossings," brings to the fore the ways in which contemporary Cuban misas modify Fernando Ortiz's idea of transculturation with racialized and sexualized spirit guides. Ortiz's conception of the negotiation of cultures in Cuba is frictive.[35] His observations illustrate how Cuban expressive culture intertwines the quotidian with the avant-garde, especially in its mobile spirituality. Ortiz, Allan Kardec, the spirit guides La Gitana, El Indio, and El Congo all serve as interlocutors for thinking through the concepts of movement and temporality in forming archives of conjure. I take Espiritismo's phenomenon of spiritual doubling and companionship, the *redoble* (doubling), as conversant with Eve Kosofsky Sedgwick's work on affect as found in Tibetan Buddhist "parallel initiations" (2003:8). My understanding of religious affect is necessarily influenced by the Latinx Cuban diaspora and queer negotiations of fleeting moments of freedom and empowered futurity that cyclically invoke the dead (Lara 2017; Muñoz 2000; Quiroga 2005:213–18). In turning initially to Ortiz's reading of Espiritismo, we see that his seminal concept of transculturation is influenced by the experience of the transmigration of souls found in the Spiritist séance.

"Crossings" thus explores how the cultural and social contexts of colonialism, slavery, and migration in the Caribbean deeply mark Espiritismo's practices in ways that challenge and expand the initial evolutionary nature of its doctrine. By revisiting Glissant's idea of a Caribbean "cross-cultural poetics," I explain how aesthetics can transform transculturation in the circumstances of interorality and ritual performance. The cultural work of contemporary Cuban spirit mediums retools positivist notions found in early writings on Espiritismo by circumventing linear ideas of spirit progression through affective, side-by-side linking of ethnic and racial difference. The spirit guides La Gitana, El Indio, and El Congo act as marked racial and sexual subjects that reveal the social tensions that create Afrolatinx spiritual signifiers. These transculturated dead disrupt the modernist tendencies of Ortiz's and Kardec's initial characterizations of Espiritismo in their fluid and rhizomatic spiritual transmigrations. As they appear side by side at misas to mediums, these racialized guides also invoke a myriad of historical imaginings that link spiritual kinship to Indigenous, African, and Romani traditions of mobility. These culturally and racially mixed traveling companions create the texture of transculturation's resonant effects on Cuban spiritual cultures as mediums memorialize and reinvent dead interlocutors. Ultimately, figures like La Gitana, El Indio, and El Congo create embodied residual transcripts that produce archives of conjure. These archives have the potential to recalibrate the understanding of transculturation as a process that *must* include the dead as active agents. This is because Espiritismo, as a practice and spiritual doctrine, created the template for how Ortiz envisioned the metaphysical components of transcultural movement.[36]

The Yoruba-inspired water divinities Yemayá and Ochún help to narrate chapter 3, "Flows." Alongside Cabrera, and a guardian spirit named La Madre de Agua, I interrogate how a sisterhood based on water provides a methodology for understanding the boundary play that is at the center of performing feminine religious creativity in Cuba. "Children of the two waters" (*hijas de las dos aguas*) is a ritual designation that devotees of both Yemayá and Ochún can carry. Rivers and seas are ecologically and spiritually connected, and relationships of reciprocity exist between practitioners and their flowing divinities. As *comadres*, the closeness between Yemayá and Ochún reveals the importance of paying attention to how aquatic forms morph into each other for rebirth and transformation. Their mutability occurs at the borders of geographic boundaries, race, gender, and sexuality.

Cabrera's published and unpublished writings about Yemayá and Ochún offer an important countercurrent for the chapter. Her stories and asides frame *chisme* (gossip) as a modality that can go unnoticed in the traditional archive. However, Cabrera's rumors about the gods' fluid sexuality and defiance of patriarchy allow for a place where LGBTQ+ and feminist versions of myth can exist on the page and in our imaginations. Often ironic, her insistence on including these "unverified" vignettes of divine rebellion and same-sex love in her work create a trail of residual transcriptions that queers the archives of conjure.

A most elucidating aspect of her queering the gods is the translocation of their queerness onto riverscapes and seascapes, watery spaces of sexual ambiguity where nevertheless the divine femininity of Ochún and Yemayá dominate.

Cabrera, La Madre de Agua, Yemayá, and Ochún make manifest water-centric epistemologies and ontologies through writing and ritual. Their messages are communicated in residual transcriptions found in the archive, created at misas, and deciphered through divination. Flow is an important kind of movement that has specific resonances in Afrolatinx expressive culture. It constitutes an openness in form and inspiration that has many manifestations in the arts, activism, and embodied practice.[37] Thus the chapter ends by looking at the intertwining of all these elements in Afrolatinx spiritual practice as a form of *creación colectiva*, a revolutionary performance strategy. By being and becoming through water, spirits and practitioners create social and cultural change on the earth.

Chapter 4, "Sirens," brings together the oricha Erinle, the Archangel Saint Rafael, drag queens, and the writing of Mayra Santos-Febres in order to investigate the relationship between gender-fluid narratives, healing, and the waters.[38] The concept of *sentimiento* (feeling) is an important affective tool in creating bonds of memory and emotion in the performance of ritual and song.[39] Storytelling reinforces trans* modes of becoming that turn violent experiences of abjection into powerful testimonies of resilience.[40] In this chapter, both ritual and narrative operate from spaces of fabulous empowerment, divascapes,[41] that render heteropatriarchy ridiculous and impotent. Conjure occurs through voice and embodiment in ways that reinforce intuition and the imagination as sites of knowing. The sea generates the rhythm of transformation analyzed in the texts studied.

In Afrolatinx religious cultures, the captivating transgendered deity Erinle is central to understanding the multiplicity of gender and sexuality. "Sirens" shows how queer Caribbean popular cultures create kinships that deeply borrow from Afrolatinx mythology and spiritual family-building where both Erinle and *transformistas* (drag queens) perform multiple subjectivities through rituals of cohabitation.[42] In reading ethnographic narratives about Erinle, along with Cabrera's stories about Yemayá, as well as Santos-Febres's novel *Sirena Selena vestida de pena*, I show how sexual and gendered forms of the sea, like mermen/mermaids, create an imaginative palette with which tales of desire, violence, and healing are performed. In particular, I theorize the lip sync of the siren-drag-goddess as a form of *oríkì* (Yoruba praise poetry) that creates an embodied merging of performer and the diva who is invoked through the act of performance. Issues of inhabitation and voice emerge as modes that destabilize universal subjectivities.

As an Afrolatinx siren, Erinle is an important deity for understanding the performance of queer spiritual kinship and the complexity of simultaneously inhabiting multiple forms of being. In Cuban rituals celebrating Erinle, the Saint Rafael is also invoked. The hagiography of the latter's movement as a healer using fish creates a fruitful associative plane with the riverine Erinle. The chapter looks at the way in which Cabrera's historiography concerning Saint Rafael and Erinle includes LGBTQ+ priestesses and practices from Havana in the nineteenth and early twentieth century that suggest multiple layers of coding, resistance, and creativity. We are able to see a continuity of artistry, elegance, and mutability in situating Erinle's ritual practices with contemporary drag performance and transgendered writing. The sea, fish, and sirens tie these elements together symbolically and literally through Glissant's transphysical poetics of the Caribbean. A nontranscendental multitemporality is asserted when varied forms of being emerge simultaneously through the waters. This denseness of time and becoming happens through Erinle and *transformistas* in the embodied fluidity of ritual and song.

The effervescence of *espuma del mar*, sea-foam, signifies the tangible yet ephemeral qualities of using conjure as a tool of inquiry. The conclusion to the book thinks through the shifting nature of the residual transcripts explored in relation to multiple experiences of modernity, science, spirituality, and materiality. Elements of our natural world are intertwined in profound ways with the spirit as we engage more and more in virtual existence and decentered notions of place. *Espuma del mar* also references the sea-foam of research—how sizzling and tickling sensations experienced during ethnographic moments leave traces of memory in notes, rituals, and stories; illustrating the ways in which some of the flows explored in this project are subtle. Archives of conjure produce the search for these traces by tracking the Caribbean poetics that shape the multiple kinds of spirituality, sexuality, and gender that might be "hiding in plain sight." In doing so, a diversity of cultural ecologies, spiritual histories, and shared ways of being come to light in ways that urge future searches, connections, and enactments. Archiving based on heightened ritual experiences expresses our need to connect with the past and the ephemeral: it is about feeling through the body in the here and now through the dead.

Weaving together different threads, this study recognizes water's movements and currents as a productive guide for understanding unapologetic mutability and sensuality. I also posit the desire for empowerment as a distinctive trait that is shared by ancestors, entities, and artists associated with the seas and rivers. The Afrolatinx cosmologies I follow are the signposts of mediums and spirits that constitute archives of conjure. These are living practices of knowledge deeply embedded in previous frames of artistic creativity and the survival of story. The vernacular transcriptions that make up residual traces change over time depending on who finds them and what they do with them, which means that a cyclic connection is created between the deities, dead, scholars, and artists who have payed attention to the residuals. Their kinship is constructed from the work, whether it be a monograph or beading, inspired by the spirits that move. The nonbiological basis for this connection is vital because it can allow for the creation of family away from eugenics, patriarchy, and colonialism. Here considerations of racial, gender, and sexual equality include the histories, stories, and vivification of the dead, even as imperfect ancestors. The frothy foam of currents charted in this book come from the siren's song for a multiplicity of motherhoods through practices like drag poetics and spiritual channeling.

As with Tomasa's and Goodison's dead, which launched this introduction, I am asking that we sit with and pay attention to the many ecologies of being that surround us. What can paying attention to the dead really do? I believe it compels us to act ethically within a larger focus of the cycle of becoming that includes endings and mysteries. The study of folk religion and belief is layered with evidence of how women and LGBTQ+ communities, in particular, create connections to spiritual entities and leave traces as residuals for future generations to conjure.[43] The residual transcriptions given to me by spirit guides like Ta José and deposited in the archive by Lydia Cabrera and Ruth Landes, for example, illustrate an intention to see future work conducted. Through unfinished notes and vague instructions, we are asked to creatively connect and complete projects that in themselves will need to be recontextualized to stay present and active.

Ultimately, we find that there is a constant dialogue waiting to be ignited through our intuition, imagination, and intent. Through collaborative engagement, we can learn from how Afrolatinx communities of practice follow their spirits in their daily lives to create art, scholarship, and change in the face of sexual intolerance, racism, and xenophobia. This work can be many things at once and may take multiple forms. Like the sea or the rivers, the flow can transport us in different directions of discovery and recognition.

1

RESIDUAL TRANSCRIPTIONS

Simple water puts out despacho *because water belongs to God.*
After I said I was an Oxúm I was told I could put my
Oxúm beads in water or just use simple water to cleanse the
way. Asking Oxúm and God.

—Ruth Landes's field notes

Here, two voices, one of Brazilian Candomblé priestess Eulalia and one of North American ethnographer Ruth Landes, discuss the spiritually cleansing power attributed to water, the deity Oxúm, and God.[1] Much of this book is about the ways that water maps routes to subjectivities and spiritualities that are slippery, fluid, yet strongly felt as currents in the experience and study of Afrolatinx religious cultures. This exchange between Eulalia and Landes was recorded in Landes's field notes from Bahia, Brazil where she engaged in studying gender, sexuality, and race with participants in the religion. I choose to begin the first chapter of this book with this quote because it reflects the reported voices from a transcript of an ethnographic moment that later became a fragment in an archive. It also illustrates the unfinished stories, suggested unofficial connections that Landes does not include in her ethnography, *The City of Women* (1994 [1947]). In this matter-of-fact recollection, Landes embraces her connection to the river goddess Oxúm and her own participation in the religion through obvious material culture markers like her Oxúm *ileke* (beaded necklace). It is the kind of advice that creates residual transcripts of ritual moments that become part of an archive of conjure that cannot be simply read on paper, but rather through clues like material culture, symbols, and a remarkably consistent imaginative spiritual memory.

An intersubjectivity between Eulalia, Landes, and Oxúm is suggested in reading this reflection from the archive. It conjures all three of them in a unique way out of the past and into the present, with the reported voices of the dead invoking gods and water on to the cleansing of Oxúm's ileke by Landes. This and other unfinished stories and their potential for thinking through the dilemma of reading transcriptions and archives of ritual work are the subjects of this chapter. The starting point is how intersubjective narratives get shared, inhabited, and repurposed through transcriptions created during ceremonies like contemporary Cuban séances, misas espirituales. During a misa, the dead tell stories, give advice, propose future rituals, and request that a variety of material culture be produced on their behalf. These mandates are communicated with/through mediums' bodies and are usually transcribed on site, copied, and then passed around. These circulated and repurposed spiritual transcripts, kept within the community as notation in *libretas* (notebooks) and archived in material culture, continue the collaborative work of ritual communion onto other social sites and modes of creative expression.

I want to consider the residual transcriptions generated by spirits and their mediums alongside the archival transcriptions found in Ruth Landes's notations of her fieldwork and personal spiritual growth in Brazil. By evaluating an archive of conjure coproduced by the dead, which includes ethnographers like Landes and Lydia Cabrera,[2] I am also suggesting a recalibration of folklore methodologies that explore the experiences of time, spirituality, and materiality. Questions to consider in evaluating different kinds of transcription include the following: What constitutes an archive of conjure? What is the relationship between a ritual object, its creation, and its inspiration? What temporalities and cartographies are stitched, beaded, smoked, and washed into the physical work that results from encounters with the dead? How does this work extend these relationships and reframe them in both visible and invisible ways?

These and other questions illustrate that taking notice of vernacular transcription helps one to consider the cyclical nature of scholarly and creative work done in Afrolatinx religious cultures that is communal. Furthermore, the texts and subjects I am addressing here are mobile and transforming. For that reason, my methodological questions reconsider what transcripts and archives are created to do. The effects and affects intentioned in residual transcriptions provoke future material and ephemeral acts of creation, ritual, and scholarship. Thus, Landes's and my own stories of interaction with spirits create mirrored archives of conjure through material culture. Our papered residual transcripts are reinscribed onto threads that bead ilekes for Oxúm and sew clothes for a spirit dolls. Each bead and stitch are connected to and vivify a history of touching the dead.

INTERSUBJECTIVITY AND INTERCORPOREALITY

Anthropologist Thomas J. Csordas discusses the ramifications of considering intersubjectivity and intercorporeality as primary experiences in conducting ethnographic research (2008). He argues that social interaction, as "objectively" observed, is the source for the experience of intersubjectivity. This is important for him to suggest as folklore studies, even in phenomenological schools of thought, may see the sharing of self in both mind and body as only relatable in "subjective" terms (Hufford 1995). Though his argument about the "co-presences" of alter egos has an empiricist bent (much like early spiritualist writings and practices in the nineteenth century exhibited in "proving" spirits),[3] his consideration of *how* intersubjectivities are collectively constructed through social interaction is productive for thinking through the Cuban misas and archival sources I explore here. One area Csordas highlights is the relational, metonymic nature of how we create ourselves through each other. This can be seen as refuting universalist theories of (inter)subjectivity that rely solely on evolutionary trajectories of development of self and society.

Where Csordas still sees a split between subjective and objective social interaction in terms of the relationship between materiality and spirituality, I see a current, a *corriente*, of connection through the senses (Otero 2016a, 2015).[4] In Espiritismo, these currents are vital energies that serve as conduits to communication with the dead through sensations like touch, hearing, vision, and corporeal cohabitation (possession). What I would like to consider is how these *corrientes* are transformed and travel through transcriptions that continue the work of intersubjectivity and intercorporeality. *Espiritistas* as transcribers, and ethnographers as ancestors, participate in acts of shared subjectivity that highlight the porous nature of the supposed subjective/ objective divide.

Scholars have considered, in different ways, the unique ontologies of spirituality and materiality that are generated by the senses and micropractices in Afro-Cuban religion (Espírito

Santo 2015; Beliso-De Jesús 2015; Pérez 2016; Ochoa 2010a). My own work thinks through how spirits produce various kinds of experiences of gender, sexuality, and race in their intersubjectivity with priestesses and mediums through storytelling and oral tradition (Otero 2018a, 2016a, 2015). The production of a misa's transcript is part of the shared creativity of the ritual communication between living and dead. These scraps of paper create unique opportunities to consider intersubjective texts as scripts, recipes, instructions or, in other words, calls to action in the world. Residual transcriptions make us aware of the alternate temporalities that archives can produce (Palmié 2014).

In Cuba, Espiritismo draws from a long history of culturally combined approaches to communicating with spirits and ancestors. One of its main components grows out of nineteenth-century spiritism as explored by French educator Allan Kardec, né Hippolyte Léon Denizard Rivail. Kardec was inspired by but also broke away from North American and British spiritualism, which combine showmanship, skepticism, and social progressivism with the practice of communicating with the dead through séances. In his *Le livre des Esprits* (2011 [1857]), Kardec presents the main philosophical components of spiritism in the form of a dialogue with spirits. Topics include the nature of the universe, the afterlife, materiality, and the relationship of spirits to human beings. The book was quickly translated into Portuguese and Spanish, and by the late nineteenth century Puerto Rico, Brazil, and Cuba became major sites of Espiritismo in Latin America.[5] The upper classes were especially drawn to spiritual work done in *centros espirituales* (spiritual centers) that sought to scientifically prove the existence of spirits through direct communication. Transcription, especially in *Le livre des Esprits*, is presented not only as a kind of documentation that proves the existence of spirits but also a means for continuing to develop relationships with nonmaterial beings.

Afrolatinx practitioners of Espiritismo incorporate their own creolized beliefs, rituals, and ancestors into the séance, and transcription continues to be an important element of extending spiritual work with the dead. Transcribing communications with spirits inspires new kinds of residual transcriptions that commemorate moments of contact with the dead. In the form of future ritual work that includes the creation of material culture, residual transcriptions serve as a testament to experiential bonds that are visual yet hidden. They are precisely residual because they incorporate traces of past encounters onto new maps of potential encounters, new destinations in mediums' futures that are being routed through them. Beads, stitches, herbs, cloth, and food are just a few examples of the raw materials used to create a textured and activated archive for and with spirits. These archives conjure clues for temporal sojourns that relate historical imaginings in an intersubjective and intercorporeal manner.

In Cuban misas, mediums reinterpret Kardec's own dialogic framework of transcribing spirits' words, wishes, and advice for and through material bodies. These inscriptions are unique in the density of cultural, religious, and linguistic bricolage they mark and also invoke. Cuban spirits have and crave *sabor*. They relish trying on the bodies loaned to them in ways that add considerations of how mediums express *spirits'* experiences of intercorporeality and intersubjectivity in their ritual performances.[6] Spirits' revelations can be compelling, lewd, humorous, and surprising. They ask for confirmation, dialogic agreement on their visionary diagnosis of the problems of mediums. "¡Luz!" Light, says the medium in affirming the accurate description of a dilemma detected by a visiting guide.

This fabric of interaction reminds mediums to consider the times outside a misa where guides may be interacting, watching, listening, and called upon. Ritual work that ensues from contact with spirits relies on sensibilities of intimacy, on building affectionate portraits of the dead that bring them closer and into everyday living. This takes effort, and oftentimes spirits' infamous love of play with humans can wreak havoc on a medium's day.[7] This can take the form of not being able to find necessary materials for ritual work or any number of inexplicable complications to completing a simple task. As my aunt and spiritual godmother Tomasa often advises me, *poco a poco* (bit by bit): the slow and steady speed of spiritual work relies on patience, especially in Cuba.

Similar kinds of affective bonding between people and spirits occurs through the creolization of spiritism and Afro-Atlantic religions in Brazil. Many of the practices and beliefs about the dead found in spiritism have been incorporated into the vernacular religious cultures of Umbanda and Candomblé. The development of unique kinds of spirits, like the Native American *caboclo* guide or the female spirit of the crossroads Pomba Gira, illustrate an attention to social tensions based on class, gender, and sexuality (Hale 2009). Both utilizing and circumventing a rhetoric of Yoruba purity, Brazilian spiritual practices have embraced spiritual proliferation in ways that illustrate the vibrancy of everyday spiritual mélange (Matory 2005:128, 248–49; Hess 1987). Espiritismo occupies a valuable space in Brazilian popular and public culture, with a variety of reimaginings of the life of Kardec (*O Filme dos Espíritos/The Film of the Spirits*, 2011), soap operas with spiritism at the center (*Além do Tempo/Beyond Time* 2015), and public monuments honoring famous mediums like Chico Xavier (Lewgoy 2001).

I mention the affinities between Brazilian and Cuban spiritual creolization in order to set the stage for the multiple contexts of transcription that I will be discussing in the rest of the chapter: ritual, archive, and material culture. The ephemeral experience of communication with spirits affords the opportunity for grounding it through clues that are the transcriptions being considered here. These clues are rhizomatic, they point to overlapping times and places. What can a misa espiritual conducted in Havana in December 2015, bits of advice given to Landes in 1938 in Bahia, and sewing a doll's clothes in Miami in 2013 have in common? These events are rediscovered by and also create residual transcriptions. Their notations point to a well-traveled road where spirituality and scholarship cross to create unofficial histories of encounter, experience, and inquiry.[8]

"DICE TA JOSÉ"

"Dice Ta José . . ." this is how the spirit guide Ta José starts the sentences he is articulating through medium José Días Casada's body. José, Tomasa, Soñia, my husband Eric, and myself are gathered in a circle in a darkened living room flickering with specks of candlelight bouncing off the clear, cool water wading in wine glasses found on the *bóveda* (spirit table, see figure 1.2). We are all smoking cigars in the hot, humid Havana December afternoon and waiting for Ta José to continue his warnings, recipes for spells, and demands for more rum. Tomasa has the unenviable task of translating and transcribing the spiritual patois that Ta José uses to communicate with us.[9] To Tomasa and me he says:

> Todo mundo habla mal de la niña . . . Ta José la va ayudar. Que le hace banderas a Sarabanda con 7 Rayo, y a Lucero. Entrégalas a los muertos de ella, que las banderas van a trabajar.

Everyone talks bad about *la niña* . . . Ta José will help her out. She should make banners for Sarabanda with 7 Rayo, and Lucero. Dedicate these to her spirit guides, [you will see] that the banners will work [to help her defeat her enemies].[10]

Tomasa writes this down furiously on lightweight sheets of paper, repurposed for the misa, with a blunt pencil.

Other stories, advice, and visions related by Ta José include a warning for Tomasa in regard to her son's new girlfriend from Santiago, who has been dusting the home with malevolent powders; a prediction of the health concerns some orichas will pronounce at a divinatory Santería session known as an *ita,* to be held for a relative in a few days; and recipes for a series of herb-based cleansings for all involved in the misa.[11] Ta José also enjoyed eating his cigar while lit, much to the ire and disgust of

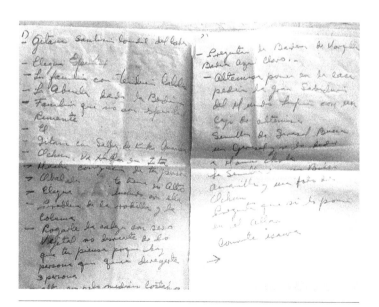

FIGURE 1.1 Tomasa's transcription from a misa espiritual, Havana, Cuba, December 2015. Photo by the author.

FIGURE I.2 José salutes the *bóveda*, misa espiritual, Havana, Cuba, May 2013. Photo by the author.

his horse, José, who does not even smoke cigarettes. It seemed like Tomasa and Ta José shared this as a private joke, with her breaking into Ta José's conversation to ask, "¿Está rico eso?" (Is that [cigar] delicious?). Ta José winks at her and says emphatically, "Síí" (Ye-es).

At the misa, Ta José directs me, *la niña*, to sew banners for Palo entities that are being invoked for protection. He diagnoses problems from his perspective as a spirit, which gives him a special *vista*, or sight, and offers spiritual solutions to the multiple interpersonal situations he senses for the participants. It is

important to note here that both spirit guides and their mediums share material and spiritual sensations in doing this intersubjective ritual work. The mediums' bodies and the spirits' sixth
sense are in constant negotiation to observe situations, make
determinations, and suggest solutions. Most spirits, like Ta José,
are very keen in detecting gossip, witchcraft, envy, backstabbing,
hypocrisy, shade, infidelity, etc. Yet, as guides, they also steer
you toward people and spiritual forces that are nourishing, loyal,
trustworthy, and so on. In asking participants to engage in future
creative work (sewing in my case), guides like Ta José invoke the
construction of further transcripts that will be the basis for other
kinds of interaction.[12] Sewing as a spiritual activity is particularly important to Caribbean, Latinx, and African diaspora
feminist traditions with regard to financial self-sufficiency, creative expression, and trauma-healing testimony.[13] Historically
and culturally, it makes sense that Ta José suggests sewing the
banners as a practice of healing, empowerment, creativity, and
as a testimonial fabric that commemorates our intersubjective
and ephemeral connection in this moment.

Ta José's and Tomasa's shared joke at José's expense is reflective of the issues inherent in relationships where spirit guides
cohabit mediums' bodies in the framework of a spiritual family.
Tomasa and José have worked together spiritually for over thirty
years. As a result, her relationship with the guide Ta José also
represents a friendship mediated through intercorporeality.
Tomasa, herself a medium who passes spirit guides, can joke
about what spirits do to borrowed bodies *with* a spirit. This ban-
ter and other moments in the misa, as when Tomasa humors Ta
José by saying, "I always have more rum for you," shows the intimacies of kin that extend beyond the limits of materiality.
Indeed, these small encounters reveal the warmth and comfort
of inhabiting a moment that bends transcendental notions of

time and subjectivity. The residual transcripts I hold from this and other misas (see figure 1.1) keep me connected to my community from miles away. The spiritual work that I create from them enacts the familial and spiritual relationships being described here.

Transcripts recall the ephemerality of Ta José's touch and words, yet they allow for a creative extension of a shared intention. These scribbled and copied notes, recipes, blessings, and warnings urge action in the world. Each person at the misa received a script with Ta José's instructions to either cleanse, plant, smoke, or sew enactments of vernacular activities intended to influence fate through their connection to Ta José as well as the world. He asked us to weave together material and spiritual *campos* (terrains) by activating the recopied intersubjective texts. The notes are not simply finished when the cleansings are done or the objects made, they are reworked into new trajectories of meanings and communication with ancestors in future ritual work. Transcripts from a misa produce affects and effects that extend and sustain relationships and foster multiple kinds of being in Espiritismo's spiritual families.

Transcribing ritual and creating its prescribed material culture begs certain methodological questions within the context of Afrolatinx religiosity. The creation of transcripts is not exclusive to misas in Espiritismo and are useful tools for divination in Ifa, Santería, and Palo traditions. For example, in Santería, the "fifíta or feícitá" acts as secretary for the orichas during *dilogún* divination whereby she/he writes down patterns laid out by the cowry shells (Beliso-De Jesús 2015:67–68; Fernández 2017). I myself have been handed written instructions from my godfather, Efun Bile, a *babalawo* from Mantilla who meticulously notes down all of the divination he performs into what amounts to a library of spiritual notebooks dating over forty years (see figure 1.3). Of special consideration in Afrolatinx religious notation is the inclusion of designs of invocation, like Palo *firmas*, that call into being entities of ancestors and the dead (Ochoa 2010b:154–57; Routon 2008:634–36). Firmas, like Haitian Vodou's *vevés*, belong to particular divinities and act as visual road maps to ritual communion with practitioners. Whether written on paper, in cornmeal, chalk, or gun powder, the firmas' notation move beyond issues of representation and signification associated with written language. They provoke an efficient and dense construction of a third dimensional space analogous to holographic and virtual experiences of connectivity between and through different material spheres.[14] Indeed, the very patterns made by the cowry shells and the *opuele* chain in Yoruba-inspired divination practices create similar kinds of dense communication that connects orichas to practitioners. Thus the methodological questions I pursue in this chapter also deal with how transcripts cocreated at the site of ritual, as in the fifita's, babalawo's, or medium's note-taking, offer instructions to practitioners as to how to proceed in the ongoing ritual work of daily life.

The transcripts of rituals like the misa are pins in a fabric, one that weaves past and future expressive acts. Residual transcripts act as reminders, but also prompt us to action. These more quotidian writings are copied on scraps of papers, carried along in pockets and purses, and reconsulted during work that continues connections with spirit guides and divinities. Like the micropractices that create the kitchen and cuisine in Santería,[15] residual transcriptions make possible the necessary, everyday texture of Afrolatinx religiosity. These written notes bridge the more dramatically marked communal rituals of communicating with spirits with the more personal, meditative spiritual work inspired by these events. Though humble and utilitarian,

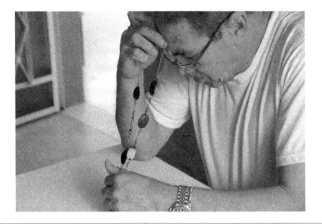

FIGURE 1.3 Efun Bile divines with the *opuele*, Havana, Cuba, December 2015. Photo by Héctor Delgado. Author's private collection.

residual transcripts leave traces of what happens in between ritual communication and spiritual work. They become a connective tissue that tell fragmented stories of intimate engagements between spiritual and material actors. The archives are particularly thorny sites littered with bits of bone, unfinished narratives. The point being that residual transcriptions may or may not reveal points of encounter between layered pasts and spiritual protagonists. They echo with the voices of partially accessible and imperfect ancestors.

IMPERFECT ANCESTORS

Archival research is an intimate yet potentially violent kind of study that requires a sensitivity toward the contexts and contents found in the paper remains of a life lived. By violent, I mean the representational and receptive damage that can occur in creating universal narratives of departed subjects. Like the pit-falls of voyeurism that can plague ethnographic accounts of "exotic" subjects and cultures, historiography based on archival work can also fall into a rhetoric that flattens in order to sell a plausible story. Work in archives of conjure disrupts the desire to create a neat timeline, to relate a linear narrative that will fall easily into recognized canons of knowledge-making in terms of the past and culture. Rather, one engages with the dead more precisely by paying attention to confusing clues and unfinished accounts in the archive. I am arguing that they (the dead) put those clues and accounts in front of the researcher, urging her to perceive, much like a spirit medium uses her vista at a séance, certain details that complicate, engage, and make manifest the archival ancestor.

In looking at Cabrera's and Landes's private correspondence, notes, poems, and drawings, I found bits of unfinished stories that suggested a scattered temporality. These snapshots of time resemble the residual transcriptions generated by rituals of com-munion with the dead, like the misas I have been discussing in this chapter.[16] Reported conversations about orichas and recom-mendations for spiritual *trabajos* (like the one suggested in this chapter's epigraph), reveal interior and personal entanglements difficult to conform to a linear life narrative but impossible to ignore. These spiritually intimate connections add a necessary layer of texture to the stories about and by scholar-practitioners like Cabrera and Landes. The residual transcriptions I found in the archive embedded Cabrera and Landes in the spiritual ontologies of Cuban and Brazilian vernacular religion in ways that emphasize these women's dependence on spirits, orichas, and ancestors in pursuing their work, relationships, and lives. Further, like Ta José, Cabrera and Landes are *muertos*, ances-tors relating stories, advice, and suggestions for further work in the clues they left behind. The circuitous pursuit of stories in an archive resembles the sensibilities present in ritual communication with spirits. In both cases, the recovery of information is serendipitous and the resulting work engages reimagined pasts and persons. Both Cabrera and Landes had deep emotional, creative, and spiritual connections to the religious communities they engaged with.[17] They developed relationships to a particular oricha that helped them navigate the waters of their own subjectivity and place within the universes of Santería and Candomblé, respectively. I discuss Cabrera's connection to Yemayá in chapter 3 of this book.[18] In the case of Landes, however, it is the deity of love and fresh water, Oxúm, that reveals herself as a guide to her work and life in Bahía. In a larger motif that dominates this book's work on the metaframing that spiritual epistemologies and ontologies do for scholars and practitioners, Yemayá and Ochún are paired in revealing routes of connection that may be unorthodox yet illuminating. Though both women were "white" in terms of their phenotype, Landes's Jewishness in pro-Nazi Brazil and Cabrera's lesbianism in both Cuba and Miami mark their alterity in ways that cannot be dismissed now, nor were they lost on the religious practitioners who collaborated with them (Landes 1994 [1947]:9–10; Cuesta 2016:13). Some ethnographers have struggled with the racial optics present in Cabrera's relationships with her interlocutors as foregrounding and perhaps limiting the possibilities of their own engagements with Black Cuban religious subjects.[19] I too have reconsidered my work in relation to Cabrera, also as an *egun*, an active ancestor looking over my shoulder. I see her as a woman who was misunderstood in so many ways and found her personal power, her *aché* in loving other women and in her devotion to Yemayá, to the sea.[20] In Landes's case, her personal

observations working ritually with priestesses like Mãe Menininha do Gantois, Eulalia, Zeze, and Sabina indicated that she
took these women and the study of women seriously.[21] In these
complicated instances, we find that the entangled transnational
politics of race, sexuality, and gender do not afford easy answers
or allegiances and that the dead and the orichas embrace dis-
harmonious bodies and subjects simultaneously.

Landes's groundbreaking ethnography *The City of Women*
focuses on the importance of women in Candomblé worship. In
the book, she forwarded a view of a matriarchal religious culture that her own archive complicates and contradicts. Sally Cole
has written extensively on the professional price Landes paid for
writing a reflexive ethnography about women in a situated context before it was popular (Cole 2003). One of the most interesting critics of Landes's work is anthropologist J. Lorand
Matory. His own work with priests of Candomblé refutes Landes's matriarchal claims, and his *Black Atlantic Religion* brings
to light and grapples with the legacies of her early work on male
religious leaders (2005:260–65). Also of significance is how both
Landes and Matory navigate sexuality in Candomblé contexts
with particular regard to male homosexual priests (Matory
2005:207–12).[22]

Landes observes the following about homosexual Candomblé priests in Bahia in the 1930s: "But as the voice of a hitherto
voiceless group, they may be path-breakers to new institutions" (1940:393). Similarly, her partner in Bahia, ethnologist
Edison Carneiro, relates the details and stress of "passing" for
straight that male homosexual priests had to perform socially
in Candomblé circles.[23] The ways that Landes and Carneiro
documented the different moments of gay male priests' partial
marginalization, ritual creativity, and ascendancy provide
useful points of comparison with similar kinds of double binds

facing gay and lesbian practitioners of Vodou and Santería (Conner and Sparks 2004; Cabrera 1975 [1954]:58–59; Strongman 2019).

Yet Landes also presents female priestesses as more "authentic" and "traditional" in their religiosity. In this regard, I must agree with Matory when he writes that Landes and Carneiro recorded "copious evidence against their own interpretive models" (2005:206). For Carneiro's notes and for Landes's essay on the subject of sexuality, I have had to read against some of the criminological language they use to describe homosexual and lesbian priests in order to comprehend the complexity of the situation both were trying to navigate in their documentation. However, I believe that Landes's and Carneiro's contemporaneous collection of data and impressions on homosexual male priests are valuable resources that open up questions about how Afrolatinx religious communities negotiate sexuality and gender in *machista* ritual and social contexts. Then and now, gay and lesbian practitioners of Afrolatinx religions like Candomblé and Santería must negotiate transnational notions of gender, sexuality, social status, and racial authenticity.

To move within all these countercurrents of race, place, gender, sexuality, and nation, I am inspired by Matory's frank discussion of his own spiritual journeying through scholarship. He acts as a guide to my discussion of Landes's spiritual awakening and the personal conundrums she faced while enacting intimate understandings of Brazilian religions. Matory's deep appreciation for the limits of ethnographic and historiographic methodologies and conceptual metaphors also aid my critique, which centers on the importance of noticing residual transcriptions (1994). In particular, his paradigm-shifting work mirrors my attenuation to the unfinished stories found in ethnographic transcription and in the archive. Landes's own spotted cartography of scholarly, spiritual, and emotional entanglements as a daughter of Oxúm recalls the ways that nonmaterial beings create signposts on these maps. Matory reflects on the crossing of oricha, scholar, and community vital to texturing the story of his scholarship: "Yemọja was the goddess who first called me to the study of Yorùbá-Atlantic religion. . . . Yet it has been the daughters of Ọṣun (in Nigeria), Oxum (in Brazil), and Ochún (in the Cuban diaspora) who have first met me in every continent and assisted my comings and goings" (2005:247–48).

Matory's words evoke a backstory rife with lived experiences and connections that open up Yemayá's and Ochún's touch on his world. The Yoruba foundational concept of *iranjo*, the journey, is at the center of both Matory's and Landes's experiences of Brazilian vernacular religion.[24] Ochún and Yemayá again serve as guides for journeys where the waters of subjectivity, in this case of scholar and believer, cross and create an undertow that spill into a larger flow.[25] These crossings leave their mark in subtle yet noticeable observations, personal reflections, and as ethnographic notations in the archive.

At the Ruth Landes Papers, letters, notes, journals, and drawings penned in Landes's hand accompany photos of great Candomblé figures like Martiniano Eliseu do Bonfim (see figure 1.8), newspaper clippings, and calling cards. These primary and secondary sources coexist side by side in neatly labeled folders, relating to each other in ways that are both intuitive and random. As with contemporary Cuban misas, this particular archive is full of sensory markers of the dead, of egun, whose layered voices and images relate multiple paths to deciphering the contents of their papered remains. Landes herself is a bit of a trickster spirit in the archive, as her field journals and notebooks are numbered in a double-sided, reverse order that are hard to decipher at first, and are full of idiosyncratic coding. Yet the denseness of her notes resembles the intimate shorthand that many practitioners of Afrolatinx religions use to condense the vast array of information, symbols, and narratives they record during divination ceremonies in preparation for future ritual work. I am interested in what these humble, coded, yet matter-of-fact observations of ritual subjects, hurriedly jotted down by Landes or by spirit mediums like Tomasa, tell us about the relationship of vernacular documentation to acts of religious creativity and posterity. How does the ethnographer-practitioner leave traces of everyday lived moments of intangible but deeply sensory spiritual recognition in the archive? The clues may be hidden in plain sight, yet they mirror how gossip, hearsay, and other forms of folk speech assist in carrying on the expressive traditions and unofficial histories of women, LGBTQ+ communities, and people of color in Afrolatinx religious cultures.[26]

ENTER OXÚM

On a September evening in 1938, Ruth Landes and Edison Carneiro visited a 120-year-old ritual compound in Rio Vermelho, Bahia, "beautifully situated" on a slope.[27] They went specifically to speak to an *ekedi*, a nonpossession priest, Juanmario. Landes was so taken with the complex, she drew the following in her research notebook:

	H6	
H5	H4	H3
	Hillside	
	H2	
	Well (H20) H1	Stream (H30)[28]

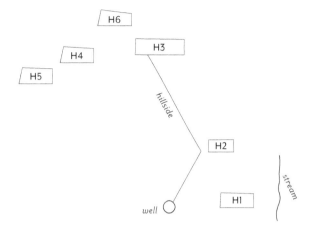

FIGURE I.4 Rendition of an archival image of Landes's map of the ritual compound. Photo by the author. The Ruth Landes Papers, Courtesy of the National Anthropological Archives, Smithsonian Institution.

The *H*s in the diagram represent houses dedicated to different *orixa*. House 1, located between the well and the stream, not surprisingly, belonged to Oxúm. Landes remarks that the house was pleasant, surrounded by trees, and that "Ed [ison] remarked that it was my santo!"[29] From almost the start of her interaction with the Candomblé houses in Bahia, Landes was identified as a daughter of Oxúm by practitioners. In this example, the making and mapping of place, houses for the divinities and especially Oxúm, reveal a mutual recognition of arrival for Landes and Carneiro. While other scholars may be interested in the very worthy information about socioreligious structures revealed by the diagram of the compound, my focus is on the encoded information included as auxiliary notations within as well as off this map.

Landes's emphatic remark becomes a residual transcript that points to a personal connection that she is developing to Oxúm through a religious-material structure in the moment. As with Matory, Landes sees Oxúm as a guide for navigating Brazilian religious worlds. It is especially important to Landes's work, however, that the community reinforced Oxúm's claim to her person, and this provided a sense of legitimacy to her work. Though it is not unusual for scholars of Afrolatinx traditions to become involved and associated with particular divinities and spirits during their research, it is rare that these relationships become the sole subject of study. This is due to the private and secret nature of such connections, as well as the supposed separation between empirical observations and subjective impressions. As my earlier discussion of Csordas's work on intersubjectivity clarifies, the relationship between the senses and recording observations are inextricably linked and indicate the collaborative nature of creating a sense of self and community. Landes's impressions of her developing connection to religious leaders and to divine beings like Oxúm situate how participant observation in Afrolatinx religions often turns epistemological authority on its head. Thus the most legible and consistent subjectivities belong to beings and ancestors present well before the scholar comes on-site or into the archive. These ever-present entities are pliable and growing, with past priests and scholars joining their ranks in memory, ritual, and the archive.

Landes constantly interacts with Oxúm in ritual celebrations, fieldwork, and divination.[30] On August 21, 1938, she travels to the compound of Sabina, a priestess she works with throughout her year in Bahia, to witness a celebration for the orixas (see figure 1.9). Landes reports that, upon arrival, "I asked to see her temple for Oxúm."[31] Noting that lots of *filhas de Oxúm* (daughters of Oxúm) are present, she brings the goddess flowers and places them among the offerings of boiled eggs and shredded shrimp.[32] "Eggs are her favorite food," says a priestess, dressed in "lovely faded corn yellow," to Landes.[33] The devotees of Oxúm then start calling out, "O-re!" in a greeting to the divinity. A song begins: "Oxúm ela e uma beleza / Oxúm, Oxúm, o ela e uma grandeza / yã yã yã" (Oxúm, she is a beauty / Oxúm, Oxúm, she is great, yã yã yã).[34]

This song hailing Oxúm's beauty and greatness follows Landes in other rituals she attends. For example, at another set of ceremonies held a month later, between September 22–25, it emerges again: "Oxum é uma beleza, Oxum é uma grandeza."[35] As these words of praise ring out, an Oxúm dances out onto the floor, crossing her hands over her chest, "placing [her] hands on [her] left hip in coquettish position," and looks into a mirror.[36]

Landes experiences the emergence of the deity in dance, taste, and song. As with the misa described earlier in this chapter, the connection to spirituality in her notes is multisensorial, registering a cacophony of voices, images, and feelings. Landes's personal observations of her interactions with Oxúm give the sense of an intimate spiritual connection. Yet these scattered sets of relations are hard to pin down in a singular narrative. They are also impossible to dismiss, as they importantly situate the deity for both Landes and for practitioners of Candomblé. Like the Oxúm dancer who looks knowingly into the mirror, the reflection one receives is one of intense self-realization.

Landes's connection to Oxúm is most evident in her relationship with her principle interlocutor, the great Candomblé priestess Mãe Menininha. Known as one of the most famous manifestations of Oxúm on the planet,[37] Mãe Menininha reinforced Landes's connection to her tutelary orixa. Mãe Menininha described Oxúm as a "lovely woman . . . calm, of golden hair, poised, agreeable" whose resemblance to Ruth Landes was unmistakable.[38] Here the mirror logics of Oxúm are at play, the mirror being one of the deity's most prized and powerful ritual objects.[39] As with divination and magic done with mirrors globally, a glass surface has the capacity to reflect a range of projections in a dialogic manner. The reliance on the visual metaphor as the mode through which observations and realizations are reflected back on the beholder also creates a reflexive dimension to the act of peering into the looking glass. As children of Oxúm are often affectionate, bright, and pleasant, they attract a lot of visual attention. This is both a strength and detriment because added visibility can bring on negativity for a variety of reasons.[40] Yet, when Mãe Menininha is looking pleasantly upon Landes and sees Oxúm, she is also reflecting her own beauty, generosity, and benevolence. As Ribeiro dos Santos claims about Bahia, "Nesta cidade todo mundo é d'Oxum. In this city everybody is Oxum's" (2001:68). And, for him, the expansive nature of religious kinship in Bahia is best described in Oxúm's pleasing touch and Mãe Menininha's smiling reflection (80). This commentary and Mãe Menininha's image in the mirror show how certain ontologies of belonging rely heavily on manifestations of Oxúm present in Afrolatinx traditions.[41]

However, focusing on solely welcoming images of the river goddess can be simplistically deceptive, as the divinity is also capable of the power to destroy, obstruct, and abandon (Abiodun 2001:35; Cabrera 1980:69–72, 89–91). Indeed, some of the roads Landes travels hand in hand with Oxúm are of loss and pain, of broken relationships and bonds. Landes's archive acts as Oxúm's mirror, albeit cracked and cloudy, reflecting fragments of unfinished stories, shards of partial information of lived experiences that the viewer touches, rereads, and reconstructs.

EDISON CARNEIRO, AN UNFINISHED STORY

One of the first items I found in Landes's papers was Edison Carneiro's calling card, a perfect example of a residual transcript of an unfinished story.[42] Landes wrote on the front and back of the card, in cursive, using a pen rather than the pencil that she usually used to produce her field notes. The writing on the front was illegible to me. However, on the back of Carneiro's card was a list of calls and responses for orixas and spirits when they manifest:

êpa <u>hei</u> = Yansan
keu-keu = Oxossi (or bark)
atolô = Omolú
Kawô = Xango
Kabiêcílé = Xango
Ria! = Caboclo[43]

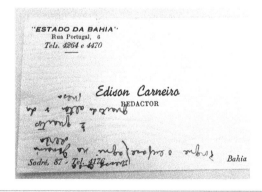

FIGURE 1.5 Edison Carneiro's calling card. Photo by the author. The Ruth Landes Papers, Courtesy of the National Anthropological Archives, Smithsonian Institution.

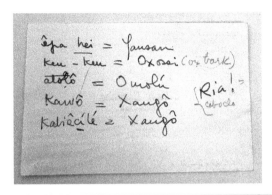

FIGURE 1.6 Back of Carneiro calling card. Photo by the author. The Ruth Landes Papers, Courtesy of the National Anthropological Archives, Smithsonian Institution.

These notes are almost an afterthought, a kind of shorthand that connects these spirits and knowledge to Carneiro through his card. The scribblings illustrate that Landes was willing to use whatever pieces of paper necessary to mark this connection, albeit perhaps unconsciously. Their casual nature reminds me of how Cabrera herself observed a "lifelong attention to the minutiae that make everyday objects magical" (Vazquez 2014:853). Cabrera doodled in her journals, providing relief for herself from "work." In so doing, she created a bridge between the worlds of research and play by writing in the margins, paying attention to the minutiae that helps the mind process with a bit more ease. Like the childlike helper spirits that appear during days of trance at Yoruba rituals to mellow the psychic tension of devotees,[44] "silly" drawings and notes that appear within the archive point our eyes to something at a remove from the center but still worth paying attention to. Landes's scribbling on the back Carneiro's calling card makes an everyday object magical. The concise dialogic call and response to the divinities of wind, forest, disease, lightning, and indigeneity act as a reminder to manifest. What do they conjure?

Matory's insights into his own processes of world-making and creating kin among religious practitioners in Brazil can offer guidance to how Landes negotiated her scholarly, spiritual, and affective relationships. In speaking about his own friendship with celebrated Candomblé priest and mentor Pai Francisco, he writes that there are "certain broad truths about group loyalties and imagined communities that social scientists must leave for poets to explain" (2005:253). Though Matory speaks to the limits of anthropology to capture certain truths, he does, however, leave his reader with a well-described set of relationships and contexts that signal some of the contours of his place within and affection for his adopted community. Furthermore, this insightful observation points to the limits of certain genres of expression in explaining the "structures of feeling" that go into creating communities like Afrolatinx spiritual families (Muñoz 2000). Matory's "broad truths" express the vivid and real nature of the affective entanglements that orixas, divinities, and the dead ask from the social lives of practitioners and researchers. Shared beliefs, experiences, and especially alliances with nonmaterial beings are difficult to express if one relies solely on academic discourses of description and discovery. Here Afrolatinx symbolic and aesthetic sensibilities are organized "de cierta manera" (in a certain way) that shapes material and ephemeral patterns of communication (Benítez Rojo 1992 [1989]: xxvi). Residual transcripts like a misa's notes and Landes's Oxúm beads may indeed be closer to expressing broadly held, but well-hidden truths for communities at risk over centuries due to racism, sexism, homophobia, and colonialism.[45]

Landes creatively reflected on her Bahian life and relationships. In correspondence, diary entries, drawings, and poetry, she outlined a deep emotional and spiritual connection with people like Carneiro and divinities like Oxúm. One of the most striking examples of this is a poem written by hand on two pieces of paper:

BAHIA, 1938–39, TIME WITH EDISON CARNEIRO

The gleaming beach of Amoreira
What [a] fitting name
It means "x lover" [sic]
X sky spread clear and dark
Above and beyond in all directions
and while we walked and loved
    as usual
a band of blacks danced and loved
    as well
Suddenly, Egun appeared and shouted
Hastily we tried to hear him
    I heard
And then we dropped, asleep
I had all to love him
Poetry and Science
Bliss, and a turn of a knife
    for eleven months[46]

The intimacy and passion revealed in the poem illustrate a sense of place. Landes's Bahia is an emotive terrain touched by love, spirits, and race. On the beach of Amoreira, she faces her own feelings of desire for Carneiro, distinctly marked by being surrounded by Afro-Brazilian people and spirituality: "and while

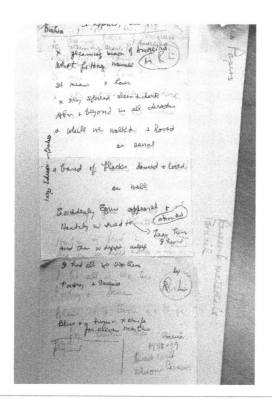

FIGURE I.7 Archival image of a poem by Landes. Photo by the author. The Ruth Landes Papers, Courtesy of the National Anthropological Archives, Smithsonian Institution.

we walked and loved / as usual / a band of blacks danced and loved / as well." She both distances herself yet approaches blackness in these lines that juxtapose dancing, walking, and loving. The romantic nocturnal scene is abruptly interrupted by an ancestor, "Suddenly, Egun appeared and shouted." What did the dead say? Did he relate something about slavery, racial injustice, or a revelation of future strife, as egun are wont to do?[47] Landes writes, "Hastily we tried to hear him / I heard / And then we dropped, asleep." She heard the message but does not tell, and the reader is left in the dark as to what the egun is conveying. Instead, the poem descends sleep upon her, her partner, and also the reader. It is noteworthy that sleep and dreaming, as discussed in the introduction, are considered dominant ways that the dead send their messages to the living. The end of the poem confesses love and pain, amid "Poetry and Science," and the end of an affair after eleven months. The temporal dimensions of the poem intertwine magical time with Eurochronology (Dinshaw 2012; Appadurai 1996; Fabian 1983). The poem ultimately relates the despair Landes felt during the last months of her stay in Bahia, as she was being actively pursued by the secret police who eventually ordered her out of the country (Landes 1994 [1947]:245).

Was Landes exotifying blackness in her academic, spiritual, and romantic life in Bahia? Did her position as a Jewish woman in Brazil's machista and pro-Nazi environment mitigate her whiteness? These questions have been explored by other scholars, and the answers illuminate the fissures and issues present in the North American academy's struggles with paternalism, sexism, neoliberalism, and racism (Cole 2003; Matory 2005). For my purposes here, I am interested in what Landes's residual transcripts of her encounters with divination, orixas, priests, and egun tell about her as an imperfect ancestor. She becomes an egun whose archive relates traces of experiences to be fleshed out in the intersection of several imagined communities: historical, anthropological, and Afro-Brazilian. Landes's movement in and out of Brazil establishes her position as a sexile ancestor, a "feminist nomadic subject," whose gender and sexuality forces her to disperse (Pérez Rosario 2014:5). Landes continues to move through her archive, where transcripts of personal ritual and divination reveal spiritual destinations that are cyclical and generative. Like the transcripts in of the spiritual misa, Landes's notes about her own ritual work perpetuate future connections with divinities, ancestors, and spirits by invocation.

MARTINIANO DO BONFIM

Martiniano Eliseu do Bonfim looms large as a figure in Candomblé's past: as a Lagosian and as a babalawo, he represents a transnational history of exchange that deepens and complicates notions of African religiosity and global citizenship (Matory 2005:46; Otero 2010). Landes appreciated his knowledge and position in Bahian religious life, and she personally sought his guidance as a believer. In particular, Landes entrusted do Bonfim with matters of the heart. In her notebook where the pages are numbered in reverse order, she details a reading she receives from him. She enters the ceremony in this manner, "I gave Martiniano three questions: 1) When to marry; 2) Will I (? Illegible);[48] 3) Shall I continue my profession?"[49] Divining with the *Jogo de Búzios* (cowry shells), do Bonfim tells Landes to marry the man she "loves best."[50] Prophesying difficulties, objections by many people because the man in question is a "mulatto," he suggests an expensive and difficult ceremony.[51] I am not sure if Landes ever completes the offering necessary to ensure a satisfactory outcome of her personal and professional dilemmas. However, this turn toward do Bonfim in such delicate matters indicates a level of commitment, trust, and vulnerability that shows the development of a spiritual kinship. More to the point, her transcript of the reading and the unfinished ritual allow for the contemplation of do Bonfim's prophecy alongside Landes's loss of the romantic relationship with Carneiro.

Do Bonfim's reading also recalls Matory's own adoption of Pai Francisco's Mediterranean and West African worldview, where negative *influências* like envy, witchcraft, and malice operate in abundance (Matory 2005:252). Like Ta José's approximation of my own problems with these kinds of forces, do Bonfim and Pai Francisco enact their roles as guides and warriors against malevolence toward adopted kin. Though Matory, Landes, and I myself may have focused on writing ethnography about the culture of Afrolatinx religions, our encounters of shared ritual work are at the heart of who we are and how we belong ontologically to the community. Works of prophesy and conjure should be taken seriously as theoretical and temporal models that rethink subjectivity and reality. Notions of will and fate are put into conversation and not in opposition in ways that highlight the pliability of existence.

There are regenerating models of being and becoming that Afrolatinx religiosity enacts. Much of the variety of the individual interpretations of these models, especially in terms of gender and sexuality, stem from purposefully enigmatic considerations of mythology, symbolism, and practice. The most intimate relationships—parents, lovers, children, enemies—are negotiated onto an affective socioreligious cartography that is transnational, transtemporal, and transcorporeal. Depth of feeling, *sentimiento*, is central to how to engage these relationships through ritual enactment. Whether it is listening to the dead at the misa or Landes washing her Oxúm beads, there is a vernacular pedagogy at work on how to be and become in the world. Can it be described in traditional academic terms? Matory opines that "the structural conditions highlighted by such models [anthropological theory] pale before the affective substance of sacred brotherhood, parenthood, and wifeliness" (2005:254). I would agree, especially with the word *substance*, in how these relationships are tangible, palpable feelings of connection that elude codification or discovery within universalist tropes of knowing. Rather, the way to relate Landes's role in her life in Bahia is to take a cue from how she also saw herself as a daughter of Oxúm. For her, this was not a flight of fancy, but a real relation, a force manifesting and helping her make sense of her most personal relationships and concerns.

Sacred wifeliness is one lens Landes also looks through in thinking about the spirituality of her relationship with Carneiro. "Menininha said that Oxúm was one of Xangó's wives, but as a king he could be with any woman he wanted," she wrote.[52] She also later remarks that "everyone considers" Carneiro's *santo* to be "Xangó."[53] Associating personal relationships through existing examples from an orixa's hagiography is a common vernacular strategy of making sense of conflicts, attractions, and behaviors in Afrolatinx religions. A dense correlation of the analogy of experience of orixa to devotee is reinforced manifold through divination and ritual, where oral and enacted frameworks are solidified between actors. However, it is the less dramatic, less hierarchical, more residual, and everyday connections that I want to emphasize in these relationships between divinities and devotees.

I would like to believe that Oxúm also truly embraced Landes in a subtle, quotidian, yet penetrating manner that shaped her life, losses, and legacy. Landes's sexual audacity and devotion to women's spirituality is certainly trademark Oxúm behavior. As in the misa that began this chapter, the layering of divinity, ancestor, and human is also found in Landes's archive of conjure through scribbled and scattered residual transcriptions. Landes's archival gossip, as with Cabrera's, reveals the necessity for taking seriously records of nonlinear, rhizomatic talk (Otero 2013; Vargas 2012). Paying attention to marginalia, material culture, nonverbal, and indirect transcripts in the

FIGURE I.8 Martiniano Eliseu do Bonfim and Ruth Landes,
August 1938. Photo by Ernesto Carneiro. Courtesy of the National
Anthropological Archives, Smithsonian Institution.

archive and in the field resonates of resistance traditions
familiar to women writers and sexual warriors of many stripes.[54]
The drawings and words on the margins of "official" sources
create potential futures through tactile and visual reflections
that recall Oxúm's mirror logics. These logics also ask the
viewer to consider the visual reflexively and indicate the importance of "reading" material culture as a stylistic guide to values
and histories incapable of being contained solely through words
(Flores Peña and Evanchuck 1994; Brown 2003; Shukla 2015).

FIGURE 1.9 Landes with Mãe Sabina, September 1938. Photographer unknown. Courtesy of the National Anthropological Archives, Smithsonian Institution.

MATERIAL CULTURE AS ARCHIVES OF CONJURE

Studies of material culture in Afrolatinx religions show the way in which the vernacular arts are rich sources of cultural history, mastery of skill, and individual creativity.[55] Constantly changing, material culture in this context acts as an archive of conjure that responds to past and present afflictions facing a religious community.[56] It serves devotional purposes in documenting relationships between practitioners and beings in ways that also visibly and invisibly mark the bodies of believers in the form of beads, scarification, ingested substances, apparel, and so forth. For example, Landes's Oxúm beads, Matory's recent exhibition "Spirited Things,"[57] and my sewn *banderas* for ancestor guides mark spiritual connections created through vernacular art. In some cases, objects are made in gratitude, seeking to please and delight divinities and observers alike.[58]

What does it mean to look at expressive culture inspired by the residual transcripts created from rituals like the misa or Landes's archive? Can we see, feel, or apprehend aspects of Ta José in the cloth, smoke, and herbs he urges participants to use after the ceremony? These questions ask for a change in assumptions on how to conduct ethnographic fieldwork and archival research. An approach that embraces the temporal arcs that residual transcripts and spiritual material culture point to is also able to grasp the cyclical nature of such work. Instead of seeing artifacts and archives as products of one decipherable ephemeral moment, objects like spirit dolls, beaded vessels, offerings at altars, and cloth banners provide invitations for revisiting and renegotiating spiritual connections repeatedly. These relationships are intimate and rely on affective bonds that are relational in nature yet deeply entrenched in the textures of racial historical memory (Matory 2018; Otero 2016a; Espírito Santo 2015; Pérez 2011). Here I am reminded of David H. Brown's observations in his rich and detailed work on Santería altars, vestments, and adornment: "Cloth's associations of loving embrace, spiritual protection, and cleansing are reiterated in Lucumí *ebós*, in which they are integral to human-divine cycles of gift exchange" (Brown 2003:243).

Ebós are sacrificial offerings to Afrolatinx entities. Brown's comments illustrate how cloth offerings invoke bonds of affection and memory between devotees and the divine. These bonds draped in cloth visibly express extended kinships as archives of conjure whose texture can tell us volumes about how vernacular history is aesthetically and physically marked by Afrolatinx religious communities. Through residual transcripts, they point us toward instinctual readings often shunned because of the deep distrust of feeling and perception inherited through some discourses of "objective" analysis that are themselves colored by unchecked Eurocentric prejudices. Yet feeling through residual readings can bring us closer to the poetics of Afrolatinx histories and experiences often overlooked in the archive or ignored because of their illegibility due to a very narrow view of what constitutes a record of the past, of what counts as a story.

But how do we "read" flowing cloth, beaded designs, and the processes that create objects dense with meaning and communication? Martin Tsang's recent work investigating the Chinese influence on Afro-Cuban sacred beading traditions for the divinity Yemayá in Regla, Cuba, sheds methodological light here (2017). His careful study of the creation of beaded vessels for Yemayá by an elder artisan priest and his apprentices pays attention to the important associations between the vessels, the human body, and designs as representative of human-divine shared subjectivity. What I take from Tsang's attention to the artistic process is an encouraging model for investigating the multiple and changing forms that spiritual materiality can take. Vessels that hold manifestations of Yemayá, as with expressive works prompted by Ta José's counsel, also require the preparation of designs on paper and several stages of planning and execution (2017:134).

Practitioners of Afrolatinx religions use similar kinds of artistry to make and keep spirit dolls. The spirit dolls' relationship with their caretakers is reciprocal: they protect the living, and we give them sustenance in return. Common offerings include rum, tobacco, coffee, flowers, and candles. They illustrate how conjure is a pedagogy that teaches through touch, intuition, and patience. Both Landes and I have dolls that were made with and for deities and their dead (see figures 1.10 and 1.11). Her doll was made by Candomblé priestesses in Bahía in 1939; I made mine in 2013. Both dolls connect to forces in the past and conjure future remembering through materially sewn paths. Each doll is significantly dedicated to an avatar of the deity of the cross-roads, Exú in her case and Elegua in mine. Thus they stand at the metaphysical intersections of the living and the dead, of leaving and arriving. They each in their unique way provide lasting residual transcripts that serve as three-dimensional road maps to and material and spiritual journeying.

FIGURE 1.10 Landes's Exú Bahiana doll. Photo by author. The Landes Collection E435081, Courtesy of the Anthropology Department, Smithsonian National Museum of Natural History.

FIGURE I.II Elegua doll. Photo by author. Author's private collection.

Landes's doll is one of a set of four Candomblé dolls that she kept throughout her life. She noted that they were "hand-made for me by cult 'daughters' in Bahia de todo os Santos, on the *terreiro* of the cult."[59] It is significant that the dolls were made by Candomblé worshippers on-site at their temple, because this indicates a high level of dedication and skill in creating these powerful objects of conjure. I examined and touched the dolls upon a visit to the archives at the Smithsonian Museum of Natural History in 2019.[60] Dressed like *iyaloja*, market women of Bahia, each is dedicated to an orixa, wearing their corresponding devotional beaded ileke and *ide* (bracelet). There are two dolls for Exú, one for Xango, and one for Yemanjá in the collection. These little ancestors are dressed in stylish Bahian cloth, with tin earrings, high-heeled shoes, and beautifully embroidered red lips. I keenly observed the care with which these elegant companions to Landes's life journey were ritually prepared.

They clearly resembled the Bahian market women Landes drew repeatedly, as residual transcripts, on scrap paper in her notes. One sketched in pencil has scrawled as a signature, "drawn by R. Landes a Bahiana" (emphasis in original).[61]

These Candomblé dolls make manifest a sisterhood that sustains Landes's connections to Bahia at a situated place in time. Landes's archives of conjure point to a specific set of stories, practices, and knowledge belonging to orixa-worshipping women of late 1930s Bahia. She participated fully in the feminine ritual work of cooking with, sewing for, and being healed by Sabina, Zeze, Mãe Menininha, Eulalia, and Oxúm.[62] The priestesses recognized her as spiritual kin with Sabina and the others, exclaiming at a gathering in 1939, "It is so clear! R[uth] L[andes] is an Oxúm! It is so [totally] clear! "[63] And, Landes herself recalls at a 1939 December celebration for Oxala,[64] "Yes, you know when a *santo* comes, for it is a kind of swooning feeling, you feel you can't find the earth under you, and you grab around for support, and can't find it."[65] These testimonies show that this sisterhood did the embodied work of speaking truths, making art, and becoming gods. They did so in the context of racial, political, and social strife, with Landes repeatedly commenting on police presence, interference, and repression at the *terreiros* in 1939.[66]

It is important then to view the residual transcripts of Landes's field notes alongside her spirit dolls because they provide a women's archive of conjure with stories of the dead that is also a palimpsest. This archive offers a layered temporal and ontological repositioning of subjects through continual revisiting. Landes joins the other egun, which include her dolls, as an ancestor in this repository. It is no surprise that the dolls for Exú are women of Candomblé. Exú is the owner of the crossroads between life and death whose female spirit form in Brazil is Pomba Gira. Pomba Gira is a female *exú* known for helping women in abusive relationships, prostitutes as well as trans women.[67] This correlation situates Landes's and the dolls' journey within a framework of allure, pain, and rebellion that belongs to a larger collective of womanist and LGBTQ+ ritual practices in Brazil.

Elegua, a cousin of the Brazilian exú, also touched my understanding of ritual and fieldwork in the form of a spirit doll. In 2013, a few months before my mother died, I was asked by an ancestor at a misa in Havana to make clothes for and dedicate a doll to an Elegua spirit guide. When I received my piece of paper to take away with me from the ceremony, I saw that the instructions for completing the work were pretty vague. I got back to Louisiana from Cuba still very much distressed by my mother's long, ongoing battle with cancer. As a way to cope, I put my mind to the task of sewing the doll's clothes by hand. Luckily, I had originally learned to sew from my Cuban grandmother, who was a consummate dressmaker and knitter. The vision I had for creating the outfit followed the aesthetics of Elegua's usual attire: a black and red shirt and knee-length pants, a hat, and a black and red beaded necklace. I also wanted to add cowrie shells and trimming in order to create a personalized visual reminder of the process. I took my pattern, doll, cloth, beads, and shells with me to Miami, where I was to spend the summer doing research. My mother was in California, and I spent most of the weeks before her somewhat sudden passing sewing and writing. In more ways than I knew at the time, the making of attire for the spirit of the crossroads that inhabited the doll, Elegua, prepared me for the rite of passage of mourning the loss of my mother. I still have the scrap of paper ordering me to make the doll. For me, it reminds me of a road map of a long, arduous journey. One made with thread, beads, and red and black satin.

This personal recollection leads me back to the connections between the Cuban misas I experienced and Landes's Brazilian fieldwork. Both journeys are sketched on papers and stitched on dolls in mobile archives of conjure.[68] This portability is experienced as both material culture to be touched and reimagined narratives to be enacted.[69] The misa's transcripts inspire future works of connectivity to an ephemeral yet sensory realm through creative works. Likewise, the artifacts left behind by Landes inspires ways of reconnecting to the potentiality of unfinished life stories through the residual arc of spiritual academic work inspired by Oxúm and the dead. The ritual work and residual transcripts explored here also reveal currents and countercurrents that rely on an unapologetic understanding of women's sexuality as a source of spiritual strength and knowledge.

While merely scraps of paper and pieces of thread, residual transcripts are rife with notations that mark and embark upon many kinds of magical temporalities.[70] Commemoration happens in a layered experience of loss and recovery where ancestors and gods come alive in community performances. By means of scribbled notes, beaded necklaces, and dolls of the dead, the devotees of Afrolatinx religions and their spirits are made through each other. Spiritual creativity and devotional art illustrate the value of reordering and reconceptualizing temporality in life, the archive, and ethnography. Focusing on vernacular points in the process, like transcripts and designs for work to be done, demystifies an overly exotified and often misunderstood set of practices that make up spiritual artisanship. Intimate religious artistry, however defined, is woven into the lives of practitioners of Afrolatinx religions in ways that create opportunities for the reconstruction of unfinished stories that in themselves evoke future retelling and remaking. The next chapter of this book explores this process of reinvention in light of theories of transculturation and transmigration.

2

CROSSINGS

Yo no soy Espiritista.

—Fernando Ortiz, *La filosofía penal de los espiritistas*

D on Fernando Ortiz's disavowal and fascination with Espiritismo is a fruitful place to start considering the interchange that exists between cultural theory and enacted religious practice. As discussed in the introduction and chapter 1, Espiritismo is an Afrolatinx vernacular religion operating in international spiritual networks that have left residual transcriptions in the archives of conjure for over a century. This chapter on contemporary Cuban séances, misas espirituales, links affect theory to interoral performative moments in Espiritismo by revisiting and revising Ortiz's idea of transculturation in light of his own attenuation to nineteenth-century spiritist doctrine.[1] I use the term *interorality* to describe how in misas, participants interact, collaborate, and quote each other to construct narratives of interconnectivity with the spirit plane. Importantly, Édouard Glissant's idea of Caribbean cross-cultural poetics can help us think through the nonuniversalist aesthetic of the oral performances expressed at the misa

(1992:97–100, 105–8). The cultural work of contemporary *espiritistas* (spirit mediums) also retools positivist notions found in Ortiz's and Kardec's writings on Espiritismo by circumventing linear ideas of spirit progression through the affective, side-by-side linking of ethnic and racial difference. Ironically, it is the practice of transculturation at misas that disrupt some of the modernist tendencies that have gone into the theorization and characterization of Espiritismo by Allan Kardec and Fernando Ortiz.

Allan Kardec penned *Le livre des Esprits* (1857) in the context of the nineteenth-century fascination with spirits generated by North American and British spiritualism.[2] The text became a nineteenth- and early twentieth-century sensation in Brazil, Cuba, and Puerto Rico.[3] The book codifies the beliefs and practices of spiritism, a religious movement that centers on mediums' communication with the spirits of the departed. Like other nineteenth-century spiritual workers, Kardec was interested in reasoning with skeptics, especially with pure "materialists," by making a scientific case out of the observations and principles expressed by the spirits in the book (Kardec 2011 [1857]:42–48; Walker 2013; Braude 1989; Tromp 2003; Chapin 2004). Kardec organized the text dialogically as question-and-answer segments between anonymous mediums and spirits (Kardec 2011 [1857]:68). The mediums' questions number up to 1,196, and the spirits' responses are recorded as direct quotations in the book. The inclusion of spirits' voices as reported speech in the text mirrors the interoral nature of spirit voices emerging in the performance of Cuban misas.

There are several concepts found in the book that are central to Espiritismo's theory and practice. One tenet that fascinated Ortiz is the assertion that souls move, cross over time and space, in a progressive fashion toward moral perfection in a process called transmigration.[4] Through transmigration, spirits do good works in the multiple worlds that exist connected and parallel to our own in order to achieve a better spiritual status. Repeatedly, spirits' responses reveal that transmigrating in the afterlife entails labor envisioned as missions: "[Spirits] cooperate in the harmony of the universe, they carry out God's design, they are [his] ministers. Spiritual life is an uninterrupted occupation, but [the work] is not burdensome as on earth, because in that one [the spirit world] there does not exist bodily exhaustion nor the agony of necessity (Kardec 2011 [1857]:331)."[5] In this quote, the afterlife is described by a spirit as a productive place where spiritual labor becomes an organizing factor. Spirits operate in a manner that is labeled progressive, imitating the social and cultural changes taking place in the nineteenth and early twentieth centuries that also influenced spiritualism, like abolition and women's suffrage (Braude 1989; Espírito Santo 205:44). Kardec's emphasis on transmigration as a socially and spiritually progressive development intrigues Ortiz and influences his formulation of transculturation.[6]

Another important element illustrated by *Le livre des Esprits* is the pliability of the soul and its ability to change and manifest itself in new ways (22). This chameleonlike quality is enhanced by the context in which transmigration occurs: inextricably interconnected material and spiritual worlds. For example, one spirit in *Le livre* asserts that "all of the worlds exist in solidarity: what is not completed in one is completed in the other" (159). Spiritism thus is action oriented, it sees the continual process of work, rather than sin and grace, as a unifying cosmological principle.[7] The role and work of mediums, then, is to find the continuities and breaks between interconnected spheres of existence as conduits of messages that are communicated through vision, energy, and sensation (19, 24–27).[8] In the contemporary Cuban séances I will discuss in this chapter, espiritistas do this affective work of linking worlds by communicating with likewise pliable spirits, while also emphasizing spiritism's founding principles of movement and labor. For Cuban mediums, the Cuban Revolution's own emphasis on labor as a strategy toward human perfection, especially seen in the image of *el hombre nuevo* (the new man), creates an important intersecting element to how *trabajo* (work) is theorized and practiced by espiritistas more broadly.

Transculturation is Ortiz's view of cultural admixture, which allows for the flow of influences back and forth between groups that create openings for new creolized cultures to emerge. As he puts it, transculturation expresses

> los variadísimos fenómenos que se originan en Cuba por las complejísimas transmutaciones de culturas que aquí verifican, sin conocer las cuales es imposible entender la evolución del pueblo cubano, así en lo económico, como en lo institucional, jurídico, ético, religioso, artístico, lingüístico, psicológico, sexual, y en los demás aspectos de su vida. La verdadera historia de Cuba es la histories de sus intrincadísimas transculturaciones.
>
> (1963 [1940]:99)

> the highly varied phenomena that have come about in Cuba as a result of the extremely complex transmutations of culture that have taken place here, and without a knowledge of which it is impossible to understand the evolution of the Cuban folk, either in economic or the institutional, legal, ethical, religious, artistic, linguistic, psychological, sexual, or other aspects of its life. The real history of Cuba is the history of its intermeshed transculturations.[9]

Here Ortiz sees cultural borrowing as a complex, relational, and ongoing process; one that has deep and varied effects on multiple facets of Cuban culture and quotidian life. Transculturation moves away from the idea of cultural synthesis, which terms like *acculturation* and *assimilation* suggest, and instead maintains aspects of cultural difference and conflict as cultures engage each other in order to reveal, in Cuba's case, a colonial historicity (1963 [1940]:98–99). This articulation of transculturation is influenced in part by Ortiz's earlier consideration of spiritist doctrine.[10]

As noted, Kardec's exploration of spiritual transmigration in *Le livre des Esprits* captivated Ortiz. One aspect that intrigued Ortiz was how spirits could move between metaphysical and cultural locations in their search for progress in building new, better worlds. Ortiz comments on the nature of these worlds and the movement of the spirit:

La vida del espíritu presupone, pues, una serie de *avatares* en uno o en varios mundos, según el estado de progreso de estos mismos, a cuyas transmigraciones el espíritu aporta su personalidad eterna vaciándola en una forma tangible y material.

(2012 [1924]:15, EMPHASIS IN ORIGINAL)

The life of a spirit presupposes, then, a series of *avatars* in one or several worlds, depending on the status of the progress of the very [spirits], to whose transmigrations the spirit transports their eternal personality, depositing it in a tangible and material manner.

Ortiz comments on the multiplicity of spiritual forms, *avatares*, and locations, *varios mundos*, implicated in the transmigration of spirits from one plane to another in the philosophy of Espiritismo. In Ortiz's formulation of transculturation, we see that encountering Kardec's idea of multiple worlds and spiritual forms, and their potential for mobility through transmigration, shapes his later emphasis on the various ways cultural admixtures can be communicated and encountered.[11] In particular, that transculturation occurs simultaneously in different registers of Cuban culture resonates with how spirits can simultaneously move through different planes (mundos). This emphasis on cultural and spiritual multiplicity and movement illustrates an attention to processes rather than artifacts or form. But whereas Ortiz and Kardec see Espiritismo's spiritual movements through a universal evolutionary trajectory, contemporary mediums transculturate spirits in performances that reveal a more rhizomatic and distinctly Caribbean terrain.[12]

In their writings, Kardec and Ortiz conceive of notions of spiritual, racial, and cultural movement and confluence in religious practice. Their work expresses an evolutionary thrust in thinking about spiritual and racially ascribed cultural movement. For example, consider the following statement by Ortiz regarding the logic of Espiritismo: "Pero el espiritismo se distingue de otros credos religiosos porque viene a ser una *teoría evolucionista del alma*" (But Espiritismo distinguishes itself from other religions because it becomes an *evolutionist theory of the soul*) (2012 [1924]:14, emphasis in original). In Ortiz's estimation, the evolutionary movement that Espiritismo ascribes to the soul also becomes progressive in its nature, developing on earlier forms toward specific ends of enlightenment.

Ortiz's admiration for Kardec's progressive, evolutionary ideas about the development of spirits is rooted in a modernist interpretation of the religious doctrine (Román 2007a:223). In Ortiz's estimation, Espiritismo is able to theorize movement on "dos escalas paralelas evolucionistas, el material y la espiritual" (two parallel evolutionary scales, the material and the spiritual) (2012 [1924]:14). Thus his understanding of Espiritismo's spiritual order in relation to the material world reinforces, yet also stretches, the limits of Cartesian thinking on materiality. The evolutionary parallelism that so excites Ortiz also creates a space where multiple movements are mirroring, perhaps even engaging each other. The layering of registers that Ortiz articulates for Kardec's spiritual transmigration reflects the range of cultural registers that inform the idea of transculturation in Ortiz's original definition. In both cases, transmigration and transculturation are articulated as processes where mobility creates new localities (Appadurai 1996:180, 182, 189, 191). Cuban historical contexts of cultural friction shape how past subjects *do* race, ethnicity, gender and labor through lateral spiritual journeying. In the course of this chapter, I will demonstrate how the localities in the performance of misa espirituales are actually created through a transcultural process that is relational and based on the spiritual community's structures of feeling (Williams 1978:133; Muñoz 2000:71).[13]

Performance studies scholar Alicia Arrizón recontextualizes Ortiz's concept of transculturation within colonial discourses of race, sexuality, and gender (2006:92). She challenges the polarities of race created by the Cuban colonial project in her exploration of the *mulata* figure in Cuba in drink recipes, songs, and poetry. This interdisciplinary work provides an important Latinx formulation for the ways in which Ortiz's concept transculturation is vexed but useful. His emphasis on friction and the multiplicity of *intrincadísimas transculturaciones* point to the centrality of in-between identities in mitigating colonial encounters. I find that Arrizón's *mestiza* approach syncs up with that of Cuban espiritistas' ritual praxis. Both remix Ortiz's idea of transculturation to confuse and reorder linear, binary colonial models of race, gender, time, and cultural "progress." In contrasting how related strands of cultural thinking on race and movement happen in different enacted contexts, we see a rearticulation of both Ortiz and Kardec by practitioners of Espiritismo that also challenges the modernist and positivist strands found in writings on the doctrine. Thus Cuban espiritistas do the important critical work of relocating race and ethnicity onto the ethnohistorical theater of the misa. These performances repurpose the ideas of transmigration and transculturation by configuring especially Afrolatinx ethnicity as portable and relational.

In a related fashion, Todd Ramón Ochoa has commented on the significant role that espiritistas play in Afro-Cuban religious culture in terms of "re-remembering" colonial experience as

FIGURE 2.1 José at a misa, Havana, Cuba, May 2013. Photo by Héctor Delgado. Author's private collection.

performances that are temporally heightened and politicized (2010a:49–50). The expression of gender, race, religion, and sexuality in misas reveal a mutual exploration of embodiment by spirits and their mediums that profoundly marks the construction of the self (Espírito Santo 2015). This coproduction happens as espiritistas perform and play with oral tradition (see also Wirtz 2014b:128, 134, 152). During misas, practitioners reinvent and quote in an intertextual fashion several genres of oral traditions including proverbs, personal experience narratives, legends, jokes, storytelling, divination, prayers, ceremonial opening/closing formulas, and song.[14] Spirits and mediums comment orally upon a colonial historical imagination through embodied expressions of becoming and seeing. The merging of bodies, consciousness, and sight occurs through the transmigration of spirits that have particular histories onto the misa. The interoral poetics at the misas reveal a vernacular Caribbean creole

FIGURE 2.2 Tomasa and Mercedes at a misa, Havana, Cuba, May 2013. Photo by Héctor Delgado. Author's private collection, used by permission.

aesthetic that mystifies official, universalist renderings of history in favor of the diversity of perspectives growing out of the fluidity of oral discourses and vernacular beliefs.[15]

CROSSING SPIRITS, MARKING FLESH

Padre nuestro, que estas en el cielo, santificado sea tu nombre. We begin with "The Lord's Prayer" and move onto songs and visitations by spirits in a crescendo of embodied experiences. Hairs stand on end, voices are whispered into ears, visions like a movie in fast-frame emerge. I am in Havana participating in misas with my maternal relatives and neighbors, who are also spirit mediums.[16] Tomasa, Mercedes, José, Soñia, and Maximina all graciously offer their expertise of over forty years of practicing Espiritismo *cruzado* in our afternoon and evening sessions.[17] We perform our *actividades* at Tomasa's residence, which is located on the outskirts of Havana in the neighborhood of Mantilla. We use a copy of the missal "Doctrina Espiritista: Colección de Oraciones Escogidas," attributed to Allan Kardec, to pray. We rely on memory and experience to sing the songs the spirits like: "Sea el Santísimo" and "Clavelitos." Sounds of blaring car horns and motorcycles from the Calzada Managua merge with our voices.

Shortly after we call upon them, spirits begin to appear: a departed grandmother,[18] Afro-Cuban *palera/os*, a Spanish *gitana* (gypsy), a *monja* (nun), a Native American, a spirit guide associated with the oricha Elegua, and a spirit guide associated with both the Catholic saint San Lázaro and the Lucumí oricha Babalu Aiye. The senior mediums engage in code-switching and cross-referencing between different languages, religious traditions, nationalities, and ethnicities while describing the spirit guides they see, feel, hear, and embody at the misas, which last approximately two hours in length.[19] Some of the spirits describe themselves as having multiethnic sources of spiritual power, for example, having both Yoruba and Congo ritual implements in the spirit world to help the living.[20]

The many spiritual voices expressed and heard at misas illustrate a performance of spiritual creolization that especially requires a tuned emotive sensibility. The Cuban and Cuban diasporic act of "listening in detail" relies on an aesthetics of affect that also hears the dead's voices (as music/songs/stories) as interoral palimpsests.[21] Afro-Cuban religions are in this manner sonically intersectional as multilayered beings are produced in rituals through sounds embedded in varying social registers and hierarchies of power.[22] Hearing how micro-performances of race, gender, and ethnicity emerge in the misa, through story and song, disturbs the experience of linear temporalities. The surround sound of contemporary Cuban noise from the street mingles with the spirits' incarnation in a way that disturbs notions of who gets to *be* heard, where, and when. What "histories" are (re)orated by such disturbances? Do the collection of discordant sounds point to a kind of temporal transculturation?

Ortiz is likewise deeply interested in how Espiritismo reveals "las discontinuidades de espacio y tiempo en la sociedad cubana" (the discontinuities of space and time in Cuban society) (Díaz-Quiñonez 1999:16). Such temporal and spatial ruptures exist in the misa as ontological moments whereby spirits co-become with a community to speak with the language of discontinuity.[23] The worlds (mundos) that Ortiz remarks upon for Kardec's spiritual journeys are then rerouted onto the misa. This temporal and spatial labyrinth performs the rifts in the supposed continuity of history as well as

emphasizing the inability to access the past. Ritual performances in a misa, then, layer representations of memory and
history onto each other, not unlike other Cuban cultural palimpsests (Quiroga 2005:21–23). However, these palimpsests are
intensely ephemeral, phenomenological, and often resist the
nostalgic memorialization of national culture found in many
other kinds of Cuban cultural performance. This is because the
voices in a misa cannot easily be homogenized, the result of visiting spirits' thrillingly spontaneous and heterogeneous cultural
discordance.

As an example of a kind of spiritual palimpsest, I would like
to highlight a moment of performative becoming for a gitana
(gypsy) spirit that visited one of the misas I participated in. Soñia
and José created the following presentation of a spirit whose
amalgamation of Afrolatinx characteristics spanned races, continents, religions, and ethnicities:

> Soñia: Ahora yo veo, desde el momento que cantamos "Los
> Clavelitos" una tendencia de gitana. Gitana, con una saya rosada
> llena de óvalos. De muchos colores. Con unas argollas grandes.
> Ella no toca castañuelas, ella no tiene castañuelas. Pero la veo
> rodando te. Con esa saya de dos vuelos y óvalos. . . . Esa gitana
> tiene tendencia de Oya, de Centella.

> Now I see, after we just sang "Los Clavelitos,"[24] a gypsy ten
> dency [a spirit with a Spanish gypsy countenance]. A gypsy,
> with a pink polka-dotted skirt. Of many colors. With large
> hoop earrings. She does not play the castanets, she does not
> have castanets. But, I see her circling you. With that full, ruf
> fled polka-dotted skirt. That gypsy has her own tendency [to
> work spiritually] with Oya, with Centella.[25]

José then interrupts, adding:

> Y donde ese espíritu que lo ves tan alegre, yo lo veo, a su vez,
> como si tenía un desdoble. Como un espíritu de una monja. . . .
> Esa espíritu la gitana como hace un redoble con un espíritu que
> es una monja. Una monja que yo la recibo vestida de carmelita,
> con la capa blanca. Como si hubiera sido una monja misionera.
> Una de Las Hermanitas de la Caridad—dedicada a ayudar enfer-
> mos, hacer obras.

> And whereby that spirit that you see as joyous, I see, as well, as
> if she had a double. Like a nun's spirit. . . . That gypsy spirit has
> a spirit double that is a nun. A nun I am receiving as wearing
> brown with a white hood. As if she were a missionary nun. One
> of the Sisters of Charity—dedicated to helping the sick, doing
> good works.[26]

The gitana spirit guide is described in both the past and present
tenses—uniting the narrative reconstruction of her living days
with the phenomenological moment of the misa. Elizabeth
Pérez sees participants in a misa as "living *bóvedas*" (spirit tables)
reflecting the idea that the self is a "dividual" rather than a "uni-
tary" being for participants (2011:355–56).[27] I would move these
suggestions further and say that the self in Espiritismo is con-
ceived as always becoming in multiple ways and attached to
diverse dimensions of seen and unseen worlds in moments that
challenge the present in layered associations. The tensions and
unresolved representations of race, ethnicity, religious difference, sexuality, and gender in the misa direct us toward contemporary issues in Cuban society that also require special attention. Like the analysis of moments of queer Latinx "utopian

performatives," the misa's moments of spiritual unity are fraught with racial, ethnic, sexual, and class-based tensions that underlie the very idea of *cubanidad* (Rivera-Servera 2012:193–203).[28] These tensions can be extended to reflect performances where a diasporic *afrolatinidad* specifically emerges from fissures created by cultural convergence. Thus the liminal space of the misa and its potential for transformation reveal some of the social and cultural sites whereby larger Latin American and African diasporas meet and negotiate cultural communion and contestation at Afrolatinx's religious crossroads and borderlands.

A brief exploration of the gitana's accompanying spiritual associations is helpful to consider here. First, I would like to discuss how the Spanish gitana, the Yoruba deity Oya, the Congo spirit Centella, and the Catholic monja are sensed as a shifting amalgam at the misa. This kind of layering is relational, associative, and reflects a complex menagerie of spiritual entities that also corresponds to different geographical and religious valences that perform spiritual *trabajo*. The different spirit guides can be experienced through and with each other in the performative moment of becoming in the misa. Their subsequent appearances and associative framing at the misa illustrate a moment of Afrolatinx transculturation that specifically comments on tense borrowings between the distinct religious and cultural traditions based on Cuba's colonial past. The flow of associations and doublings also creates a spiritual palimpsest that reflects cultural and political attitudes toward the past particular to said Cuban colonial contexts.[29]

The Spanish gitana, rather than "whitening" the performance of Afrolatinx spirituality, actually presents a different manifestation of afrolatinidad whose site is rooted in the Black Atlantic in several ways (Gilroy 1993:25–32; Linebaugh and Rediker 2001). Gitanos, a Mediterranean population related to the Rom, are a nomadic and persecuted group in Europe who are racially coded as dark-skinned and culturally tropicalized in specific ways to suggest their alterity (Aparicio and Chávez-Silverman 1997:10–13; Silverman 2012:48, 243–44, 260). As R. L. Román uncovers, while looking at espiritistas in Cuba's Republican era (1901): "Not only do African orishas masquerade as Catholic saints, . . . but seemingly European spirits also 'camouflage' their hybridity in a variety of guises" (2007a:235).[30] I would argue that the gitana's position in Espiritismo's spiritual universe represents this kind of slippage in terms of being a racial, religious, and culturally hybrid figure in the misa.[31]

The addition of the Yoruba deity Oya and the Congo-inspired entity Centella represents an intraethnic and cross-referenced Africanization of the gitana spirit guide. Both Oya and Centella are already linked to each other in various forms of symbolism and combined ritual practices in the religions of Palo and Santería that illustrate a deep history of mixing in Cuban vernacular religious performance.[32] These creolized Afro-Atlantic crossings and additions to the gitana's spiritual universe represent a kind of afrolatinidad that carries with it a density of potential spiritual work that can be done with the gitana through these associations. In other words, references to future performances of misas and trabajos based on these spiritual palimpsests are embedded in the descriptions of the figures, especially in the emphasis of their spiritual *poderes* (powers).[33] Here Cuban spirit mediums are temporally extending and culturally creolizing Kardec's initial configuration of spirits' work in the afterlife through their ritually stylized performances. The interoral nature of how José and Soñia build upon each other's sensations of these powers create an ephemeral tapestry that invokes how interrupted listening and remembering create an important component of Caribbean poetics (Glissant 1992:104–7,

124–27, 229, 237; Vazquez 2013:5–12, 19). Thus the cyclical, poly-phonic, and polyvocal rhythms of the misa mirror other orally inspired genres of Caribbean narration in fiction, poetry, the-ory, film, song, and historiography that emphasize postcolonial concerns like race, gender, and sexuality.[34]

José's addition of the companion monja spirit to the gitana further marks the religious efficacy of the associated spiritual guides. The monja represents a figure of empathy and of healing that also is connected to a specific Catholic religious order, the Sisters of Charity. Her appearance creates a *redoble* (double), as José puts it, to the gitana in terms of signaling another kind of nomadic aesthetic, albeit in this case one that operates within Catholic representations of sanctity and sacrifice. I also see the monja as a celibate sexual subject that adds to and interrupts the sultry, exotic depictions of la gitana's imagery.[35] The gitana's sex-uality is embedded in a symbolic order of desire by her mixed racial position, much like the mulata figure in Cuban transcul-turation (Arrizón 2006:88–89).

A majority of the dead that conjoin with mediums in the misa clearly emerge out of the performance of the legacy of slavery and race in Cuba. Guides like Ta José, Mica Ela, and Francisca appear out of the context of a remembered and spiritually per-formed slave past that is also marked by specifically Congo and Yoruba religious references.[36] Yet I would argue that these spirit guides manifest as Afro-Cuban Congo and Yoruba religious workers, culturally creolized and ambiguous in their associa-tions to both an African and Cuban past. The process of trans-culturation especially touches Afro-Cuban spirit guides as they appear with their companions of multiple religious, racial, and ethnic origins. The mobility of transmigration is impli-cated in their emergence at the misa, however their ethnic and racial conglomerations complicate the routes of the spirit world as theorized by Ortiz and Kardec.

The redoble spirits in a misa create dense cultural and religious textures that touch the mediums through the senses.[37] There are several definitions of the word *redoble* in Spanish—to reinforce, intensify, redouble. These multiple meanings come into play while looking at the multiple ways spirit guides stand next to each other in Espiritismo. None of them are completely merged into one image, but, rather, they act as separate yet connected forces revealing themselves to the material world in different acts that are felt, especially in the body.[38] As José clarifies, in one instance,

> Y no te equivoques. [Diciendo te que] <<tengo que ir al médico porque tengo problemas en los huesos.>> Y, no [señala que no con el dedo]. Ya sabes que es la propia acción del espíritu que es un protector tuyo. Muy fuerte. Que a la vez es *nganguluero* [y] me hace un redoble con un indio.

> And don't make a mistake [Saying to yourself], "I have to go to the doctor because I have problems in my bones." And, no [waving no with his finger]. You already know that it is the very act of the spirit that is your protector. [He is] very strong. He is at the same time a *nganguluero* [and] appears to me as a redoble with an Indian [spirit].

Here, José is specifically referring to how the medium in question suffers from pains in her feet, and it is the spirit and his redoble that are communicating with her through that very cramping.[39] He also reconfirms that certain symptoms of ailments in the body may also have spiritual rather than material causes and that multiple interpretations of that feeling of pain should be explored. In this manner, then, communication through embodiment does not solely occur through spirit possession of the head per se. It can also be focused on different parts of the body that may hold specific meanings and intimate connections infused with cultural and historical significance.

For the protector spirit who is identified by his ritual work with Palo traditions in Cuba, the movement side by side with a Native American companion relates to historical tropes of spiritual work in nature and parallel colonialisms in the Americas. The foot as the site of their communication with the medium is connected to West African and Afro-Caribbean beliefs, which see the ancestors entering their horses through the left foot specifically, as the dead live inside of the earth.[40] The pain in the foot also insinuates a shared pain of enslavement, of the shackling of the foot being relived by the medium as a reminder of the spirit's past life as a Congo living in Cuba. Since the spirit himself is seen as a palero who works with a *nganga* (spirit cauldron), he also has his own dead he attends to and is affected by.

On considering the side-by-side aspects of redoble spirits, as well as the shared sensory experiences between mediums and their guides, Eve Kosofsky Sedgwick's concept of "parallel initiations" comes to mind. In *Touching Feeling*, she looks at the pedagogical implications of affect in Western interpretations of Buddhism. For her, the "parallel initiations" found in Tibetan Buddhist views of the reincarnated subject also promote the construction of a "transindividual" self, albeit through affective spiritual pedagogies (2003:8, 17, 21, 158–60). I would argue that José's revelation of the redoble spirits and their physical effects on the medium's body relate a similar logic of affect whereby the spirits are working side by side to touch a specific part of the medium's body to attune her to their shared existence through both *touching* and *feeling*.

The boundaries of the material and physical plane are constantly shifting in transindividual performances that extend beyond the misa and spill into the daily life of mediums. In terms of multiple incarnations of the dead, the nganguluero protector spirit has his own dead inhabiting and touching him from another realm. This multiplicity resembles the infinity of reemergence that Sedgwick reveals for her consideration of Tibetan monks' densely layered existence. Similarly, redoble and other spirit guides are constantly touching the mediums through temporal and phenomenological planes. In Espiritismo, spirit guides push for recognition of their side-by-side existence with and in the body of practitioners through sensory stimulation. The interoral aesthetics of the performance of cultural and historical interpretations of migration, colonialism, slavery, and disenfranchisement shape the very texture of that touch.[41] The sensory reminders that spirits inflict on their mediums in and out of the misa also offer a kind of pedagogy as to how to continue working and living with very specific notions of the past.

Spirits reflect a complex set of social relations in their emergence in misas and other Afro-Atlantic rituals of cohabitation with practitioners' bodies and consciousness.[42] The biographies and temporalities that accompany spirits in rituals implicate them in various kinds of religious, racial, and historical registers that complicate any neat notion of performative or cultural context. These registers fool with the ability of ontology, language, and history to recognize and/or a recover a stable social subject, especially in terms of the traditional anthropological project of producing cultural knowability.[43] Misas thus demonstrate a relational logic of mobility and presence that makes participants attuned to both the larger ritual experience (phenomenology) and the sensory nature of participating in that experience (affect). As Kardec and his nineteenth-century North American spiritualist counterparts also suggest, when thinking about communicating with spirits through bodies of mediums, the dichotomy emphasized between material effects and ephemeral affect becomes not so much false but misguided (Kardec 2011 [1857]:19, 24–27; Chapin 2004). Or perhaps, as the moments in the misa suggest, these seemingly opposed elements are actually co-penetrated in ways that traditional social science cannot grasp as part of its own very specific world-making project. It would seem that the cultural and spiritual work that Espiritismo does is promising specifically because it generates an affective methodology for traveling certain routes between the material and the ephemeral.

This interplay between experience and feeling in misas creates productive frictions similarly found in other Latinx and Latin American performances where the elasticity of ethnicity and race are negotiated (Dávila 2012; Broyles-González 2002).[44] The spiritualities that emerge in the performance of misas are marked by their Afrolatinx textures. Latinx performatives express, according to Ramón Rivera-Servera, "moments where the aesthetic event becomes, temporarily, a felt materiality that instantiates the imaginable into the possible" (2012:35). Misas create new worlds and potentialities that combine the material and ephemeral products of Latinx performatives. For example, the emergence of the redoble Ngaguluero/Indio spirits in ritual creates a moment where the "imaginable" not only becomes possible but is speaking and being felt directly. In other words, misas not only allow for a temporary materiality, literally for some attendant spirits, but also allow for a supple and shared materiality in mediums' experiences of bodies, consciousness, and time. Thus, Afrolatinx spiritual performatives redefine the nature of possibility in terms of what constitutes peformative efficacy as well as which experiential plane is affected by a performed ritual activity.

At the heart of this spiritual work is the challenge to see the potential for community building in fleeting moments that are also reflective of racial, social, and cultural contestations. Espiritismo seeks to heal, but also confront, communities of affect through performances of rituals that do not homogenize, but rather expose conflictive pairings. The performance of multiple kinds of blackness and indigeneity in the examples given earlier are embodied through translocating ethnicity, place, and religious registers. Both the mediums and the spirit guides at the misa complicate static racial and religious positions by performing a kind of transculturation that purposely crosses multiple boundaries. Misas are sites where the spiritual and social routes of different registers of race and ethnicity emerge, combine, and clash.

The interoral and hybrid aspects of performances that create these spiritual "borderlands" are central to how mediums construct their narratives and interpret the sensations they are experiencing.[45] Interorality also encourages linguistic spontaneity and experimentation at the misas as mediums codeswitch from speaking in Spanish to Lucumí, to Kikongo, and in dialect. Bodily enactment of postures and facial expressions also include afflictions and particular physical attributes of spirit guides.[46] It is important to think through how mediums perform this polyvocality *with* the spirits. The shared expressions of embodied cultural and religious terrains illustrate performative emergence and aesthetic creativity (Bauman and Briggs 1990; Wirtz 2014a; 2007). Thus we can historicize the creative flow of visions, feelings, perceptions, and embodiments, in Glissant's terms, as "an imposition of lived rhythms" (1992:109). These lived rhythms are deeply connected to Cuban patterns of orality, move to a polyphonic beat that may at any time also include aspects of transculturated African, European,

Asian, Semitic, Rom, Amerindian, Caribbean, and Latin American punctuations. The vernacular aesthetics of the misa, then, necessarily express a desire for the variegated because of the fluid, spontaneous, and ever-transformative nature of spiritual and material co-manifestation. Practitioners' preference for this kind of a nonlinear ritual approach also resists the kinds of transcendence implied in Ortiz's progressive characterization of Espiritismo.[47]

Ritual performances like the misa also tap into a Caribbean poetics that resist universalizing. The emphasis on presence, on an orality that expresses supramaterial relationships, creates a tapestry of voices that cannot be neatly codified in historical or anthropological terms. Here the vernacular aesthetics of the oral perpetually emerges in spite of "official" dismissals or silencing in the archive or ethnographic record. As Glissant declares, incredibly, in *Le discours antillais*:

> Mais un autre passage a lieu aujourd'hui, contre lequel nous ne pouvons rien. C'est le passage de l'écrit à l'oral. Je ne serai pas loin de croire que l'écrit est la trace universalisante du Même, là où l'oral serait le geste organisé du Divers. Il y a aujourd'hui comme une revanche de tant de sociétés orales qui, de fait même de leur oralité, c'est-à-dire de leur non-inscription dans le champ de la transcendance, ont subi sans pouvoir se defender l'assaut du Même. Aujourd'hui l'oral peut se préserver ou se transmettre, et même de peuple a peuple.
>
> (1997 [1981]:330–31)

But another transition is taking place today, against which we can do nothing. The transition from the written to the oral. I am not far from believing that the written is the universalizing influence of Sameness, whereas the oral would be an organized manifestation of Diversity. Today we see the revenge of so many oral societies, who—because of their very orality—that is, their not being inscribed in the realm of transcendence—have suffered the assault of Sameness without being able to defend themselves. Today the oral can be transmitted and preserved from one people to another.[48]

This passage presents us with a subversive temporal ordering of how history and culture is communicated. Glissant's association of futurity with the oral anticipates much work on imagined communities, ethnoscapes, and virtual ethnography (Anderson 1983; Appadurai 1996; Lau 2010). His emphasis on orality invites us to explore associations blossoming outside a single material location or historically universalizing notion of community. In particular, his focus on an "organized manifestation of Diversity" (*là où l'oral serait le geste organisé du Divers*) undoes the work of representing oral cultures as scattered, unorganized, outside of time, especially with regard to the Hegelian exclusion of Africa in transcendental history.[49] It is clear that Glissant includes colonial reinterpretations of Caribbean cultures in thinking through the "revenge" of the oral by invoking the sound of specificity of voice. The emergence of the indio and nganguluero spirits in the misa likewise suggests an atemporal and inappropriate rupture. Here two subjects travel together who do and do not "belong" to the present moment of the misa historically and culturally.[50] Their push into the misa reveals a shared imaginary of subjugated colonial subjects doing the rebellious work Glissant is suggesting here. The rebellion is one against a universal ordering of the past: where it belongs in terms of experience as well as how we recognize, hear, and name it. These moments archive conjure and conjure archives. Further, the shared mobility of racially and ethnically diverse spirits resembles the organized diversity Glissant attaches to an aesthetics of orality. In this manner, spiritual performatives in the misa draw on broader Caribbean poetic traditions of resistance geared specifically to derail neat categorizations of temporality, materiality, and location. Misas and other rituals reorder temporal and material relationships, revealing an ongoing tension between experience and representation pointed to by archives of conjure.[51] Yet the creation of transcendental history is not without its own mysterious performatives of the past, not without its own ritualized world-making behaviors. In a reflexive consideration of the work that transcendental historiography cannot do with Afro-Cuban ritual, Stephan Palmié considers whether to "historicize is to ritualize" (2014:238). Glissant also links the writing of universal history to an elite "esoteric and magical art" that archives "pseudo-information" (1997 [1981]:332, 1992:101). Surely toward different ends, yet similarly inclined in this regard, both Palmié and Glissant critique the flattening of cultural and aesthetic specificity that the conjuring of universal histories requires.[52] Thus the temporal logics that universalism naturalizes obscures nonlinear expressions of the past. Whether these are performances of ritual, story, or even material culture, moments of "temporal hybridization" reveal that there are a variety of subject positions on the chronological continuum (Palmié 2014:220).

As discussed earlier, redoble spirits express multiple layers of subjects and temporalities, which reveal connections to other global spiritualities, like Tibetan Buddhism, that rely on relational rather than linear notions of existence. These comparative considerations of temporality illustrate that historical transcendence is not so universal after all and that it takes quite a bit of belief in its magic to make the rebellious voices Glissant reminds us of disappear. Though the traditional Western archive may not or cannot contain these performances, due to its own epistemological framework, voices like that of the indio and ngaguluero nevertheless create unorthodox, ephemeral, and living repositories that are built upon repeatedly. These repositories signal that archives of conjure rely on ritual as an epistemological mode of world-making.

Ortiz's exploration of transmigration in Espiritismo invokes a universal transcendence that sees spiritual movement as an evolutionary development. When we compare this consideration of the movement of spirits to the enacted practices of contemporary espiritistas in Havana, we notice both continuities and departures. For both Ortiz and espiritistas, transculturation in Cuba is embroidered in a complex tapestry whereby ephemeral and experiential worlds, spiritual beings, and ritual temporality provide the texture.[53] For example, Ortiz seriously contemplated the ramifications of transmigration's material and temporal fluidity in regard to Cuban culture. He speaks directly toward the effects that living in an "inter-human," "inter-spirit," and "meta-terrestrial" society might suggest (84). Though he initially articulates cultural and spiritual movement according to linear logics, he later complicates this depiction of mobility, I would argue, because of the slippery relationship between temporality and culture. Ortiz effectively names Cuban spirits as important actors in perpetuating the cyclical nature of mobility and materiality in Cuban society.

Ortiz's description of the process of transculturation purposely challenges the top-heavy theories of acculturation popular to North American anthropology in the 1940s. Indeed, anthropology's own consideration of time relies heavily on marking presence, as the ethnographic present, in elusive ways that compare to historiography's ritualizing performatives of authority.[54] Localities and local subjects are produced and performed through dynamic and relational "rites of passage" (Appadurai 1996:179). Ortiz does this traditional anthropological work of constructing presence and location by also confounding the task at hand: transculturation scatters temporalities, directions, and forms of cultural exchange toward multiple social directions, registers, and sites. The theory can be applied broadly as a disorganizing principle. It does so specifically because it derives its sense of momentum from Ortiz's own attenuation of the dead's movements in Cuban ritual practice. Thus, behind transculturation's tense conglomeration of race, ethnicity, gender, and culture is an archive of conjure that Ortiz's writings on Espiritismo both reveal and occlude.

José Estaban Muñoz sees Ortiz's take on the Cuban satirical practice of *choteo* as instrumental to understanding cultural play as political commentary. Thinking through Ortiz's Yoruba etymology of the term, especially the creolized Lucumí term *cho*—to keep watch—Muñoz defines an optic with which to understand performances by Carmelita Tropicana usually characterized as camp.[55] Following Ortiz, Muñoz agrees that the aesthetics of Cuban ironic play is "imported from African culture as a mode of being, a style of performance, a practice of everyday life" (1999:135). This turn toward a performative Afro-Cuban understanding of choteo is significant. It firmly situates the power of queer representational dexterity and societal critique within the realm of Afrolatinx experiential knowledge and embodied practices. I propose that we understand spiritual actors like la gitana and el indio in a like fashion, as adept performers of a watchful choteo and disidentification at a misa. They, like Carmelita Tropicana, are larger-than-life commentators and cultural critics that use ritual embodiment, and the play that it affords, to frame the dynamics of Cuban cultural discordance and amalgamation. Here spirits, mediums, scholars, and performers all participate in undoing transculturation as a discernible cultural product. They reveal that transculturation is an incomplete process of cultural analysis that works as a challenge to singular subjectivities. This challenge is grappled with through social rituals of embodiment that are unapologetically fragmented and reflexive, like the misa.

Espiritistas are marking and performing multiple locations of religiosity, race, ethnicity, and temporality by revising transculturation at misas. Arjun Appadurai sees "locality as a structure of feeling" that creates vernacular sites and mobilities (Appadurai 1996:181). This invocation of Raymond Williams's work on affect urges us to consider how specific historical and cultural matrices inflect Cuban transculturation.[56] Some of the more painful structures of feeling found in Cuba's localities include colonialism, slavery, genocide, and indentured servitude. The creative and conflictive emergence of spirits at a misa perform these localities in new ways that extend their temporal resonance, that make the legacy of these structures of feeling pertinent in spiritually intimate ways. Embodied practices, feelings like pain, become archives of conjure here. These spiritual performatives are expansive localities as associations with beings leave Cuba and stretch across the globe. The side-by-side movement of figures like La Gitana, Oya, Centella, La Monja, el nganguluero, and El Indio from the spirit world to the ritual site of the misa relate affective bonds that undo linear conceptions of spiritual movement and manifestations. Moreover, the texture of the songs and narratives at a misa occur in polyglot oral formulations that are dense and confound notions of linguistic and cultural purity. Thus espiritistas take transculturation and complicate it further by highlighting the lasting supernatural ramifications of colonization, immigration, and creolization. The spirits' voices engage in this rebellious remembering through an interoral aesthetic that connects them to larger Afrolatinx, Caribbean and Latin American enacted histories (Glissant 1997 [1981], 1992:122–24; Taylor 2003:18, 21).

Similar performances in Latin American, Afrolatinx, and Caribbean contexts engage in repurposing transnational figures from a shared historical imagination in ways that disrupt and reorder colonial pasts.[57] The performance of the ritual of the misa employs a temporal and experiential bricolage that complicates Cuban performances of history in terms of where it is accessed. If we "listen in detail" to the voices in the misa, we would note the transnational backbeats and nomadic aesthetic that connect these performances to histories enacted by music, dance, and feeling (Vazquez 2014:36, 135).[58] In this chapter, I have invoked Ortiz, Kardec, and Glissant as my main interlocutors along with the spirits and mediums I experience in my fieldwork and religious practice. Though differing in approaches in their assessment of Afro-Cuban and Afro-Caribbean cultures, their considerations of history and culture reinforce a nomadic aesthetic as well. Their shared resistance to certain kinds of universalizing features of historical and anthropological discourse illustrate the necessity of disordering—indeed moving—accepted paradigms that obscure temporal and cultural fissures. As a result, we find that enacted history and culture resist reducibility. Residual transcripts are the vestiges of these moments that can bring us a more whole yet scattered picture.

The complex affective textures of Afro-Cuban ritual performances create a myriad of sensations and representations. Misas have moments of joy and laughter, but the communion with spirit guides is taken very seriously. Instances where mediums are touched and inhabited by different racial and ethnic spiritual entities are made *with* the spirit guides and not *for* them. The interoral aesthetics and practices of these performances also ties them to deep values held in the community's understanding of vernacular culture and folk belief. Thus I want to complicate the representation of Espiritismo's mixed-race performance of Black affective spiritual communities to a kind of spiritual "blackface."[59] That being said, I also see that the transculturation taking place in the misas analyzed in this chapter moves race, ethnicity, religiosity, and sexuality in multiple and conflictive directions. Ritualized cultural mixing provides us with affective and experiential links to historical components of Cuban performance that reflect the enduring nature of race and ethnicity as a central concern for Cubans. The misa also behaves as a spiritual disidentification of embodied racial and ethnic codes, expressing how these attributes also move between bodies and metaphysical planes in a way that lasts beyond "liveness" and spills over onto the dead (Muñoz 1999:189).

Thinking about misas in this manner has implications for translocating performances of Cuba globally. Since spiritual interlocutors arrive as doubles, multiraced, ethnically ambiguous, and religiously promiscuous, they question and push against an isolated and "authentic" Cuban nationalism. Spirits and mediums thus also form transnational communities that confound boundaries of nation, place, race, and becoming. They serve as living, performed archives of conjure that leave traces of future connections to be made. The next chapter explores how salty and sweet waters provide epistemic clues for navigating Ochún and Yemayá's own fluid and unbounded archives of conjure.

3
FLOWS

Con el agua del río, con el agua del mar, con el agua del río,
yo me llevo todo lo malo.

—Merceditas Valdés, "Cantos Espirituales Cubanos"

Through YEMAYA Y OCHUN the door to an enchanted
land is opened for us; that of the primordial waters, the salty
and the sweet, placed by the lucumís under the domination of
these two water goddesses.

—Pierre Fatumbi Verger, *Yemayá y Ochún*

The sisterhood between the water deities Yemayá and Ochún is rooted in fluid metaphysical crossings. Their porousness spills into narrative, personal relationships, and ritual practice. As explored in the previous chapter, spirituality, materiality, and the contours of Afrolatinx cultures are tensely bound together. The fluidity of Yemayá and Ochún directly addresses how gender and sexuality play a crucial role in expressing a sensuality of the spirit. Their well-known sisterhood provides an allegorical methodology for understanding the boundary play that is at the center of religious creativity in Cuba.[1] Lydia Cabrera's nomadic queerness and unflinching penchant for irreverent play in the name of Yemayá situates this religious creativity within the spectrum of Yoruba deep knowledge, *ìmò jinⵁ*,[2] that must be excavated in layers to be accessed. Along with Cabrera as an ancestor, this chapter vivifies the voice of a spirit guide, Madre de Agua (Mother of Water) from a misa whose realm joins the two waters. Thus the dead's waters flow together with Yemayá and Ochún in epistemic countercurrents that frame the reading of gender and sexuality in Afrolatinx archives of conjure.

Las hijas de las dos aguas (daughters of the two waters) is a ritual designation that devotees of both deities can carry.[3] Yemayá is the great mother, the divinity of the seas. Ochún is the river goddess of Oshogbo State in Nigeria, where she rules over female reproduction, beauty, and sensuality.[4] The title of *hijas* reflects a fluid kinship between the two divinities and their devotees that carries over into practice, knowledge, and the performance of religious storytelling. Being a child of the two waters creates a set of relationships based on discourses of incorporation that deeply affect practitioners' religious work. The close mythological and ritual connection between Yemayá and Ochún and their children also reveals a level of religious interaction that performs at the borders of geographic boundaries, race, gender, and sexuality. Both Yemayá and Ochún provide adherents with avenues for opening shared ritual interaction between these orichas as well as manifesting a range of embodied subjectivities. Though other orichas also allow for similar kinds of cooperation and boundary play,[5] the two water divinities here represent a specific kind of symbolic affirmation for recognizing the important role that women and water play in Afrolatinx religious cultures.[6]

I am an hija de las dos aguas. As a child of Ochún, and with a given name that invokes the sun and sea, I was not surprised to have my deep affection for the two waters affirmed by divination, initiations, and séances. My earlier work with the Olókùn house in Lagos as a graduate student over two decades ago was the first sign that I had many kinds of water to contend with and to protect me.[7] In Africa, Cuba, and my home state of California, my connection to the sea and rivers shapes the flows of my writing, religious work, and relationships with people. Santería, Espiritismo, and Palo allow for such connections to be named and developed in a manner that makes the creation of the self a constant negotiation with the environment and one's spiritual community. For me, it was a huge gift to know vernacular discourses and practices existed that would help me refine these connections. Talking to others who had similar connections to the salty and sweet waters enriched the ways that I have come to understand the intersections of religiosity, narrative, public culture, and ritual in Cuba. These relationships and conversations also necessarily reoriented my own understandings of race, gender, and sexuality in a manner that reinforced the importance of considering new taxonomies emerging from non-Western epistemologies—or at least creolized epistemologies and ontologies that take into account very real, lived, and traditionally nonparadigmatic modes of being and becoming. Living conscientiously with the waters creates opportunities for reflection, change, and renewal.[8]

Tita is a priestess of Ochún who lives in in the neighborhood of Santa Amalia in Havana and was crowned over forty years ago.[9] She is married to a popular Ifa divination priest, and her son and grandchildren are also babalawos. She is constantly witnessing the male-identified practices of Ifa worship in her home, but holds strong to her identity as an *iyalocha*, a mother to the gods. In my conversations with her, which started about two decades ago, she constantly talks about being a child of las dos aguas. Our discussions have taken on the form of formal interviews as well as informal chats about the gods, godchildren, and the role of Ifa in shaping her life. Tita was even present when I received my *ikofá*, Ifa's protection and the determination of Ochún as the oricha of my head, my guiding deity. I remember she exclaimed loudly, with a laugh, "¡Lo sabía!" She knew it! Ever since, Ochún is a connection we share when we talk in her living room in between rituals. We informally invoke the river goddess's energy as a welcome vibe in an otherwise heavily macho-oriented household.

I want to examine how Tita, as a daughter of Ochún, understands her relationship to Yemayá through interoral traditional narratives and vernacular criticism of these narratives.[10] Interoral storytelling practices found in Afro-Cuban religious cultures create spaces where spiritual creolization happens during ritual work (Otero 2015; Argyriadis 1999).[11] Interoral narration, like intertextual narration in writing, generates story arcs that contain many voices, a range of genres, and modes of interpretation.[12] Santería, Espiritismo, and Palo create especially rich avenues for understanding nonbinary and nonlinear modes of being through telling.[13] Thus, looking at the story worlds Tita creates, and the way in which she interjects her narration into the fieldwork process, invites us to consider the dynamics of world-making as well as creative self-making through discursive interjections (Rivera-Servera 2012:21–24; Allen 2011).[14] These vernacular aesthetic sensibilities, as metafolklore and as a form of oral literary criticism, abound in the performance of Afro-Cuban traditional narrative and ritual.[15]

During a 2009 interview in her home, Tita told me a *patakí*, a traditional sacred narrative that exemplifies the relationship between Yemayá and Ochún. In her version of the story, the two

FIGURE 3.1 Tita, Havana, Cuba, May 2019. Photo by Efun Bile. Author's private collection.

water deities are sisters who borrow physical attributes from one another.

Ochún era una mulata muy linda, tenía un cuerpo muy elegante, muy bonita. Pero, no tenía pelo. Ella tenía el pelo muy cortito, no tenía pelo, no. Entonces, ella le dice a Yemayá, <<Mira, tan linda como yo soy, y sin embargo no tengo tu pelo.>> Yemayá tenía el pelo largo, [muestra a la cintura], y de lo más bonito. Y Yemayá le dice, <<Mira, para que seas feliz completa yo te voy a dar mi pelo.>> Y le da el pelo a Ochún.[16]

Ochún was a very beautiful *mulata*,[17] she had a very elegant figure, very pretty. But, she had little to no hair. She wore her hair very short, she really didn't have any hair. One day she says to Yemayá, "Look at me, even though I am considered beautiful, I don't have your hair." Yemayá had long hair [gestures down to her waist], and [it was] really very beautiful.[18] And so Yemayá tells her, "Look, so you can be completely happy I will give you my hair." And she gives her hair to Ochún.[19]

Part of the context of the story included Tita giving me a figurative response to my too direct and literal line of questioning about the relationship between the two water deities. Tita was teaching me a lesson about Yemayá and Ochún, as well as guiding me pedagogically on the kinds of questions that would be more fruitful to ask. She understood, much better than I, that the answers I was seeking would be in the stories and their layers of meaning. Her redirection of the ethnographic interview into a storytelling session helped me witness the important work done by shifting modes of authority.[20] Her choice of reframing the conversation to highlight a performative interchange through storytelling had me listening in a way that would inspire more storytelling and listening.

Tita's story has many layers, reflects the use of reported speech, and also uses ritually coded symbolism to represent different components of Yemayá and Ochún. Charles Briggs has commented on how reported and quoted speech in narration play important roles in creating multiple avenues for visible and invisible authority (1996:27). Within the brief story she told, other myths and beliefs are referenced that add various levels of quoted authority stemming from Afro-Cuban oral tradition (Cabrera 1980:70, 83; Castellanos 2001:37–38; Barber 1999).[21] For example, daughters of Ochún, for the most part, are instructed by their godparents to keep their hair long, as this is a way to invoke the *aché* or vital force of the deity.[22] Rather than question which came first—the belief in the aché of long hair for daughters' of Ochún, or the tale of Yemayá's and Ochún's exchange—I want to offer a symbiotic reading of both. That is to say that story, belief, and practice refer to each other simultaneously in instances of their enactment by practitioners.

The directional change of an ethnographic interview to a storytelling session acts as a performative[23] that realigns access to traditional authority and knowledge (Wirtz 2007:245–46). Tita's break into story offers perspectives on time, history, and the nature of religious values in Santería. Pataki narratives are often layered with advice, warnings, and behaviors to emulate or avoid. Later in this chapter, I examine similar kinds of work that ritual storytelling at a misa espiritual suggests. However, I first want to explore negotiating the flow of authority and sacred knowledge in the less heightened, albeit significant, context of the ethnographic interview and storytelling session. The intimate politics of negotiating the authority of knowledge in the ethnographic interview are also connected to and embedded in the "grander" performances of narration in possession rituals. Within both contexts, gender, race, and sexuality are marked expressions of a sacred yet accessible reenactments of the past in terms of imagery and embodiment.

Audiences allow for moments of reflection, meditation, and self-rerendering in order to interpret potential readings of tales told about and by spiritual beings. The elusiveness of finding a sole, dominant meaning in a pataki or a divinatory tale allows for a palpable shift of not only how to listen to a story but also how to order the world. The etymology of the term *pataki* comes from the standard Yoruba word *pàtàkì*, meaning important (Abraham 1958:546). In Cuba, patakís are the stories of the orichas told in formal ritual circumstances and in informal conversation. At the heart of the meaning of the term *pataki* is the importance of creating a pedagogy for living in complex and shifting circumstances through story. The tales conjure the deities into our imaginations and invoke instruction and reflection that is both communal and deeply personal. In performance terms, the pataki allow for audience members to co-construct the meaning and impact of narratives as active participants in creating a religious world. This is especially so because Afro-Cuban pataki are meant to be unpacked in various ways. The tales' multiple versions and meanings create a rich tapestry with which to hone critical listening practices.

In Tita's tale, Ochún's position is one of indebtedness to Yemayá in terms of giving her the attributes that "perfect" her beauty. The long, beautiful hair that Yemayá gives to Ochún is related to both deities' manifestations as mermaids, water sirens, and aquatic sprites (Cabrera 1980:79). Physical attributes of mermaids found in folklore from all over the world carry over into Cuban folklore. According to Stith Thompson's *Motif-Index of Folk-Literature*, motifs for both dark-skinned (B81.9.5.2) and fair-skinned (B81.9.5.1) mermaids are found in Indo-European folklore and mythological traditions (1955–58:371). These stories contain motifs where mermaids have physical attributes like large breasts (B81.9.2),[24] long flowing hair (B81.9.0), and "wooly" hair (B81.9.1) (1955–58:371).[25] In Africana studies' debates surrounding the mermaid form of Mami Wata, there is much discussion as to the origins and aesthetic characteristics of this water spirit.[26] In all these instances, female water deities have multiple characteristics that make a systematic classification of their attributes elusive at best.

I want to turn to the postcolonial symbolism expressed in Tita's story, as she begins with a description of Ochún's beauty, body, and *mulatez*.[27] Her representation of Ochún is typical of how both practitioners and Cuban popular culture describe the river deity. Representations of the mulata do the symbolic work of negotiating Cuban national identity by embodying race and gender in specific ways since the colonial era (Kutzinski 1993:5, 75, 165–66, 174–79; Arrizón 2006:101–6). Ochún's location as a mulata in Tita's story demonstrates a particular kind of hybridity because of the range of racial, cultural, and religious associations she symbolizes. As a mulata, she is mixed race. As Ochún, she is both Cuban and Yoruba in terms of culture. As associated with La Virgen de la Caridad del Cobre, she is actively present in the vernacular Catholic register of practices on and off the island. It is significant to note here that La Virgen de la Caridad del Cobre, the patron saint of Cuba, is represented as a mixed-race virgin in church iconography (Murphy 2001:87–101; Rodríguez-Mangual 2004:110). In terms of Ochún's hybrid subjectivities, I am inclined to see her body in Tita's story as a site that is shifting, as a project that Yemayá helps her to reconfigure and recreate.

Another important valence to uncover here is the way that race is negotiated in the story through the coded imagery of hair. The long, flowing hair of Yemayá provides an allegorical opening for the idea of how she gives her more "European-looking" hair to Ochún and, in a sense, completes her mulatez. The act of placing this crown of hair on the site of Ochún's head also symbolically connects this part of the story to initiation rites where the head is shaved and crowned to create new links between divine and human subjects. Thus the story's crowning of the mulata Ochún by the dark-skinned Yemayá is a performance of mythic memory. This recollection traces the cultural and racial transference that is the legacy of slavery, creolization, and transculturation in the religion. Rather than understanding this moment as a "whitening" of Ochún, I would suggest that the story reveals, through the interorality of its internal dialogue, a space where Cuban cultural friction and racial ambivalence is remembered and retooled.[28] In other words, Tita, as a daughter of the two waters, is opting to recast the reality of racial friction in Afro-Cuban religious history and practice within a framework of affect that also pays attention to difference.[29]

Through this story, I want to suggest that mulatez can be a potential source of agency, rather than a solely racialized, sexualized, and gendered subjectivity that always does the work of reinforcing colonial, racial, and patriarchal hegemonies. Mulata embodiment can work as "a hybrid body, which can *perform* whiteness and blackness" (Arrizón 2006:117, emphasis in original). In this formulation, the body disrupts the stereotypical racial dyadic by reinscribing mulatez in a manner that disidentifies the binary categories that seek to make it solely transgressive, to mark it as a racial abjection (Muñoz 1999:31–33). This observation also calls to witness the relationship between mulata and Latinx hybrid subjectivities. Thus this reading of the historical legacies of racial rupture and ethnic reconfiguration are rearticulated as a hybridity, where, "the mulata's subaltern agency becomes a reinscription of the divided and hyphenated self" (Arrizón 2006:117). Clearly, this kind of mulatez does *not* implicate a raceless or "whitened" subjectivity. Rather, mulata, Afrolatinx, and Latinx performances of multiple racial valences illustrate the complexity of selves that mark the important history of racial struggle and cultural transference in the hemispheric Americas. This means embracing disdained Latinx female figures, like La Chingada (La Malinche), La Llorona, and La Mulata as sites of empowerment and recognition of kin.[30] That these figures are particularly dangerous to the establishment and continuation of patriarchal, heteronormative, and dyadic racial orders only illustrates the importance of thinking through hybridity within the lens of disidentification.[31]

Disidentification in this pataki resignifies the colonial marking of the mulata by shifting her body, power, and representation into the realm of sacred narrative and vernacular knowledge. Ochún's multiplicity is incorporated by her devotees, where embodying the goddess becomes an act that necessarily disrupts questions of personhood, especially for male devotees of the deity, in terms of another kind of disidentification. The mulata body, and the kind of mulata body Ochún represents in Tita's story, needs to be rethought with these considerations in mind when it comes to vernacular religious folklore, practice, and discourse. This is because the contexts in which practitioners are negotiating living texts are also a shifting terrain of hybrid subjectivities and negotiations.[32]

Tita's story offers a mythological configuration of how attributes like generosity and beauty might be handled, shared, and understood by the community through the orichas' example. Also seen as cautionary tales, the story worlds of pataki tell of what not to do: what to avoid by observing the mistakes made by the deities (Cabrera 1980:117–99; Wirtz 2007:253). This story, like others found in Afro-Cuban religious belief, gives us a model for thinking about ritual reciprocity between the deities as well as between adherents. For Yemayá and Ochún, the vernacular concept of las hijas de las dos aguas acts as a guide for the kinds of reciprocity to be replicated in ritual and material culture. For example, through this idea, believers utilize the symbolism of the mermaid or bring offerings specific to both deities to sites where the two waters meet.[33] Tita describes the characteristics of those who share a ritual responsibility to Ochún and Yemayá in this manner:

> Y, por la mayoridad, nosotras hijas de Ochún queremos mucho a Yemayá. Nosotros la tenemos que cuidad la mucho, y adorar la mucho. Mírame a mi por ejemplo, todo lo que le ofrezco a Ochún, quién es mi mamá, le tengo que ofrecer a Yemayá. Es como si fuera mi mamá. Y así es, las dos aguas son una y iguales. Muchas veces yo tengo que ir dónde el río y el mar se encuentran para rezarle a Ochún y Yemayá, y eso es dónde yo pongo mis ofrendas. Allí es dónde uno puede adorarlas. Allí es dónde uno puede encontrar las dos, el agua dulce y el agua salada.

> And, for the most part, we daughters of Ochún care greatly for Yemayá. We have to really care for her, really have to adore her. Take myself, for example, everything that I offer to Ochún, who is my mama, I have to offer to Yemayá. It is as if she were my mama. And that's the way it is, the two waters are one and the same. I often have to go to where the river and the sea meet in order to pray to Ochún and Yemayá, and that is where I put my offerings. That is where one can worship them. That is where you can find both of them, fresh water and salt water.[34]

Tita provides examples of mutual devotion, ritual reciprocity, and a connection to the natural domains of the sea and rivers. Santería's spiritual ecologies ask practitioners to see the natural world, its cycles, materiality, and dynamism, as vital guides to contextualizing human-divine relationships. As a devotee of both kinds of water, Tita feels it is her duty to respect, honor, and give joint offerings to the water deities at sites where their elements merge. This makes sense since, as she says, "the two waters are one and the same." I take this to mean that the differentiation between these two orichas can become blurred, combined, and creatively conjoined in narrative, ritual, performance, and the construction of material culture honoring them.[35] This kind of geographical confluence and connectivity between orichas in general is an integral part of how devotees make sense of natural and spiritual worlds in a global context. Transnational Santería communities deploy movement in (often urban) space, as ritual praxis and the performance of sacred narrative, to create a place where supernaturally extended families can form (Otero 2007a:179–80, 189–91; Beliso De-Jesús 2013a, 2015).[36] The creativity of spiritual work done in and with both waters offers a discursive countercurrent—one that blends genres of ritual acts and oratory performance to conjure a kind of intercontextuality, a form of place-making based on the fluidity of water that is portable and reproducible.

Like Tita, Cuban folklorist Lydia Cabrera also finds a mythological transformation between the two kinds of water when she describes the patakí of how Yemayá turns the salt waters into sweet waters for her sister Ochún (Cabrera 1980:82–83).[37] Another variant, from Cabrera's unpublished notes, has Yemayá handing over to Ochún not only the fresh waters she has made but also all the riches inside of the rivers.[38] In this version, Cabrera interrupts herself by placing reported speech into the description of the exchange, code-switching into a vernacular mixture of Spanish with Lucumí (Cuban Yoruba),[39] creating in her papers an oral texture that refers back to the voices of her collaborators in Cuba. For Cabrera, the avatars of Ochún Akuara or Ochún Ibu,[40] manifest between the waters: "[Ellas] vive[n] entre el mar y el río" (They live in between the sea and the river) (1980:70–71). Accordingly, Cabrera also quotes the *santero* Gaytán's relation of Yemayá Akuara's home in the juncture between river and ocean,[41] where "se encuentra con su hermana Ochún" (she meets with her sister Ochún) (1980:22, 29).

Ochún's and Yemayá's sisterly bonds appear in Cabrera's papers, where I found the following handwritten note, a residual transcription:

Oshún [sic] tiene su *ilé* en el río. Quien sabe adorarla allí le lleva una bandeja de frutas, de dulces naranjas de china, -*orómibó*—o las golosinas que más le gustan. En el río guarda sus joyas, sus manillas de oro famosas, sus corales y ámbares, metidas en calabazas . . . su tesoro. . . . Tanta riqueza se la debe a su hermana Yemayá que hizo los ríos y se los dio. <<La hizo dueña de Omí *dudú*, del agua dulce.>> Calazán y otros nos cuentan que Oshún no podía sufrir el fuerte olor de mariscos que respiraba a veces en las playas, y por esta razón Yemayá le hizo el río para bañarse y recrease en su canoa. "Cuando necesitas dinero," le dijo Yemayá que es muy esplendida . . ."tómalo de mi baúl."[42]

Oshún has her home in the river. Those who know how to adore her take a tray full of fruits, of sweet oranges from China, -*orómibó*[43]—or her favorite candies there. She keeps her jewels in the river, her famous golden bangles, her corals and ambers, [she] places them in calabashes . . . her treasure. . . . She owes this great wealth to her sister Yemayá who made the rivers and gave them to her. "She made her the owner of Omí *dudu*, of the sweet waters." Calazán and others tell us that Oshún could not stand breathing in the strong smell of shellfish that is sometimes found by the seaside, and for that reason Yemayá made the rivers so that she could bathe herself and rest in her canoe. "When you need money," Yemayá who is very generous said . . ."take it from my [treasure] chest."

This scribbled patakí by Cabrera, like Landes's notes about Oxúm, reveals an archive of conjure that connects transnational spiritual and academic terrains through personal musings about Yemayá and Ochún. Overall, this montage of exchange between Yemayá and Ochún reaffirms how boundary play between the two deities, and their unique kinds of water, opens up possibilities for ritual and narrative reciprocity. As I read Cabrera's notes, and look at her drawings and doodles, I see how she interweaves stories, beliefs, and voices in processing organically the relationship between the sister orichas (see figure 3.2). She utilizes the inclusion of reported speech, dialogue, interruption, and code-switching in ways that illustrate a textual intersubjectivity and interorality. As we get to know about Ochún's riches and Yemayá's generosity, we hear the voices of Calazán and Yemayá performing words that emphasize these qualities. We also get a picture of Yemayá's central position in owning and creating all the waters, the treasures they hold within them, and also who gets access to their respective salty and sweet powers. Her indulgent behavior toward her younger sister Ochún establishes the parameters of their relationship.[44] Yemayá often takes care of Ochún's mistakes, forgotten children, and discarded lovers (Castellanos 2001:37–36, 42–43; Cabrera 1980). Thus, the rivers and the oceans share a topographical space imbued with sacred meanings, especially with regard to women's relationships to each other, that is ritually enacted in Santería. The kinship ties between Yemayá and Ochún, and their children in religious communities, are complicated, layered, and in constant renegotiation through practice, narrative, and social performance. In places where Yemayá and Ochún merge, as where the river spills into the ocean, their subjectivities are also merged, and this enhances the kind of aché they emit into the world.

FIGURE 3.2 Drawing of cover for *Yemayá y Ochún* by Lydia Cabrera. Photo by the author. Courtesy of the Cuban Heritage Collection, University of Miami Libraries, Coral Gables, Florida.

The stories that Tita and Cabrera tell about Yemayá and Ochún reveal a level of meta-analysis offering a discursive agency that is participatory for audiences and for the characters in the narrative. The dialogue they insert into the patakís creates a space where the storyteller and the deity inhabit the story collectively.[45] The listener/reader hears the duality of these voices and responds with their own active interpretation of how the narrative relates to their own situation. In addition, creating and sharing knowledge about Yemayá and Ochún in the form of stories allows for the opportunity to name various divine subjectivities and temporalities. Yemayá and Ochún encourage a level of co-ownership with the very elements of salty and sweet waters in the patakís as well as in ritual practice. Storytellers like Tita and Cabrera understand that the fluidity of the worlds Yemayá and Ochún inhabit are created through the ontological boundary play between the waters, *entre las aguas*, where their shifting ways of becoming are explored.

A similar kind of ontological boundary play is enacted through the performance of narratives and selves in misas. Espiritismo's practices incorporate and also play with the borders found between Amerindian shamanistic traditions, vernacular Catholicism, African beliefs, Asian spirituality, European folk religion, and Kardecist spiritism.[46] In Cuba, many different cultural elements are recast and reperformed in Espiritismo's rituals. As discussed in the previous chapter, misas are gatherings where spirit mediums communicate with spirit guides, guardian angels, the dead, and with family ancestors through visions, possession, and intuition.[47] Misas illustrate a site for mediums to access a spiritual bricolage that also highlights different mediums' divinatory talents. Both communal rites and individual mastery are emphasized in a misa. What stands out about the performance of the misa is the transculturation of the many ethnicities of the spirit guides as well as the blending of the different religious traditions that Espiritismo draws from. Here I am referring to Fernando Ortiz's concept of transculturación, discussed at length in the previous chapter, to think about how the misa provides a site for performing the historical frictions of social, gendered, and cultural mixing productively.[48] This does *not* mean, however, that racial and ethnic distinctiveness of spirit guides are watered down, vanished, or ignored by practitioners. In fact, the performance of racial difference can be a central component of rituals with the dead, with varying social and cultural results.[49]

CLEANSING WATERS, VISITING SPIRITS

In the summer of 2013, Cuban spirit mediums Tomasa, Devit, José, Mercedes, Soñia, and Maxi decided upon spiritual investigation that several misas needed to be conducted.[50] This was especially the case as my mother was very ill and approaching the end of a long bout with terminal breast cancer. I was distraught, and my religious family saw that I needed assistance and comfort. The initial séances were investigations into the general spiritual condition of participants, with one of the masses being held specifically for my grandmother, who passed away years earlier quite suddenly. With her blessing and the blessing of other ancestors and guardian dead, we conducted more misas, which eventually lead to my ritual *coronación* (crowning) as a medium (see figure 3.4). It is not the goal of this chapter to provide a thick description of that ceremony, which is private and belongs to the community. However, I *do* want to discuss some intersubjective and interoral moments of those performances, narratives, and rituals where spirits and mediums cocreate a tapestry of worlds, meanings, and spiritual goals. My descriptions and discussion of mediums' and spirits' dialogue are given with the approval of both types of participants.

For the misas I attended that summer, a *bóveda* was set up with colorful flowers, glasses of fresh water for the spirits, rosaries, candles, tobacco, perfume, and prayer books for the ancestors and spirit guides who were coming to visit (see figure 3.3). A bowl full of water with fresh flower petals was placed at the foot of the table for cleansing before the start of the ceremony. Those who had immediate ties to the dead were given a clear glass of water to place under their chairs. The bust of a Native American spirit held two rosaries at the head of the bóveda, a symbol that reflects how Amerindian spirits are represented in

FIGURE 3.3 *Bóveda*, Havana, Cuba, May 2013. Photo by Hector Delgado. Author's private collection.

Afro-Atlantic spiritual work from New Orleans to Brazil to Cuba (Wehmeyer 2007).

As mentioned in the previous chapter, espiritistas do the important work of engaging the dead in an ethnohistorical "theater of possession" (Ochoa 2010b:49–50). This is poignant, as the arriving dead can represent the legacy of slavery and race in Cuba. The misa's religious historical work creates a temporally heightened and politicized context. I have repeatedly experienced the emergence of ritually collapsed moments, in terms of the past as repossessing the now and as renderings that reorient notions of being and becoming in misas. Most of the spirits' messages and advice are transcribed and, as discussed in chapter 1, create an archive of conjure that generates ritual work and connections with the dead outside the misa in daily life. Working with the transcripts and the debriefings among participants after a misa involve the interpretation of stories and the symbolic meanings of messages in relation to the individual medium these were addressed to. This collective discussion delves into the meaning of embodiment and the construction of the self with regard to spirit guides.[51] As discussed, the dead often require further ritual work of participants as a way of deepening relationships with the living, outside the misa's performative frame. Here performance as ritual work allows for the development of a portable liminal frame that can transform space and temporality according to spirits' instructions. It makes manifest their presence and intention in the material world through creativity with nature, material culture, and sympathetic and contagious magic.

Misas are deeply collaborative enactments. This includes the *misa de coronación* that signifies an important initiatory event. They help to provide a forum where mediums can coconstruct interoral narrative events. Of import to note here is that the practice of Espiritismo is dominated by women and sexual minorities in Cuba.[52] Thus it provides a location for the creation of spiritual authority and voice for the participants and spirits involved. Generosity and reciprocal acts of kindness, as expressed in the Yemayá and Ochún stories of sisterhood, are at the heart of the ethics of the tradition. Espiritismo also has a status as an open religious practice that generates little to no income for its practitioners, which makes it a unique religious culture in Cuba. Espiritistas do not claim one kind of religious purity or require participants to hold an authentic racial, ethnic, or national identity.[53] However, ideas of religious authenticity and authority are certainly negotiated within the misa, especially in the citation of certain specific cultural practices to describe and create life histories for the arriving spirit guides. After the guides reveal themselves to be raced and gendered figures, like La Ngangulera (female Palo practitioner), or El Indio Chamán (Amerindian shaman), the mediums then build on their narrative histories to make connections between seemingly disparate cultural practices to create a mosaic of story worlds and selves for the guides (Wexler 2001:92; Wirtz 2014b; Romberg 2003).[54]

I experienced an instance of this kind of spiritual confluence with regard to being a child of the two waters during a misa that difficult summer. My Afro-Cuban spirit guide, who works in between two female Palo entities associated with salty and sweet water, Madre de Agua,[55] appeared to José and Mercedes. She was also cross-referenced at this misa with Santería's Yoruba deities Yemayá and Ochún. Madre de Agua is a ritual specialist in working, as José and Mercedes put it, "entre las dos aguas," between the two waters. They observed the following:

José: Se presente también una acción, de un espíritu de mujer, una prieta ella, más bien gorda, mediana de estatura. Que se deja ella conectar con las dos aguas. . . . Y es ese mismo espíritu que le está dando *la corriente* de Yemayá y Ochún, porque ella trabaja con las dos aguas—con Madre de Agua y con [Mama] Chola. Porque ese espíritu se dedica mas bien a la parte fuerte de la religión. Porque ese espíritu se me presenta vestida de guingán azul pero con un vuelo así abajo del vestido que parece como una ola del mar. . . . Y allí ella atiende sus cosas, de su prenda, su *nganga*, sus cosas. Y, ella, [hace] el trabajo de brujería. Porque trabajaba fuerte. . . . Y hay veces, porque ella me da todo esto por las dos aguas. . . . Ella se debe de respetar, era fuerte.

Mercedes: También veo ese espíritu de Madre de Agua cantando [canta] <<campana en la misa se rompió, cuando mi nganga compone>>. . . que viva Madre de Agua.[56]

José: There also presents itself an action, of a woman's spirit, she is dark-skinned, heavy-set, of medium height. She lets herself be connected to the two waters. . . . And that very spirit is giving one the current of Yemayá and Ochún, because she works with the two waters—with Madre de Agua and with [Mama] Chola. Because that spirit dedicates herself mostly to the strong part of the religion. Because that spirit presents herself to me dressed in a blue gingham dress with a ruffle below the dress, like this, that looks like a wave from the sea. . . . And there she attends to her things, her *prenda*, her nganga, her things.[57] And, she [does] the work of *brujería*.[58] Because she worked with strength. . . . And there are times, because she is giving me all of this [information about her] through the two waters. . . . She should be respected, she was strong.

Mercedes: I also see that spirit [who is] Madre de Agua singing [sings] "the bell breaks during mass, when my nganga composes [a verse/conjure]" . . . long live Madre de Agua.

In the transcript, José and Mercedes jointly concretize the image of the spirit guide who works between the waters through description, backstory, and song. The guide herself is a complicated being who crosses boundaries between the different religious traditions of Palo and Santería through her creative magic work in the salty (Madre de Agua/Yemayá) and sweet waters

(Mama Chola/Ochún). As José paints the *cuadro espiritual* (spiritual portrait), he emphasizes her use of the *corriente* (current), the flow of the waters, to connect Santería entities with Palo spirits of the dead. José also quotes religious knowledge from the creolized spiritual practices of Palo with Espirtismo *cruzado* as he layers the personal qualities and ritual actions of the guide.[59] Mercedes's performance of the very voice of Madre de Agua through song uses, in turn, indirect speech, sonic emphasis, and lyrical quotation to flesh out the image they are both receiving in the misa. It is important to note here that Mercedes is a Yemayá priestess who also sees herself as a hija de las dos aguas (Otero 2013:95). Through these performances, the aforementioned metaphors of exchange and borrowing between the waters marks the spirit guide as connected with the waters in a similar way. Mercedes and José relate the vernacular belief in the efficacy of ritual work performed between the two waters as a metaphor that encourages religious admixture and cross-association.

As with Tita's story about Ochún and Yemayá, the image of Madre de Agua is gendered and raced in specific ways. Visiting spirit guides at misas are described in terms of physical appearance, dress, ritual implements, and religious attributes. José sees the dos aguas spirit in a manner that associates her with the oricha Yemayá. He describes her as "una prieta" (a dark-skinned woman) wearing a blue-and-white gingham dress with a ruffle resembling a wave, clearly connecting her to Yemayá's colors and her domain, the sea (Cabrera 1980:20–21, 122). Following this vision of the spirit, it is useful to note that, in Cuban Santería, Yemayá is also characterized as being dark-skinned, corpulent, and maternal.[60] Such representations have led to the analysis of the repercussions of incorporating this image into transnational Black understandings of Yemayá, with the ongoing critique of how the mammy stereotype may be evoked in such depictions (Pérez 2013:9–42; Wirtz 2014a).

Similarly, the association of *brujería* (witchcraft) with the spirit guide also marks her in terms of gender, race, and ethnicity. It creates a picture of female blackness that is efficaciously dangerous. Indeed, José says that she works "la parte fuerte de la religion" (the strong part of the religion), a coded phrasing that indicates that she works in Palo, sometimes called the "left hand" of Santería.[61] As with Tita's rendering of a mulata Ochún, José's description of a "prieta" Madre de Agua/Yemayá reveals the complex layering of race that emphatically marks female figures in Afro-Cuban religious cultures. Both the mulata and the prieta are representations that suggest multiple readings and appropriations, some of which can subvert the stereotypical and flattening frames that help to construct these very images. Here the poetry of Audre Lorde and Nancy Morejón provide examples of work that powerfully recasts images of Yemayá and *la mujer negra* in ways that fight historically negative representations of each (Lorde 1978:6; Morejón 2001:226–27).[62]

José's spiritual sight draws upon his own archives of conjure, stored as religious knowledge formed from a fully developed performative repertoire. He illustrates his discursive creativity and spiritual adeptness as a medium at the misa. His artistry allows him to expose the in-between and nonbinary position of the dos aguas spirit guide. The spirit guide's perceived religious versatility shapes how mediums see her mobility through established categorizations—i.e., Catholic, Yoruba, Lucumí, and Congo. The demonstration of fluid and coded trespassing of spiritual boundaries comes very close to how Cabrera's coded and transgressive writings on Afro-Cuban religions are especially "queer" (Quiroga 2000:75–80; Cabrera 1980:44–45).[63] Also, like Cabrera, José's non-normative sexuality adds a subtle personal dimension to how he receives and creates links to spiritual figures that break through rigid religious categories. José's use of the oricha Yemayá to perform multiple forms of "queerness" connects this ritual moment to places in Cabrera's *Yemayá y Ochún* where Yemayá is ambiguously framed in terms of gender, sexuality, and religious boundaries (Otero 2013:98–99, 2015; Cabrera 1980:44–45). Further, we will see how Cabrera's work comments on the content and form of Cuban vernacular religious storytelling and queer residuals in Yemaya's archives of conjure. She does so by emphasizing the use of coded messages and metaphorical layering when speaking about gender and sexuality in *Yemayá y Ochún*. The use of nuanced language exists for many aesthetic, social, and cultural reasons, including a history of social persecution for both queer and Afrolatinx religious groups, especially for those who move in between these communities.[64]

The Madre de Agua spirit guide is described in both past and present tenses, connecting the narrative memory of her living days with the lived moment of the misa. Her entrance into the liminal frame of the gathering creates a temporal palimpsest that allows for the perception of different kinds of time. Perception here is subtle, and spirit guides illustrate that attention to sensory detail is vital for communicating with them. That is why the very idea of materiality takes on a different perspective when defined by spirits. Consider the following interaction between a spirit and a medium from *Le livre des Esprits* illustrating the book's own potential for generating archives of conjure:

[Spirit]: "Nevertheless, matter exists in states that are unknown to you [humans]. It can be, for example, so ethereal and subtle that it causes no impression on your senses. With everything, there is always matter, although for you it may not be."

[Medium]: What definition can you give of matter?

FIGURE 3.4 Devit, José, Mercedes, Soñia, Maxi, Tomasa, and the author at a *misa de coronación*, Havana, Cuba, May 2013. Photo by Hector Delgado. Author's private collection.

> [Spirit]: "Matter is a link that chains the spirit; it is the instrument that the spirit serves and over which, at the same time, [the spirit] carries out its actions."
>
> (KARDEC 2011 [1857]:82–83, QUOTED SPEECH IN ORIGINAL)

Le livre des Esprits provides a dialogue between spirit guides and mediums in the form of questions and quoted answers. The unnamed mediums and spirits discuss lofty topics like the nature of god, matter, the universe, humankind, and the afterlife. This quote comes from a line of questioning about matter, science, and the senses. Here the spirit guide is suggesting that there are many different kinds of matter, some that humans cannot perceive, and that matter and the spirit are tied in unique bond of actions and processes. Using a similar sensibility of materiality, José and Mercedes are capable of perceiving the many valences of matter that the Madre de Agua spirit emits and moves through. They tap into the spiritual assemblages carried by the spirit guide while paying attention to the energy current she emits through matter.[65] These examples illustrate an understanding of materiality and spirituality that is unopposed, complimentary, and developed alongside the Manichaean split between body and spirit. Espiritismo's vernacular, messy, and unofficial beliefs and practices create unique opportunities to examine alternative approaches to the ontology of self and community.[66]

The difficulties, tensions, and unresolved representations of race, ethnicity, religious difference, sexuality, and gender that Madre de Agua, Yemayá, and Ochún direct us toward illustrate contemporary issues in Cuban society that also require special attention. As with the cultural performance of latinidad, Afrolatinx religiosity promises moments of unity that are fraught with racial, ethnic, sexual, and class-based frictions that underlie the idea of cubanidad and afrolatinidad (Otero and Martínez-Rivera 2017; Rivera-Servera 2012:193–203; Aparicio and Chávez-Silverman 1997:5–7, 11–4). These tensions reveal that the dead understand and engage in struggles for different kinds of justice and that their pasts are raced and gendered. Histories of spirit guides' own experiences with slavery, colonialism, and disenfranchisement are also revealed in misas. In voices that are doubled and quoted, mediums like José and Mercedes show that the dead are watching, listening, and asking us to engage with power, personal and social, in visceral ways.[67]

Raquel Romberg has referred to the creative work done within Espiritismo as a kind of "ritual piracy" that reflects a "creolization with an attitude" based on the conflicts found in the religious colonial history of the Caribbean itself (2005: 199–201).[68] I would add that on top of cultural "poaching" (Romberg's term), mediums are also actively creating phenomenological openings where religious creolization is being negotiated *in consultation* with spirit guides. Spirit guides borrow the body and voice of mediums in ways that confound singular understandings of their origins and leave residual transcripts on bodies, memories, and places that constitute a living archive of conjure. Further, the representation of subjectivity is pluralized when spirits cohabit with a medium's body. The medium also presents cases of ethnohistorical transculturation as existing in the spirit plane, as Madre de Agua's Yoruba and Congo properties and associations suggest. Even within intraethnic African cross-fertilizations, there exists a continual process of reassessing ethnic, racial, gendered, sexual, and religious difference and tension.[69] Espiritismo, as its own set of religious practices, creates sites whereby religious and sociocultural boundaries are pushed to their limits and, in so doing, are reconstructed through metaphors of ethnic commemoration. As a source of controversy and strength, then, Espiritismo disrupts the supposed authority found in the symbolic and material economies of Santería and Palo. It does so because it so boldly mixes claims of ethnic, racial, and religious authenticity through its ritual and narrative boundary play.[70]

Interpreting Madre de Agua relies on accessing a historical imagination and narrative of the past similar to how historians create "official" (read: universal and empirical) histories using their culturally inherited historical imaginations (Taylor 2003: 19–20, 33, 173; Palmié 2013:17, 107–8). Images of similarly creolized passing spirits in misas signal to gendered, raced, sexed, and ethnic tensions echoing from the experiences of colonialization, transnational immigration, indentured labor, and slavery.[71] The trabajo the spirits come down to do in the misa and on earth, which they then ask mediums to engage in during and after the ritual, connects causes and effects on various planes. Within these considerations of the movement of power through ritually creative action are national and transnational spiritual economies. Exchanges between spirit guides, mediums, and clients may also mirror the type of work done especially by people of color, women, and sexual minorities, and which they continue to do, spiritually and physically, in producing certain kinds of experiences for foreigners.[72] Here I am thinking about the ways that sex and religious tourisms are embedded and at times conjoined in Cuba's vernacular economies, which also impact Afro-Cubans and youth.[73] However, at the misa where Madre de Agua emerged there were productive cultural frictions and ethnic boundary crossings taking place within a context that was translocal and transnational between Cubans and Cuban Americans. The attenuating tensions and caveats still apply to a certain extent, although it was important for mediums and spirits at the misa to perform their different kinds of cubanidad for each other. Here negotiations of transnational spiritual economies are retooled by emic aesthetics, nationalistic affects, and diasporic longing.[74]

CABRERA'S COUNTERCURRENTS

Cabrera's *Yemayá y Ochún* resonates with the uncovering and occlusion of certain kinds of information, tensions, and connections found in Afro-Cuban religions. This balance of revelation and erasure works as a countercurrent that is pervasive in archives of conjure. Her narration of the goddesses' mythic worlds creates a rhizomatic maze that brings audiences to open-ended and unexpected locations. Cabrera's textual performativity exposes the discursive similarities between spoken and written narratives that use Cuban vernacular speech as their texture.[75] The interoral sensibilities that frame Cuban spoken genres clearly mark the ways that Cabrera creates her layered, queer texts (Quiroga 2000:77–79). Like the shells and pebbles left on the shore, Cabrera's writings serve as residual transcripts of prolonged interactions with Afro-Cuban imaginaries. This has the effect of bringing audiences with different degrees of ritual and lexical literacy into actively unpacking the meaning of narratives, cocreating the work of her archive of conjure with every reading of Cabrera (Otero 2007b:64–66; Bakhtin 1981:324).[76] As with the interpretive frames that Tita's story and the misa's narratives generate, modes of telling and listening interrupt each other in frictive yet productive and collaborative ways in her writings. Cabrera, then, with her fieldwork-inspired "speakerly" practices, pushes her audiences to reinterpret vernacular speech acts onto the site of the written page in order to develop textual aural literacies.[77]

In *Yemayá y Ochún*, Cabrera describes the two water deities as sisters. She sees Yemayá as the elder sibling who cares for Ochún (Cabrera 1980:70, 83). Cabrera's writing often combines a range of narrative forms: ethnography, archival history, reported speech, folktale, *chisme* (gossip), and mythology. Cabrera's mode of negotiating these different kinds of voices incorporates the interoral strategies of communication of Cuban vernacular speech genres. Cultural critics like José Quiroga and Edna Rodríguez-Mangual have analyzed the writing in Cabrera's seminal work *El monte* with regard to her polyvocality and genre boundary play

(Quiroga 2000:76–78, 80; Rodríguez-Mangual 2004:96–104).[78] Here I want to offer a closer reading of *Yemayá y Ochún* and the important early work it does in locating a queer religious historiography of Santería through the storytelling and mythology of an archive of conjure. This archived history of queer Santería requires readers to conjure connections between ancestors, gods, and events otherwise undisclosed in canonical homophobic and patriarchal renditions of Santería hagiography.

Yemayá y Ochún contains patakí that illustrate the fluidity of sexuality and being in Afro-Cuban religion. In stories about Yemayá's love affairs, Cabrera gleefully reveals the sea divinity's relationships and travails with same-sex-loving manifestations of the orichas Obatala, Orula (Orúmbila), and Inle (1980:44–45).[79] In one telling, Orula, the macho deity of divination, leaves Yemayá for the even more macho divinity of Iron, Ogún, much to Yemayá's dismay. Cabrera further explains: "It [same-sex love] is not such a terrible mark of shame for Orúmbila" (45).[80] These assertions about Orula are certainly scandalous and antithetical to the patriarchal and homophobic framework of babalawo priesthoods in Cuba.[81] Yet Cabrera's insinuations perhaps also reveal an open secret to readers. In the following chapter, I look at one babalawo's interpretations of adodi (gay men) through religious storytelling about Inle and Orula, which complicate and corroborate Cabrera's residual reading of sexuality among the gods being discussed here.[82] For Cabrera continually destabilizes her description of standardized patriarchal and homophobic norms in Afro-Cuban religion by adding statements like, "Pero la homosexualidad no es siempre un estigma en el santero sino en muchos casos el influjo de la feminidad de su oricha" (But homosexuality is not always a stigma for a santero, but in many cases is an influence of the femininity of his oricha) (Cabrera 1980:241). In adding this caveat, she opens up the consideration of alternate histories of Santería that move beyond heteronational renderings of Afro-Atlantic religious traditions into transnational queer religious frameworks.[83]

Though subtle, Cabrera's inclusion of the importance of gay priests and lesbian priestesses in the religion's history appears in both *Yemayá y Ochún* and *El Monte*. For example, she mentions the nineteenth-century lesbian priestesses of Erinle, La Zumbão, and the great santero Lorenzo Samá (aka Obadimeye) as legendary figures responsible for influencing religious traditions and public culture in Havana (Cabrera 1975 [1954]:58, 1980:241). In a set of practices where speaking and doing create status, becoming *legendary*, in both religious and LGBTQ+ vernacular contexts, is dependent on spreading story. Cabrera clearly spreads the stories of queer orichas and practitioners in her own unauthorized way, which resembles the work that *archechisme* (archival gossip) does in creating unofficial histories. As Deborah Vargas observes, "hearsay, murmurs, and silent gestures" create a site for the expression of queer and feminist histories and experiences (2012:56). I would argue that Cabrera creates her own queer and feminist *archechisme* of conjure that includes and also generates deities, practitioners, and even ritual work in her corpus. *Yemayá y Ochún* provides a specific case study of how this alternate history flows through the current and vernacular logics of las dos aguas, the two waters. Further, Cabrera's riff on the leitmotif of salty and sweet water illustrates a kind of fluid attenuation akin to Cuban music's own "unpredictable currents and accompaniments," which also suggests "the necessity of secrets" (Vazquez 2013:9, 21). In other words, what Cabrera does and does not tell us requires a kind of listening that destabilizes the expectations of the "knowability" of Santería, its entities and practitioners. Yet, she does so in an ironic manner that also has roots in *choteo*, a Cuban kind of mockery of authority, that decidedly calls upon race, sexuality, and gender as sources of disidentification, especially in diaspora.[84]

Along these lines, we can explore the connections and fissures between Cuban vernacular speech's linguistic form and Cabrera's texts. Chisme is a consistent linguistic genre that Cabrera utilizes in order to interrupt herself in an intertextual fashion that feels interoral and performative. Chisme generates its own residual readings and retelling that connects it to rituals with the dead, and the work of archives of conjure, by emphasizing the importance of speculation, a necessary stage for the metaphysical work of brujería or witchcraft (Ochoa 2010b:27). One arena where chisme is especially helpful to Cabrera's conjuring of an alternate religious history is in discussing the ambiguous nature of sexuality and gender among the orichas. As discussed earlier, Cabrera's talk about sexuality takes on the form of reported speech and gossipy asides that break into the conversationally ethnographic description of deities, priests, and ritual praxis. The genre of chisme is often a queered and feminized form of "talk" in which women and gay men provide volatile and "unverifiable" information that destabilizes official narrative arcs.[85] Chisme is a seductively powerful and quick form of storytelling that works specifically because it plays with the boundaries of secrecy and the impropriety of revelation. It also acts as a performative of residual transcriptions that are often transgressive. In Afro-Cuban religion this is an especially sensitive subject because of the importance of secrecy and oath taking to the establishment of knowledge, kinship, and ritual efficacy. Yet play with these boundaries is a strategy that many practitioners avail themselves of in expanding their own spiritual becoming. Indeed, Todd Ramón Ochoa has remarked that discursive modes of allusions and rumors are efficacious in magical work with the dead among seasoned *paleros* (Ochoa 2010b:2). Thus chisme and rumor provide a space where the unspeakable is spoken in ways that reframe historical, temporal, and epistemological possibilities in Afro-Cuban religious discourse, especially where the dead are concerned.

Chisme is a polyvocal performance; it inserts multiple voices into its telling (i.e., "friend of a friend" sources, the use of reported speech, hearsay). Cabrera reinscribes chisme by writing it into *Yemayá y Ochún* in ways that mimic the vernacular rhythm of chisme's interruptions and asides as well as mirroring the echoes of marginalia in the archive. Moreover, Cabrera's chisme is juicy: its contents are a forbidden territory that is infectious and irresistible to ignore. Besides content, chisme and gossip are popular and pleasurable ways of imparting vernacular versions of the past that rub against official histories because of their porous, unverifiable, and often subversive narrative frames.[86] As Abelove has shown, "deep gossip" allows queer readers and critics to reframe canonical texts, community history, and modes of discourse (2003:xi–xviii). I would also offer that the passing on of chisme creates an aesthetics of intimacy.[87] The lowering of the voice, the vow of confidentiality, the moving closer of the body to *chismear* constructs a bond through the shared performance of this unique kind of speech act.

Santería, Palo, and Espiritismo all avail themselves of the immediacies and intimacies of chisme in their modes of narration—embodied, written, or oral. Cabrera's texts illustrate how we can listen in the gossip of the gods, spirits, and practitioners in ways that both reveal and occlude.[88] In a similar manner, Tita's tale about Yemayá and Ochún also felt like chisme when I heard the story as a confidant. Chisme is talk that is passed on between sisters, lovers, and friends. It flows between the waters, crosses the boundaries of propriety, and relates keenly feminist and queer modes of knowing.[89] Archives of conjure are riddled with the dead's chisme, the kinds of residual clues and insinuations that also clearly mark Cabrera as ancestor with her own stories to tell through and with the gods.

Vernacular ways of knowing are intertwined within chisme's narrative structure and flow. The stories embedded in chisme's performative frames invite subsequent and multiple interpretations. Chisme opens up suggested narratives, themes, and concerns in ways that simultaneously construes and distorts the subject at hand. This is either done through a negation of authorial origin for the chisme (i.e., indirect information) or another means of disassociation between the bearer of the gossip and the gossip itself.[90] For Cabrera, chisme's authorial ambiguity is especially useful for imparting what would be considered scandalous information about the orichas' sexual orientation and cross-gender identification.[91] As she states before talking about gay and lesbian tendencies among the orichas, "No omitamos una versión que pretende que . . ." (Let us not leave out a version that pretends that . . .) (1980:44–45). This distancing opens up possibilities for coming closer to taboo subjects.

In more than one instance, Cabrera partakes in chisme where Yemayá performs her own queerness: "A Yemayá le gustaba cazar, chapear, manejar el machete. En este camino es marimacho y viste de hombre. . . . Yemayá es a veces varonil hasta volverse hombre" (Yemayá liked to hunt, to cut, to wield the machete. In this *camino* she is *marimacho* and dresses like a man. . . . Yemayá is at times [so] masculine that she becomes a man) (1980:45–46).[92] Here Yemayá displays a range of female masculinities that connect her to multiple traditions of performing and playing with noncisgender displays (Halberstam 1998: 1–43, 267–73). Cabrera's use of one particular term, *marimacho*, tomboy or butch-masculine woman, especially connects Yemayá to Chicana feminist traditions of reshaping gender and sexuality in Latinx art, writing, and spiritual practice (Díaz-Sánchez 2013; Anzaldúa in Arrizón 2006:158). This chisme about Yemayá's fluidity of gender and sexuality is an apt discursive weapon for Cabrera's personal archive of conjure. Among her handwritten notes, I found several instances where Cabrera remarks on Yemayá's amazing ability to be the great mother at her masculine best. In one example, Cabrera describes the avatar Yemayá Okutí(é) as a "Yemayá tan macho como cualquier macho y tan hembra como la que más" (Yemayá as macho as any macho and as feminine as any [woman]).[93] Another set of notes from a handwritten, torn page also mentions this road of the sea deity, "la varonil Yemayá Okuté es compañera del orisha Oggun, caza con escopeta, maneja el hacha y el machete (the manly Yemayá Okuté is companion to the orisha Oggun, [she] hunts with a shotgun, handles an ax and a machete).[94]

Yemayá's masterly performance of different kinds of masculinity allow her to own and maneuver male ritual tools usually reserved for warrior orichas: guns, machetes, axes. Such correlations mix up the gendered and sexual logics of patriarchal forms of Santería in terms of how aché is distributed and wielded—allowing for a metaphysical reordering of energies and possibilities. For Cabrera, the avatar of Yemayá Okutí can provide this kind of productive destabilization by being both ultramacho and ultrafeminine.[95] Yemayá Okutí's subjectivity presents us with a kind of disidentification that moves her away from the rigid binary schemas of gender created by human beings toward a third space that plays with the very stereotypes about gender and sexuality generated by societies and cultures.[96] However, the powerfully rebellious images that we gather from Cabrera's chisme remain coded and only partially revealed in both her published and unpublished work. As the introduction to this volume discusses at length, reconsidering Yemayá and Ochún in light of residual transcriptions and archives of conjure also invokes an ecofeminist, speculative critique that shifts epistemologies and ontologies toward the necessary incorporation of nonhuman material and spiritual beings as kin through collaborative frames of existence.[97]

Cabrera's personal connection to Yemayá is necessarily informed by her life as an artist, writer, investigator, and a lesbian. Cabrera, like Yemayá, moved between forms of being and becoming in her creative life as well as a Cuban exile living unhappily in Miami (Vazquez 2014:854–57). She crossed the ocean to find herself writing *Yemayá y Ochún* from a space in her imagination where spirits and her past resurfaced in multiple forms of storytelling, including ethnography, fiction, and, yes, chisme. Cabrera, like Yemayá, provided comfort and inspiration for gay and lesbian writers, artists, and practitioners in exile all over the world.[98]

One poignant example is Cabrera's relationship with Cuban author Reinaldo Arenas. Cabrera and Arenas were close, sharing an affectionate and ongoing correspondence. Many of the letters illustrate a level of frustration and sense of alienation with living in the U.S. For instance, in a letter dated July 15, 1982, Arenas asserts: "Este país esta controlado por la estupidez y la barbarie" (This country is controlled by stupidity and barbarism).[99] Yet, in the same letter, Arenas later touchingly pronounces that "mientras tanto reciba como siempre mi admiración y mi cariño incesante, por gente como usted vale la pena seguir viviendo" (In the meantime receive as always my admiration and incessant affection, life is still worth living because of people like you).[100] Arenas committed suicide in 1990 because of his pronounced suffering from living with AIDS. I want to consider his words of admiration, acknowledgment, and hope as a space where Yemayá worked to inspire healing and acceptance through this friendship between two exiles that loved whom and wrote what they pleased powerfully, rebelliously.

Both Cabrera and Arenas place the sea at the center of their published work as a means of invoking their past or as a way of creating newly surreal, spiritual, and bawdy versions of Cuba.[101] They are archival redobles, traveling ancestors, important to LGBTQ+ ways of imagining belonging in exile. The rhythm of memory marks their letters as the waves of the sea shape the shore. Cabrera's archive produces residual transcriptions that locate her companion dead as they transmigrate through correspondence. In this movement, Arenas acts as an undertow in Cabrera's archive, drudging out *cariño* amidst an ocean of loneliness and complaints. Scholars reading this correspondence become mediums in mediating layers of meaning in the dead's words. The paper trail left behind makes Cabrera a "textual *madrina*," a godmother in this process of uncovering secrets and tales (Tsang 2019: 63).

Cabrera's connection to the sea and Yemayá is part of the slippery historical discourses that surface in waves and currents about non-normative sexualities, genders, and embodiments in Afro-Atlantic religious cultures.[102] These aquatic bits of the puzzle act as symbolic markers, as sites of commemoration and residual transcripts between the waters, that mark a place for communities to imagine a history, a home, a future from a diasporic and queer perspective. The different levels of Cabrera's "outing" in *Yemayá y Ochún* encourages community-building reading practices for fluidly sexual scholar-practitioners of Santería and other Afrolatinx religious cultures. And her use of chisme illustrates a subversive mode of world-making that cannot be verified nor entirely denied by convention.[103] Again,

Cabrera's consideration of Yemayá performs alternate versions of pataki that resist heteronormative and patriarchal characterization of the deities. Yet this reading and unpacking of a queer positioning of the orichas is not work limited to her coded writings. Rather, Cabrera gives us clues as to how to read the variegated nature of the presentation of gender and sexuality in Afro-Cuban religious communities in a range of religious genres and contexts. On a personal level, this means inviting the ambiguity of the two waters into my spiritual practice, my writing, and the multiple families I belong to.

Vernacular logics in Afro-Cuban religions are expressed in a plethora of genres of expression: personal experience narratives, rituals, material culture, ethnographic writing, divination, fiction, plastic arts, and even videoscapes as a kind of ethnoscape.[104] Cabrera mimics the multifaceted approaches that Afro-Cuban religious boundary play affords through the incorporation of interoral performative frames in her ethnographic writing that serve as seminal feminist, queer archives of conjure.[105] In work that Cabrera's writing anticipates, anthropologists of Afro-Cuban religions are now embracing ethnographic writing that shares the authority of knowledge and invites performative listening, imagining, and world-making for readers.[106]

The religious workers that I have introduced in this chapter are committed to world-making projects within different religious registers that are cross-referenced in specific ways that signify racial, ethnic, and religious marking and copenetration. In the misa, the pain of loss, the sweetness of reunion, and the promise of future spiritual agency open moments where ritual and narrative converge to expose sites where memory, existence, and creativity can be witnessed as an archive of conjure. The misa's conjuncture allows for the voice of the postcolonial subject—sometimes subaltern, sometimes divine—to interrupt the present via the body of an adherent. Through advice, admonishments, and blessings, the residual transcriptions of the dead are interlaced in a present moment that becomes a densely layered chorus of interorality. This interorality signals to the multiple and transnational origins, diasporas, and routes of circulation traveled by adherents and spirits in Afro-Cuban religious becoming. These routes are well traveled in the space between the waters, where cultural and spiritual currents move in unexpected ways.

My own becoming as an hija de las dos aguas also happens inside the waters that Ochún and Yemayá share. This journey between the salty and the sweet is not solitary or solely my own. It is conjured with practitioners like Tita, José, and Mercedes and with ancestors like Madre de Agua and Cabrera. All of us are bound in spiritual and social collaborations that are revelatory and ongoing, as the dead and gods require constant spiritual and material activation and recognition. The labor of Afrolatinx spirituality happens in the everyday spaces of kitchens,[107] gardens, library reading rooms, and workrooms. The task of piecing together residual transcriptions into an archive of conjure is activated by a reflexive creativity. Add to this consideration that the process of making a spirit doll, sewing a banner, telling a story, or performing a cleansing is not performed in a vacuum. Thus I believe that Afrolatinx spiritual communities exhibit the values and aims of *creación colectiva* (collective creativity), a Latin American art-making process. The Latinx all-female performance collective, Teatro Luna, understands creación colectiva as "radical collaboration; relationships; authentic storytelling; honoring roots while challenging static notions of identity; extending grace; and understanding limitations while not giving up on dreams. Art is honored as a radical expression of being" (Acosta and Mena 2015:12).

Cuban mediums', ancestors', and spiritual sojourners' everyday ritual work honors these artistic truths in a culturally unique way that also participates in the broader political concerns over self-governance, neocolonialism, and freedom of expression that Teatro Luna's manifesto expresses. In the misas and narratives explored in this chapter, "a radical expression of being" includes a multiplicity of selves, temporalities, and locations of existence that resist culturally dominant discourses of materiality and subjectivity. These radical ways of being live on in archives of conjure that vibrate with traces of spiritual awakening waiting to be animated. In the next chapter, we follow the radical epistemology emulated by transformistas and the orichas when they inhabit the divine feminine through sirens and the sea.

4

SIRENS

Ce qui existe par totalité relativisée.

—Édouard Glissant, *Le discours antillais*

What stories are told about materially fluid beings in archives of conjure? In this chapter, I investigate how hybrid bodies are understood in Afrolatinx mythology, folklore, and literature using a Caribbean ritual poetics. I show how these poetics destabilize universalizing subjectivities by paying attention to feminist and queer expressions of sexuality. In Afrolatinx religious cultures, the captivating transgendered oricha of Erinle (Inle) is central to thinking about these considerations.[1] By investigating traditional narratives and the fiction of Mayra Santos-Febres, a complicated set of attitudes and aesthetics emerges, revealing components of sexual violence, desire, trauma, healing, and ethnic connotations of difference. Taking this legacy of "reading" further, this chapter also discusses how figures like Erinle continue to influence Caribbean queer folk and popular culture in ways that emphasize the deep relationship between mythology and performance.[2] I am using *queer* here to express nonheteropatriarchal

forms of expression and becoming, especially in public sphere
performances that emphasize feminine verbal agility and
stage presence, like Yoruba *oríkì* and *transformista*'s lip sync
traditions.[3]

Erinle is an ancient river divinity hailing from Nigeria. He is
recognized as the tributary of the Ọṣun River, which supplies
most of the water to Oshogbo state (Drewal, Pemberton, and
Abiodun 1989:156). His name is translates to *erin*, elephant, on
ile, earth (Mason 1994; Abraham 1958:162–63).[4] He was the first
oloba (king) of the town of Ilobu, where Erinle's shrines hold
smooth river stones in clay vessels to commemorate his riverine
origins (Abraham 1958:304; Drewal, Pemberton, and Abiodun
1989:167; Adepegba 2001:104). In Nigeria, devotes of Erinle are
known by their names that start with *omí*, water, such as Omíy-
alé, "water rushes into the home" (Abraham 1958:474). Abata is
a divinity of the marshes and swamps that is closely associated
with Erinle, sometimes as an (androgynous) partner, in Nigeria
and Cuba alike (Abraham 1958:474; Tsang 2013:116; Ramos
1996:63; Conner and Sparks 2004:78; Cabrera 1980:88).[5] In Africa,
Erinle's fluidity is centered on how the deity moves between the
forest and the river in an amphibious manner. Oral tradition tells
of how Erinle, a skilled hunter and fisherman, saves the town of
Ilobu from Fulani invasion and later returns to live in the river
named after him (Drewal, Pemberton, and Abiodun 1989:167;
Abraham 1958:164). He is associated with great traditions of
sculpture, with male ritual traditions surrounding the hunt, and
with female ritual traditions of healing with river water. Erinle's own archive of conjure illustrates a scattering of affects where
he crosses borders and creates alliances based on transgression.

Lydia Cabrera describes Erinle (Inle) as, "Médico, cazador y
pescador, es para muchos una divinidad andrógina, Inle Ayayá
vive en la tierra y en el agua" (Doctor, hunter, and fisherman, he

is for many an androgynous divinity, Inle Ayayá lives on the earth and in the water) (1980:87). Erinle's fluctuating nature inspires an array of interpretations in Afrolatinx religion linking the deity to the orichas Yemayá, Ochún, Ochosi, and Ifa. As Cabrera asserts, in Santería he is primarily known as *el médico divino* (the divine doctor), who can heal maladies and is closely linked to and ritually works with the Archangel Saint Rafael (Pérez 2015:282; Ramos 1996:63; Conner and Sparks 2004:78; Lawal 1996:31).[6] Erinle has a wide array of qualities that make him the patron of hunters and fishermen. In the oral tradition of the pataki, Erinle has intimate relations with Yemayá of the sea, Ochún of the rivers, and Ochossi of the forest (Tsang 2013:118; Cabrera 1980:271). Erinle's dynamic and alluring qualities, according to Martin Tsang, a respected Erinle priest, artist, and scholar, are due to his "sexual ambiguity and homosexuality," "androgynous appearance," as well as to a "refined beauty and elegance" (Tsang 2013:121).

Erinle's residual transcriptions, in snapshots of stories and myths, map beauty in ways that are visceral yet irreducible to dyadic structures. Like stones gleaming under river currents, rippling, his archive of conjure may only be perceptible under certain kinds of light. Erinle's mutable and multiple aspects, especially in his *camino* or road of Inle Ayayá, frames a way into the "transphysical poetics" of creative work that incorporates Afrolatinx religious aesthetics in the Caribbean.[7] Transphysical poetics, according to Édouard Glissant,[8] is aesthetic expression that is "open to change" and allows for the "domain of the unseen" to become part of the narrative that creates history, literature, and knowledge. The transphysical poetics that characterize Erinle's interactions with various orichas demonstrate how fluidly presenting bodies and subjectivities do the important work of ritual transformation. These transformations are dynamic, and the metamorphosis of gender that occurs relies on moments of recognition, disavowal, and desire.

The connections between the deity of divination, Orula, and Erinle run deep in how some religious practitioners understand sexually malleable bodies in Ifa divinatory traditions. Babalawo Tony Vilches told me a pataki about Erinle that also "queers" Orula, by association, in interesting ways. He related the following story while drinking a *cafecito* one afternoon in his living room in Havana:

> Orula estaba caminando por el desierto y estaba perdido. No tenía agua. No tenía comida. Al fin, se desmayó de debilidad. Erinle y otros seres bellos—que eran entre hombres y mujeres—lo recogen y lo salvan. Orula se despierta y ve que esta gente lo han salvado. Desde entonces Ifa tiene que respetar el *adodi*. Hasta cierto punto.[9]

> Orula was walking through the desert and he was lost. He didn't have any water. He didn't have any food. In the end, he fainted from being so weak. Erinle and other beautiful creatures—who were between [being] men and women—pick him up and save him. Orula wakes up and sees that these people have saved him. From that time Ifa has to respect the *adodi*. Up to a certain point.

Tony speaks of Erinle and the androgynous beings Orula encounters as "beautiful creatures."[10] This depiction echoes Tsang's own elaboration of the oricha as containing in-between sexual characteristics that are alluring and demonstrate an ambiguity of gender. The tale also reaffirms vernacular beliefs about Erinle being a healer, a divine doctor. In this story, he brings the powerful deity Ifa back to health. Erinle does not work alone, however. He has an entourage of helpers, other healers who make up a community of fluidly gendered beings devoted to this kind of work. According to Santería's cosmology and ritual logics, these helpers would be the androgynous Abata(n), the orisha of the marshes and swamps, and Otin,[11] a river in the Ọṣun division of Ibadan who in Santería is considered to be one of the four "wives" of Erinle.[12] Cuban scholar and priest Dr. Miguel Willie Ramos puts it this way: "Together with Abatan . . . and Otin . . . Erinle administers the cure while Abatan and Otin supervise the patient" (1996:63).

We can enrich Tony's story based on this fleshed out and contextual information using Afrolatinx, queer, and Caribbean imaginaries that relate directly to transphysical poetics.[13] By inserting Otin and Abata(n) in the description of Erinle's entourage, it makes specific the connections between the entities in the story and its larger mythological framing. In so doing, Glissant's poetics become an aesthetic mode of narrating and reading that is "open to change" with the addition of diverse "unseen" elements. Transphysical poetics works away from materialist understandings of history and transcendental notions of metaphysics precisely because it allows for the addition of languages, cultures, characters, details, and beliefs in the mind of the audience. Tony's story is thus an invitation to opening various interpretations that change and transform with each retelling and listening.

The terms *adodi*, *ado*, and *adé* refer to same sex male eroticism in Cuban Santería and Brazilian Candomblé (Cabrera 1980:45; Matory 2005:189, 206; Pérez 2016:119).[14] These terms are a part of the religions' vernacular speech and popular consciousness.[15] When Tony uses *adodi* in the above story he code-switches from Spanish to Lucumí dialect in a manner that indicates he is touching upon a delicate subject for babalawos in particular. Ifa priests have taboos against being sexually or

FIGURE 4.1 *Inle* by Alberto del Pozo. Courtesy of the Cuban Heritage Collection, University of Miami Libraries, Coral Gables, Florida.

spiritually penetrated by another being, including the penetration of possession by an oricha.[16] This avoidance plays into the homophobia and sexism found within certain interpretations of Cuban Ifa.[17] However, as Cabrera points out, the flip side of Ifa folklore reveals an open secret about Orula, "Yemayá se disgustó con Orula porque descubrió que era *adodi* . . . que la abandonaba por Ogún" (Yemayá became upset with Orula because she discovered that he was an *adodi* . . . that he abandoned her for Ogún) (1980:45).

As discussed in the previous chapter, Cabrera's irreverent rendering of two of the most macho of the orichas as lovers brings an alternate narrative tradition to light. It uncovers a receptive practice that is becoming more and more prominent as LGBTQ+ communities reimagine their claim to Afrolatinx religious legitimacy. It also illustrates that folklore fosters tales of taboo behavior as irreverent versions of sacred history. Elsewhere I have written extensively about Yemayá's role as caretaker and warrior for LGBTQ+ children of the saints.[18] What I want to point out in the two examples about Orula and the adodi is the intimate connection between disavowal and the appropriation of power of the transgendered and transphysical (poetic) subject in particular. It is telling, then, that Tony concedes that Ifa priests need to respect the adodi "up to a certain point." In asserting the connection between Orula, Erinle, and the adodi in a manner that reveals admiration, desire, wonder, and denial, Tony is indirectly acknowledging the close connection between the three figures.

The transphysical *divine* subject, with its ability to change (genders/sexualities), is a global figure found in multiple cosmologies and mythologies.[19] What interests me about Erinle is how the connections he embodies between gendered/sexual mutability, desire, violence, trauma, and healing run thematically through Afrolatinx queer cultural production, starting with literature. Archives of conjure are found in Afrolatinx literary works where residual transcriptions are generated and made possible through an exploration of the kinds of irreverent histories that mark women's and LGBTQ+ actors' emotive, sexual, and spiritual becoming through performance.

Mayra Santos-Febres is an acclaimed Afro–Puerto Rican author who writes openly about sexuality, gender, and race through the transphysical poetics of Santería in many of her poems and novels. For example, in talking about her historical novel *Nuestra Señora de la Noche* (2008),[20] she says:

> Se me ocurrió que Isabel [la protagonista/una Madama] para mi era como una Virgen. El problema es que las Vírgenes no son putas. Eh, pero yo quería una Virgen puta. Ahora, ¿qué pasa? Que en Catolicismo no hay esa posibilidad. Pero en la Santería sí. ¡Yemayá! Ochún sobre todo. La Caridad del Cobre, Ochún, sobre todo. Que es una Virgen que a la misma vez es seductora . . . es Venus, es Afrodita, es el símbolo de la feminidad y de la seducción.[21]

> It occurred to me that Isabel [a Madame / the protagonist] was for me like a [holy] Virgin. The problem is that Virgins are not whores. But, I wanted a Virgin whore. Now, what's the issue? In Catholicism that is not a possibility. But in Santería it is. Yemayá! Ochún above all. Our Lady of Charity, Ochún, above all. She is a Virgin who is at the same time a seductress . . . is Venus, is Aphrodite, is the symbol of femininity and seduction.

Santos-Febres makes it abundantly clear that the transcultural traditions found in Santería, and their gendered and sexual tensions, mark the aesthetics of her writing.[22] Indeed, Cabrera's informants echo Santos-Febres's own creative choices that connect the divine to sexual pleasure: "Ochún, La Virgen de la Caridad, es coqueta, enamoradísima y correntona" (Ochún, Our Lady of Charity, is a flirt, love-struck and gay) (Cabrera 1980:69). It is no accident that Santos-Fébres sees Yemayá and Ochún as cosmological models of divine sexuality that can inform layers of her storytelling through allusions, incantations, and symbols. In Glissant's articulation of poetics in the Caribbean, oral tradition, music, and ritual are central to the development of transnational literatures and histories that bring an auditory, lived element to narrative. Both Glissant and Santos-Febres assert the instrumentality of storytelling to the future of the regions of the Caribbean and Latin America in ways that demystify evolutionary depictions of culture, writing, and narrative performance from these areas. As discussed in chapter 2, Glissant sees a futurity in the oral that repositions the relationship of writing to performance in a manner that reorders the basis for creative progress away from universality toward specificity and diversity (1997 [1981]:336–40, 364–66).

Santos-Febres's novel *Sirena Selena vestida de pena* (2000) brilliantly explores the desire for an enigmatic gender mutability that Erinle embodies.[23] The title of the text refers to the Homeric sirens and their symbolic connection to the main character, Sirena Selena. Sirena is a sixteen-year-old Puerto Rican drag queen, former prostitute, and chanteuse who travels to the Dominican Republic to reinvent herself with her drag godmother Martha Divine. The story depicts the rise of Sirena's professional and romantic success with "straight" business mogul Hugo Graubel and creates an ethnographic-like tapestry of drag culture in Puerto Rico, New York City, and the Dominican Republic. As with Tony's story about Erinle and Orula, Hugo relies on Sirena's mutable body for pleasure and healing (Santos-Febres 2000b:59, 256, 258; Castillo 2001:20, 22). The novel acts as a performative archive of conjure that enacts an Afrolatinx transnational history of drag. In doing so, it also critiques neocolonial attitudes toward gay and trans cultures of color by North Americans, especially tourists.[24] Santos-Febres's narrative, then, touches upon the connections that exist in folk belief between

Yemayá, Ochún, Erinle, scintillating water creatures, the crossing of aquatic borders, and the contested expression of global queer folk cultures.

The pervasive fluidity of gendered pronouns that Santos-Febres deploys in the original Spanish version of the novel cannot be overemphasized, as it allows for a multiplicity of Sirenas (sirens) to emerge. In this chapter, I will switch between masculine and feminine pronouns, as Santos-Febres does, in order to best capture Sirena's fluidity as a character. I see Sirena's mutability as being informed not only by the Greek mythology Santos-Febres clearly invokes as a leitmotif in the narrative but also by Santería's myths and rituals where magical kinds of embodiment expand the human form to include elements of spirits, nature, and animals.[25] For Sirena is not just an illusionist, a performer with an enchanting voice that can bring out your deepest emotions and memories, but she is "la viva imagen de una diosa" (the living image of a goddess) (56). Yet this goddess also displays the needs of a boy-girl who is haunted by the loss of a childhood, sweetened only by the memories of a doting grandmother who taught him boleros while cleaning homes for wealthy Puerto Rican families (43–47).

It is Selena's *abuela* that first spoke to him about the safety and sweetness of a lesbian relationship in the family, Crucita and Finín, "dos mujeres que se querían y vivían juntas en la calle Las Delicias" (two women who loved each other and lived on Delicias Street) (164). She emphasizes the power of that relationship to heal the wounds of previous abuse and violence. Sirena learns about emotion, performance, and healing from his grandmother, who humbly but powerfully points toward a moral compass that relies on a genuine sensibility of affect. The rhythm of Sirena's abuela's memories is punctuated by the labor of cleaning, lyrically laced with boleros.[26] As abuela observes and sings,

Mira cómo está el trapo sucio en este *hamper*. Coge tú esa canasta
y yo cojo la colorá. Lo que pongamos en la tuya va para la lava-
dora y lo que vaya en la mía, para la tintorería. *Cuando se apartan
dos corazones, cuando se dice adiós para olvidar. . . .* A mí me encantaba vivir en Campo Alegre.

(45)

Look at how dirty this rag is in this hamper. You grab this bas-
ket and I'll grab the red one. What we put in yours will go to the
washer and what goes in mine will go to the cleaners. *When two
hearts are separated, when one says goodbye to forget. . . .* I loved living in Campo Alegre.[27]

The bolero abuela sings is "Ausencia" by the great Puerto Rican
composer Rafael Hernández. Hernández wrote his love songs
to Puerto Rico from a space of longing and diaspora in New
York (Glasser 1995). This rendition of the song takes place in
a flashback, making temporality fluid in the novel. Likewise,
throughout the chapter, Sirena and abuela's speech interlace as
Santos-Febres does not distinguish who is speaking in their dialogue. The singing of "Ausencia" interrupts and accompanies their
conversation and the cleaning of the home. Like Hernández,
abuela and Sirena simultaneously inhabit multiple spaces through
music. Abuela uses the song as an entry into another flashback,
her own memory and retelling of life in Campo Alegre where she
grew up. The lyrics of the bolero, "Cuando se apartan dos corazones, cuando se dice adiós para olvidar" (When two hearts part,
when you say goodbye to forget), accentuate the feeling of loss
and the passage of time present in abuela's stories as well as fore-
shadowing her separation from Sirena because of her early death.
The doing of work, song, and story embrace in a dance, with a
rhythm that binds their bodies, voices, and memories as one.

The worlds of memory, longing, hope, and desire create the aesthetic texture of the bolero. The bolero genre has been characterized as "a form for that last dance before during after love eros separation" whose recorded renditions reveal the "underground economies of love, desire, and escape" (Vazquez 2014:83, 170). Thus the intimate and performative memory of cleaning with abuela while singing boleros creates for Selena a conduit for expressing deep longing. This longing, like the larger sociocultural context of the novel and the sites of Erinle's patakís, is layered within a matrix of race, class, gender, and sexual access. Thus abuela's singing is an act of personal expression that resists the flattening of her experiences or the silencing of her voice. It also points to abuela's archive of conjure, one in which her vernacular pedagogies of doing housework while singing boleros teach Sirena how to enact intimate and resilient conduits for passing down emotive histories.

Sentimiento is an important Latinx and Latin American value attached to performance, especially to song, that creates "affective territoralities" located through sound, memory, and feeling.[28] Feeling here creates kin and this kin recognizes itself across nations, time, and embodiment. Afrolatinx queer familymaking on the part of transformistas like Sirena Selena, has made performance, especially of the bolero, central to their traditions and values.[29] Sirena Selena's boleros are a performative of memory that is ephemeral yet palpable for those who hear her voice. Like the song of Homeric sirens, Sirena Selena lures her audience into inescapable places that render them helpless, in this case with emotion (Santos-Febres 2000b: 221–26).[30] Sirena Selena's boleros have mutable qualities that can bring out deep desires filled with pain and sweetness. Thus Sirena Selena performs with the transphysical poetics I have been discussing in this chapter in a manner that both transports and binds audiences together in a kind of "memoryscape" (Vargas 2012:55). Consider this general response to one of Sirena's siren songs:

> Los testigos recuerdan haber oído el mar enredado en aquel piano de visión. Las mujeres se llevan ansiosas las manos al pecho de y reviven deseos que una vez tuvieron a la orilla del mar ... Los hombres no podían dejar de agarrarse el vientre, les dolía la presencia de aquella Sirena, de aquel ángel que translucía bajo sus ropajes de fuego y hielo seco, fuego y hielo seco ... Recuerdan cómo escaparon, años corriendo cimarrones por las calle y la casa de citas de la calle Duarte ... El público anclado en su incertidumbre, en su doble perdición del tiempo. No sonaba ni un solo corazón, ni una sola gota de sudor contra la piel. No se multiplicaba ni una célula mientras Sirena cantaba. El tiempo obedecía a su voz, su voz era la única prueba de que la vida transcurría.
>
> (224–25)

The witnesses remember hearing the tossing sea behind the notes of the piano. The women anxiously put their hands to their hearts and relive desires they once had at the edge of the sea ... The men couldn't help grabbing their bellies, they were pained by Sirena's presence, by the presence of this angel, translucent beneath her vestments of fire and smoke ... They remember how they escaped, spent years running as fugitives through the streets and the houses of ill repute on Calle Duarte ... The audience anchored in its uncertainty, in its double betrayal by time. Not a single heart beat, not a single drop of sweat formed on the skin. Not a single cell multiplied while Sirena sang. Time obeyed her voice, her voice was the only proof that life was unfolding.[31]

Sirena Selena's performances resonate with the emotive power of oral traditions that also create routes to alternate and vernacular histories found in queer Afrolatinx archives of conjure. The bolero, like Santería, is a transnational cultural expression that invites translatinx cross-fertilization as music, performers, and staging constantly traverse borders.[32] Song and memory are deeply intertwined in the Afrolatinx bolero as musical representations of the past that serve as individual and communal temporally "orienting back-beats," especially for queer communities across this cultural spectrum (Vazquez 2013:36; Quiroga 2000:155–56, 162).[33] In listening to Sirena's voice, the women and men in the audience are transported to different periods of time by accessing their desire viscerally, clutching their bodies in emotion. Note how Santos-Febres switches her reference strictly to Sirena here, again recalling sirens, mermaids, sea divinities like Yemayá and the hypnotic quality of Erinle's allure. Time stops, or at least it bends to the emotive and communal framing of the bolero's "intimate and distant, close and far away longing" (Vazquez 2013:130). This inspiration of sentimiento creates a unique Afro-trans-latinx imagined community of affect in that ephemeral instant by the sea.[34] Here Sirena, a Boricua working-class hustler, sings a bolero, a genre born in Cuba that came of age in México, to her upper-class Dominican audience.[35] As readers, our reorientation of time and emotion behaves reflexively, and we "deploy and reconstruct borders" with the bolero's sentiments, which are "sung to no one in particular, or to someone always on the outside" (Quiroga 2000:155). Of note is how the bolero variously affects men and women, with women reliving their desire and men aching physically from their want.

The bolero in Latin America and the Caribbean is a genre that bends patriarchal gender dynamics by reversing the sexual-social order so that male emotional vulnerability and ambiguity emerges within machista social contexts.[36] Yet this reading of the bolero may be expanded by considering how women and transformistas perform their own non-normative sexual and gendered subjects, behaviors, and desires.[37] The performance and poetics of the bolero in *Sirena Selena vestida de pena* allows for gender mutability and transferable desire in ways that resonate with other invocations of the bolero in Latin American performance and literature. From the sentimental writing of Manuel Puig to the daring performances of Chelo Silva,[38] the bolero allows for a space where sexuality and feeling are explored in ways that can challenge patriarchal control over queer and feminine bodies.[39] As opposed to the *corrido*, a Mexican borderland music genre known for its rugged masculinity and nationalism, the bolero allows for "critical counter-histories" to emerge as sentimental, intimate, and dramatic enactments that are decidedly cosmopolitan and transnational in nature (Vargas 2008:173).

As with Sirena's breathtaking performance, boleros become a vehicle for accessing and reframing the residual transcripts that remember, lament, and challenge the past, where social norms often squash the songs' forbidden love. At the moment of performance, a space is created in which hidden and deeply held desires come to life in the songs' lyrical texture and context.[40] I would say boleros conjure memories archived in music in ways that are subversive to heteropatriarchal social structures in their emotive punch, and that their elasticity allows them to travel across national, sexual, and gendered borders. Boleros perform experiences and allegiances based on feeling where "passion" becomes a "historical modality" (Vargas 2008:175, 178). Again, the relationships mourned in the bolero are often socially inappropriate pairings of class and race that can easily be extended to include gender and sexuality.[41] The impossibility of love is a standard condition expressed in the bolero, and this impossibility is surmounted by the performance of the bolero, which "spiritual-izes the urgency of physical desire" (Campos 1991:640).[42]

Spirituality, desire, and artistry take place as embodied expressions in both the bolero and in Afrolatinx religions. These are embedded within larger contexts of vernacular knowledge as the enactment of a bolero or a divinity refers to accompany-ing narratives, symbolism, and histories. The contexts in both the bolero and in Santería, for example, follow a uniquely trans-national route that links the Caribbean to Latin America in mul-tiple manifestations of music and practice. The nature of differ-ence felt and lived through the inhabitation of a racialized queerness, as Sirena performs them with boleros, also has reso-nances in how sexualized, often Black, spirituality is enacted in Afrolatinx religions' affective economies of embodiment.[43] Soul-ful desire, sex, race, spirituality, and gender are performed in both the bolero and rites of cohabitation as the interpreter of a song or a spirit rely on being able to *sentir* (to feel) and transmit the ephemeral in their craft. Their unique enactments also behave as transnational sites and experiences of imagined community making, as we see in Sirena's moving interpretation of song. Rit-ual performance, in these instances, draws from the Americas' historical palette of colonialism, slavery, Black and Afrolatinx modernities, migration, and multiple revolutionary wars.

The *bolerista* pays homage to the lyrics and musical score in a manner that honors the composer and yet also uniquely makes it their own (Pedelty 1999:43; Vargas 2008:185). Performances of boleros are considered "interpretations,"[44] versions that are made great by artists with very specific stylistic signatures. Famous female interpreters of the bolero like Chelo Silva, La Lupe, Olga Guillot, and Sylvia Rexach create profoundly dramatic and emo-tional renditions of standards, reinventing them as new experi-ences with every listen. Still, audiences are aware of the bolero as authored, and composers like Augustín Lara, Isolina Carrillo, Consuelo Velázquez, Ema Elena Valdelamar, and María Grever are as lovingly remembered as the interpreters of their music.[45] In some instances, the composer and interpreter, like Sylvia Rexach and Ema Elena Valdelamar, are one and the same.

Audiences often sing along and collaborate with live and recorded performances in their own practices of simultaneously inhabiting the worlds of the bolero and their memories. This participatory and open process indicates a vernacular and popular transphysical poetics of interpretation and embodiment that make the bolero a significantly mutable and regenerative performative practice. Enactment of the bolero crosses temporalities, nationalities, generations, sexualities, and genders (Monsiváis 1997, 2004:17–18; Pedelty 1999:50–54; Quiroga 2000:149). The bolero is then a chimera that draws out emotion, ambivalence, and alterity as modes of community building. Its power is fueled by the intertwining of sexual and spiritual tension. Like Erinle, the bolero is both male and female, moves between topographical locations, and embodies a righteous elegance born from pain.[46] Thus Sirena, Erinle, and the bolero enact mobile ways of becoming that have the potential to aesthetically resist patriarchy and heteronormativity.

Like the interpreters performing familiar boleros that transform listeners to different temporal and sensory worlds, spiritual leaders generate new realities out of ancient beings made manifest through the artistry of cohabitation. The most famous spiritual workers interpret particular inhabitations and expressions of orichas, muertos, and other entities in memorable and aesthetically consistent ways. Scholars are now taking the artists-priests, spiritual workers, and divine beings they enact as models seriously for rethinking the performance of history, social spectacle, and ontological Blackness in Afro-Cuban religious cultures.[47] Embodiment and discourses performed by recognizable actors from other temporalities and planes of existence influence the cultural analysis of both time and the collective sensual experience of the ephemeral.[48] As with the bolero, experiences of a familiar yet unique manifestation of an entity through a great interpreter/priestess create the condition for negotiating time, feeling, and the possibility of touching a reality that is in many ways intratangible as well. Great spiritual leaders like Fermina Gómez, Omi Tomi, Mãe Menininha, Chico Xavier, among many others, bring beings and communities to life in their enacted and recorded ritual work.[49] Archives of conjure suggest a transformational site for retracing the context, inspiration, and limitations of work with the dead as interlocutors and active kin. Also like the bolero, spiritual enactments and collectives in Afrolatinx archives of conjure are enlaced within the social and cultural context of the Caribbean and Latin America, with all the accompanying racial, gendered, and sexual "ideologies of embodiment" that these postcolonial sites imply (Wirtz 2014a:130–34). Thus the expression of racial, social, sexual, and cultural tensions in the interpretation of a bolero or a divinity become irreducible to universalist renderings of temporality and transcendental metaphysics.[50]

Elegance and beauty are specific characteristics that Erinle and Sirena Selena share in their interpretation of the mystical and the sensual (Tsang 2013:121; Santos-Febres 2000b:71). In narratives that connect spiritual artistry and gender ambiguity with the healing of sexual trauma, the oricha and the transformista create unique spaces in the imagination for their work, divascapes.[51] Divascapes act as important trajectories in Afrolatinx archives of conjure. They are performative locations where patriarchal and machista orientations of the nation, the family, and the body are challenged. The residual transcriptions created by participants in a divascape note emotive transformations that operate as ritual. These changes occur in ephemeral and affective realms that live in the body as memory, as the audience's reaction to Sirena Selena's performance suggests. Divas enact sensuality as "high life" and perform sexuality as potently divine: "Mujer, mujer divina, tienes el veneno que fascina en tu mirar" (Woman, divine woman, you have the poisonous look that fascinates) (Monsiváis 1997:72).[52] Divas are not nice little ladies that conform to notions of respectability. It takes reflexive artistry and verve to create divas' illusion and wonder. As curated embodiments of powerful femininity, divas perform desire and vengeance with an emotional authority that heals the community they are performing for and with.[53] In doing so, divas disidentify projections of danger and destruction that their non-normative subjectivity poses to the patriarchal subject.[54] This supposed threat is one of the main rationales for the perpetuation of sexual violence and death on queer, lesbian, and sexually transgressive figures.[55] Divas defy this violence by voicing their own version of the life story and death of a relationship. In so doing, they often enact elements of spirituality, magic, and nature within the aesthetics of sensuality.[56] Like muertos in archives of conjure, divas retell history within subversive frameworks that disorder official narratives of the past.

For both Sirena and Erinle, the power of their sensuality and beauty to transform and heal is connected to the sea. They inhabit multiple sites of being and becoming in water, on land, and through their embodiment. The imagery used in their narratives reveal an interconnected set of "scapes" already discussed: memoryscapes, divascapes, and, especially, seascapes. These relational sites are constructed through each other in ways that illustrate, as Arjun Appadurai notes, that "locality" is reliant on the mechanics of the rites of passage and the affective logics of structures of feeling (1996:179–81). Thus the multiple scapes that Sirena and Erinle perform come into being through ritual temporalities and emotive entanglements. Consider the opening of *Sirena Selena vestida de pena*, which behaves as a praise song to the ocean, desire, and divas:

Cáscara de coco, contento de jirimilla azul, por los dioses di, azucarada selena, suculenta sirena de las playas alumbradas. Bajo un *spotlight*, confiésate, lunática. Tú conoces los deseos desatados por las noches urbanas. Tú eres el recuerdo de remotos orgasmos reducidos a ensayos de *recording*. Tu y tus siete moños desalmados como un ave selenita, como ave fotoconductora de electrodos insolentes. Eres quien eres, Sirena Selena . . . y sales de tu luna de papel a cantar canciones viejas de Lucy Favery [sic], de Sylvia Rexach, de la Lupe sibarita,[57] vestida y adorada por los seguidores de tu rastro . . . [58]

(2009:11)

Coconut shell, melancholy and restless, from the gods you came, sweet Selena, succulent siren of the glistening beaches; confess, beneath the spotlight, *lunática*. You know the desires unleashed by urban nights. You are the memory of distant orgasms reduced to recording sessions. You and your seven soulless braids like a *selenita* bird, like a radiant bird with your insolent magnetism. You are who you are Sirena Selena . . . and you engage from your paper moon to sing the old songs of Lucy Favery [sic], Sylvia Rexach, La Lupe, sybarite, dressed and adored by those who worship your face . . . [59]

In this passage, Santos-Febres creates a visual and aural link to the ocean that also includes Santería's mythological resonances. The coconut shells that birth Selena from the gods reflect back on the *obí* divination done by Santería priests. And, like an oríkì praise poem, these lines open the book by celebrating Sirena's sensual, mystical, and artistic qualities in layers of language that serve as an incantation (Barber 1991).[60] Each consecutive line connects Sirena to mermaids, the moon, and the water divinity Yemayá. Two significant details are the invocation of Yemayá's sacred number seven and of the Yoruba symbolism of birds, representing women's power to hurt or heal through the powerful female entities known as Ìyámi Àjé, "my/our powerful mothers."[61] The obvious Homeric illusions found in the passage mingle with Yemayá's imagery to create an interactive mythological pastiche. Later in the novel, Santos-Febres refers back to this opening connection to the sirens of the sea when she writes that Sirena "deja su cola junto al mar / Allá de orillas" (Leaves her tail near the ocean, there on the shore), before performing her songs (2009 [2000]:221). The opening incantation in the text singles out a whole array of residual connections that readers are invited to interlace.

Sirena's own singing voice is described as part of a sonic seascape that enraptures all who hear its song with memories of past divas and desires. The space is ritually prepared by Sirena through rehearsal, choreography, and set design to create a topography of mystery and sensuality. Sirena's performances conjure up connections between the sea, the stage, song, and sex. The mention of recorded music behaves like memory by suggesting residual sounds and images of great *intérpretes* under the spotlight like "Lucy Favery, Sylvia Rexach, La Lupe." It invites us to recall their existence on celluloid and vinyl—archives of ephemeral performances conjured through a mediation that traces the affective passion of their art. Indeed, recordings, played through computers, televisions, jukeboxes, and radio stations,[62] are an important aspect of experiencing a "performing" archive of conjure (Vazquez 2013:170; Monsiváis 2004:17; Taylor 2003:110–13).

The term *oyentes* (listeners) in Latin American entertainment parlance connotes the loyal fandom of radio audiences and may be applied here to aficionados of the bolero. Santos-Febres is especially inviting the transnational, cosmopolitan, and media savvy bolero oyente into the novel. Her allusion to Harold Arlen's "It's Only Paper Moon" (1933) beckons the bilingual reader to recite the song's opening lyrics—"Say it's only a paper moon / Sailing over a cardboard sea / But it wouldn't be make believe if you believed in me"—before entering into *Sirena Selena vestida de pena*'s story world.[63] We are asked to surrender disbelief, to believe in that paper moon, cardboard sea, and play in the performance of the novel. The ideas of "phony" and "true" are irrelevant to the broader emotive logic of the novel, which endorses instead a value system based on depth of feeling. I would argue that Santos-Febres is invoking Glissant's notion of *relativisée* by showing a deeply fluid and specific kind of (Caribbean) existence through *Sirena Selena*.

This invitation for dialogic play between reader and novel is connected to the inspiration for adopting performative play in Yoruba and Caribbean ritual enactments of the sacred that also embrace aspects of humor, sexuality, and intellectual dexterity.[64] The transformista and the oricha likewise use the performative frame of play as a way to communicate and build worlds with their public or community/audience. There exists a metatheatrical aspect to how different bodies, personalities, and expressive modalities are performed in ritual artistry and artistry as ritual. In the contexts of Santería and transformista performances, this reflexivity allows for the cocreation of events and meaning relying on specific strategies of engagement, like interorality,[65] that grow out of Afrolatinx and Caribbean religious beliefs like divine sexuality.[66] Play here is a skill that is developed to allow for the expression of contested meanings, ironies, and productive tensions, especially during the heightened moments of performance. However, a philosophy of invention, imagination, and productive work with illusion spills into daily strategies of self-making that are resourceful in moments of stress, trauma, and alienation for both Afrolatinx women and transformistas who face violence because of an unapologetic use of sexual expression as a source of personal power. Mobility and creativity often develop hand in hand for sexiles like, for example, the Puerto Rican poet Julia de Burgos and our heroine Sirena Silena, both viewing the sea as the source of their inner strength and struggle.[67] These lived and imagined artists' raw portrayal of desire, emotion, and *mujerista* sexuality creates a basis for both public exaltation and social alienation that feeds into their becoming through wanderlust and lyricism.[68]

Divine narratives about the sea as a site, and as an oricha, tell of sexual violence and trauma that lead to journeying. Archives of conjure collect these tales of travel in the many versions of myths recited in daily life and on the page. These stories reveal creativity, and also cruelty, with respect to Yemayá and Erinle. Consider the following pataki:

> Yemayá amó locamente a un andrógino, el bellísimo Inle. Para satisfacer la pasión que el joven dios le inspiraba, lo raptó, lo llevó al fondo del mar y allí lo tuvo hasta que, sacando del todo su apetito, se aburrió de su amante. . . . Inle había visto lo que ninguna criatura divina o humana. El misterio insondable del mar, lo que oculta en lo más profundo. Y Yemayá, para que Inle a nadie lo contara . . . le cortó la lengua. Adviértase que es Yemayá quien habla con Inle en el Dilogún.[69]

(CABRERA 1980:45)

Yemayá was madly in love with the androgynous, gorgeous Inle [Erinle]. In order to satisfy the passion the young god inspired in her, she captured him, took him to the bottom of the ocean and kept him there until she was completely satisfied and then bored of her lover. . . . Inle had seen what no divine or human creature had ever seen. The bottomless mystery of the sea, what happens at the deepest of depths. And Yemayá, so that Inle would not tell a soul . . . cut out his tongue. Note that it is Yemayá who speaks with [for] Inle in the Dilogún [cowry shell divination].

This tale unveils layers of passion and violence that complicate the relationship between Yemayá and Erinle. Yemayá's overall image of the benevolent mother turns into that of the devouring, monstrous feminine, a type of maternal subjectivity that connotes aspects of unbridled, dangerous sexuality (Otero 1996; Kristeva 1980; Beliso-De Jesús 2013b).[70] In most versions of the narrative, Erinle's relationship to Yemayá is intimate yet abusive and constitutive of his ability to appear and speak to initiates ritually (Tsang 2013:118–21; Brown 2003:136, 141; Conner and Sparks 2004:78–79). Erinle acquires the secret knowledge of the depths of the ocean by being physically transported there by Yemayá. Later his tongue is removed by Yemayá because of what he has witnessed mystically and sensually. Here the sea gives but also takes away voice, reaffirming her awesome and mysterious power over sound and divination. It is noteworthy that Santería's cowry shell divination, the dilogún, comes from the ocean and that Yemayá dominates Erinle's ability to speak through this marine artifact.

There is something uncanny about Yemayá's desires turning violent when her truths would be exposed by a young transgendered love object. This is a situation of violence and exploitation all too familiar to the character of Sirena Selena as well as to many transgendered youth (Santos-Febres 2000b: 90–95).[71] I want to suggest that Santería's mythological corpus is ample and adapts to contemporary forms of vernacular oral literary criticism.[72] These tales are being told and read in the current Afrolatinx and Caribbean social contexts, and it is in these spaces in which Erinle and Sirena Selena speak to transgendered youth through their beauty, performativity, and experiences of abuse. The pataki, then, touches upon and warns against the institutionalized frameworks of power, especially between older and younger generations, that abuse access to ambiguous sexualities and gender performances.[73] Therefore, Santería's narratives incorporate new contexts and become relevant, resistant, and vigilant sources for developing community ethics that preserve life and personal dignity.

Yemayá's angry removal of Erinle's tongue also invites us to consider some intriguing parallels and reversals to Santos-Febres's framing of Sirena Selena's voice. For example, Sirena's voice was "given" to him by his mother and developed in song by his grandmother (Santos-Febres 2000b:45). As indicated, in divination it is Yemayá who "speaks for" Erinle. Like the performative tradition of the lip sync, where transformistas honor divas by inhabiting them through enactment, the shells ring out with a Yemayá's voice to express what Erinle wants to communicate. It is no coincidence that Yemayá, being the protector oricha of queer folk, often "speaks" for male deities when they have no voice.[74] Yet her violent treatment of Erinle, and of her favorite fowl, *el pato* (the duck), illustrates the nondyadic, dangerous, and complicated nature of her patronage.[75] Of note is how both Erinle and el pato pay with their voices for potential and enacted transgressions of secrecy.[76] In the case of the latter, Yemayá strangles the duck, damaging his voice forever. Of course, these cautionary tales underscore the central importance of secrecy in Santería. Yet, on another level, when read in an Afrolatinx queer folk context, they also indicate how multiple forms of violence manifest real consequences for not keeping the most delicate and damaging of sexual secrets. It is telling that Sirena experiences the violence and exploitation of prostitution, but also finds the courage to transmit her own voice and emotional truth through song.

Issues of inhabitation and voice play with different ends of the aesthetics of the lip sync, an important performance practice for transformistas.[77] Lip sync enactments play with the framing of performance by enhancing, usually one-upping, the voice recording of a popular song with heady vernacular theatrics. The lip sync negotiates voice in a relational matter. Similar to the transphysical poetics present in how spiritual copresences enact with bodies, the voice in a recording inhabits the lip sync virtuoso who then (silently) amplifies the song being transmitted through them. These voices belong to larger-than-life personalities (like bolero divas), which come with a rhizomatic array of affective and material associations.[78] The transformista creates story worlds for her performative selves out of associations that add to the emotional and imaginative depth of her performances. For example, a transformista develops and is inhabited by named personas with a history, like the Boricuas Sirena Selena, Nina Flowers,[79] or Martha Divine, which reverberate with how muertos' personalities manifest in spiritual masses. As with the medium's performative symbiosis with the dead, the transformista as diva and the diva on the recording are perpetually reinvented through each other. And, also like ritual work with spiritual copresences,[80] the body and consciousness of the transformista must be meticulously prepared for the enactment of the lip sync. This includes investing in complex physical transformations and mastering techniques of illusion.[81] Add to these considerations that informed audiences act as immediate critics and respondents to performances that make the drag show intensely collaborative, like Caribbean ritual play. Thus the recorded voice in a lip sync acts more like a musical score arranged by the transformista as a conductor, assembling moving parts to create a multifaceted performance. These performances *are* rituals that create kin whose residual memories of enacted moments are important traces to accessing queer Afrolatinx archives of conjure.

Transformistas take these skills of orchestration into their everyday lives where they have to negotiate precarious social contexts. Consider how on the surface it seems that Santos-Febres writes the character of Sirena Selena in a manner that breaks the drag-performative mold of the lip sync because Sirena uses her own voice to transmit the boleros she interprets. Yet Sirena enacts the aesthetics of the worlds of drag and the bolero in a manner the merges the two terrains. This is a significant move Santos-Febres makes in aligning Afrolatinx feminist, gay male, and transgendered cultural production in the novel. The text creates a distinctly nonheteronormative space that is critical of patriarchal control over multiple kinds of bodies, especially through cultural, social, and physical violence. The novel also reveals the relationships of these kinds of violence to neocolonialism, racism, and the effects of globalization in Puerto Rico and the Dominican Republic. The complexity of the geopolitical relationship between these two neighboring societies is mitigated in the work through the representation of transnational yet localized queer and drag cultures that emphasize the heterogeneity of Latinx LGBTQ+ experiences. Thus queer kinship plays a central role in providing a means to economic, emotional, and physical survival.[82]

Creativity *as* kinship, through performance, allows for Sirena Selena to survive a brutal rape by a john at age twelve. After Sirena's first drag mother, La Valentina Frenesí, finds him bleeding in the street, she "lloró, lloró con él. Lo levantó de entre los escombros, se lo echó al hombro. De dos patadas, botó los tacos mientras corría" (cried, cried with him. She lifted him up from the rubbish, and put him over her shoulder. With two kicks, she flung off her high heels as she ran) (94). La Valentina then finds a gypsy cab that takes them to the hospital. When the driver, El Chino, asks what she will say when the authorities ask for Sirena's documentation as a minor, she responds: "<<Nada, mentir>>. . . mentir como jamás había mentido. Tirarse el *performance* de su vida para salvare la suya a su amiguito" ("Nothing, lie." . . . lie like she never has in her life. Throw herself into the *performance* of her life in order to save her beloved friend) (94, emphasis in the original). Here the intensity, danger, and precariousness of Sirena Selena's existence as a child prostitute is confronted with swift creativity by La Valentina: kinship and performance act hand in hand. These passages show how unofficial ways of becoming family are based on relational and affective bonds, "structures of feeling," that are consciously enacted rather than genetically produced, especially in queer Latinx communities.[83] La Valentina nurses Sirena Selena back to health before she dies of a heroin overdose herself, illustrating the bittersweet and short-lived nature of their small family. The story of Valentina's performance, one that saves Sirena inside the novel, is its own residual transcription where imagination as memory is encouraged of the reader.

Creole religious practices play an important role in the construction of Afrolatinx queer kinship transnationally. Artists, transformistas, activists, and writers find inspiration for creating chosen, nongenetic families from the incorporative ritual kinship practices of religions like Santería and Espiritismo. For example, in an interview conducted by Gloria Anzaldúa, Yemayá devotee Eduardo Mejía explains that, in New York, "you visit any Hispanic drag queen's apartment and what do you see—a grand altar!"[84] And José Vigo, Eduardo's friend, adds that drag queens in New York read the "caracoles (cowry shells)" and "work the *obra* (craft)."[85] As noted earlier in this chapter, rites of passage create lineage, communities, and localities based on relational social performances that include the invention of tradition.[86] The Afro-trans-latinx and queer traditions of drag, altar-making, divination, and casting spells, according to Eduardo and José, illustrate a continuum of creative kinship practices that address the interconnected nature of ritual to quotidian practices of place that can be traced as residual transcripts.

Queer kinship relies on the transformative liminality found in rites of passage. Like the archive, the stage and the altar are two important ritual sites constitutive of queer family.[87] It is important to note that ritually prepared sites, like altars, thrones, and bóvedas, are essential components, I would even say participants, of Afrolatinx religious performances. These sites frame liminal spaces where connections to extensive, often ephemeral kin can be developed through multiple performance practices: naming, singing, embodied motion including dance and material culture. The stage and the altar also mark areas where transformistas and practitioners imbue material culture with imagination in a transformative manner that also plays with time. The work of folklorist Cory Thorne on the ways that drag queens perform the orichas in Havana gay bars suggests new inventions of traditions that blur the localities of the stage and altar.[88]

In merging the stage and the altar, orichas and divas share legendary performance status.[89] Afrolatinx transformistas' renditions of deities also suggest a kind of "reading" that acts as vernacular metacriticism. Performances of inhabitation allow for the fleshing out of great figures and songs through unique, personalized renditions. Transformistas' homages to divas like La Lupe, Celia Cruz, and Lucy Fabery behave like oríkì, Yoruba praise poetry that calls down deities or celebrates heroes through elaborate wordplay. In Nigeria, women are the true masters of oríkì, performing with lightning speed the satire, punning, and play that can both exalt and sting the subject of the verses (Barber 1990, 1991). In a similar fashion, a transformistas' ability to play multiple kinds of "lip service"—through "reading" as well as the "lip sync"—is vital to her social standing among other queens.[90] Thus verbal agility is a central aesthetic for praise performers, whether they be oríkì singers or transformistas. Both sets of artists seek to reveal multiple manifestations of legendary and immortal figures through their performative work. Spiritually and sensually infused movement, dance, and words are arsenals of expression that illustrate the intimate historical and cultural connections lying within Afrolatinx worlds of performance. Again, the organizing principle of a transphysical poetics of being and becoming allows for the body to become malleable and open to copresences and transmission.[91] The marriage of these different yet adjacent traditions of vernacular expression create a unique opportunity for locating queer Afrolatinx and Caribbean sites in multiple genres of artistic work, including literature, performance, and ritual practice.[92] These sites constitute overlapping archives of conjure.

Ritual and spectacle performances directly connected to Erinle illustrate unique examples of feminist and queer Afrolatinx site-making through Santería. On October 24, the Catholic feast day for Saint Rafael, LGBTQ+ practitioners, mainly women priests, in Cuba pay homage to both the archangel and Erinle by lighting a straw fish full of firecrackers on the street.[93]

Before thinking through this ritual, however, I would like to refer back, residually, to the story of Saint Rafael and Tobias found in the book of Tobit, a Hebrew narrative that also exists as a Greek apocryphal text (Sundermann 2008:155–56). The biblical legend gives us a basis for examining the creative admixture of correlative Yoruba and Catholic symbolism found in Afrolatinx vernacular religious rites, narratives, and symbolism. For both Saint Rafael and Erinle are conjured through each other in ritual work, memory, and creativity without losing their individual spheres of resonance and healing.

Tobias was the son of Tobit, a blind and faithful Israelite merchant who fell on hard times due to hostilities with the Assyrian king. Tobit sends the young and inexperienced Tobias on a journey toward the ancient Persian town of Rey to collect money from a former business partner. Along the way, Tobias meets a helpful traveler, Azria (son of Ananis), who is accompanied by a small dog, and they decide to make the journey together. What is unknown to Tobias is that the traveler is God's own "archangel of healing," Rafael, who has disguised himself as a human being.[94] They travel to the east, and when they get to the Tigris River Tobias catches an enormous, monstrous fish. Azria (Rafael) tells Tobias to keep the fish's liver, gallbladder, and heart for their healing properties. Upon reaching Ecbatana, they stay with Tobit's cousin, Ragouel. Tobias wants to marry his cousin Sara, but she is the victim of the demon Asmodaios's curse. As a result, Sara's last seven bridegrooms have all died. Yet Rafael knows how to vanquish the demon with his alchemical skill and tells Tobias to prepare the heart and liver of the fish and burn it in the bridal chamber after the marriage ceremony. The smell of smoked fish drives Asmodaios away,[95] and Rafael captures the demon in upper Egypt and binds him there for "all eternity."[96] Tobias collects his father's money and returns home, where he heals his father's blindness with a remedy made from the magical fish's gallbladder. At this point, Rafael reveals his true identity as an archangel and returns to heaven. Tobias and Sara return to her father's land and live out their days.

This story illustrates the many residual transcriptions that connect Saint Rafael to Erinle. It also shows how vernacular Catholic religious hagiography acts as an archive of conjure. This unofficial tale opens up the logics of Afrolatinx cultural assemblages that embroider together seemingly disparate narratives and rituals. Foremost, the biblical tale shows how Saint Rafael and Erinle share properties of healing sourced through a river, and with fish in particular. (Recall that Erinle is known as a healing deity that resides in a river, and is the patron of fishermen in Nigeria and Cuba.) Like Saint Rafael's vanquishing of the demon for Tobias and Sara, Erinle of Ilobu fights invaders to protect his people. These similarities create a rich spiritual, ritual, and narrative resource in which new spiritual kinships can be constantly extended beyond and across multiple boundaries.

What I want to emphasize here is that the interweaving of Saint Rafael and Erinle in Cuban Santería illustrates a deep knowledge of both Catholic hagiography and Yoruba mythology. Elsewhere I have written about the reductive nature of explanations that depict Catholic saints solely as "masks" for Yoruba deities in Afro-Cuban religions.[97] Though I appreciate the anticolonialist thrust of such arguments, the result is a flattening and dualistic misreading of how expansive Yoruba and Afrolatinx religious traditions actually work on the ground. For deities, angels, and spirits merge and move in ways that conflate and reformulate their symbolic universes based on Afrolatinx, heterogeneous, and nonbinary logics that also embrace new racial, gendered, and place-making manifestations. This is where queer spiritual kinship comes into being in terms of a kind of creative audacity, or *nerve* in gay vernacular, to expand family in ways that especially destabilize patriarchal and heteronormative nation-building projects.[98] In other words, the transnational, polylingual cohabitation of Saint Rafael and Erinle in ritual acts, speech, and the imagination makes them and their devotees kin in ways that destabilize and circumvent religious and cultural essentialisms. Catholic hagiography, symbols, and rituals are recontextualized physically and ritually in Afrolatinx vernacular practice, especially in Cuban public spaces like el Rincón de San Lázaro,[99] in a defiance that clearly lays claim to a Black vernacular Catholicism based on Yoruba-inspired religiosity.

Public rituals for Erinle and Saint Rafael share the symbolism of fish and water through the Caribbean transphysical poetics I have been highlighting in this chapter. The yearly displays of commemoration for the oricha and the archangel also create connections to ritual moments imagined as part of Santería's past through vernacular history and chisme as archives of conjure for these two beings.[100] According to Cabrera, celebrations date back at least to the nineteenth century, where, on Saint Rafael's Feast Day in el Barrio de Ángel,

> por la noche se quemaba un pez de pajo relleno de polvo y con cohetes en la cola; la procesión y los fuegos artificiales resultaban espléndidos.
>
> (1975:58–59)

during the night a fish made of straw filled with gunpowder and with firecrackers sticking out of its tail would be set on fire; the procession and the resulting fireworks were splendid.

Cabrera goes on to relate how the majority of celebrants were same-sex loving practitioners devoted to Erinle.[101] For example, she also gossips that one priestess of Erinle, a seamstress named La Zumbão who organized the procession in 1887, was part of the "sociedad religiosa de Alacuattás" (the religious society of Alacuattás) (1975 [1954]:58).[102] *Alacuattá* is a Lukumí term used to refer to same-sex-loving women. Erinle is also described as imperious, strict, *fuerte* (strong), and *misterioso* (mysterious) with his devotees (Cabrera 1975 [1954]:58–59). It is significant to note how Cabrera's secondhand descriptions of rituals and followers devoted to Erinle and Saint Rafael invoke a historic framing that includes active participation by alacuattás in public religious work.

The Lukumí terms *alacuattá* and *adodi* suggest some productive difficulties, considerations, and caveats for considering the historical contexts, taxonomies, and cultural translation of Afrolatinx queer kinship. The question here is how to understand the work that these terms do in shifting contexts where they are simultaneously legible and illegible. I want to point to how the use of these terms allows for Cabrera to relate a historical imaginary that includes Afrolatinx public ritual as a site for creating and expressing queer kinship as a residual transcript of hearsay. They are legible yet perhaps also problematically flattened with that recognition. However, Cabrera's use of chisme to pass on this information suggests a looser kind of marking that does not carry the weight of institutional pinning. Her gossip also allows for an alternative register for passing on a history, contained within and generated through archives of conjure, both infectious and unverifiable. One must also remember that Cabrera herself is a trickster of sorts whose writing sits between the storytelling modes of ethnography and fiction. Thus readers either relish or are rankled by the unverifiability of her content and the ironic mischievousness of her discourse.

The shared symbolism between the Archangel Saint Rafael and the oricha Erinle allows access to a Caribbean imagination that is based on a historically, culturally, and symbolically layered "series of relationships" (Glissant 1992:139). These relationships are surely marked by the colonial realities of slavery and racism, but also spiritual pliability and resilience. Here I want to emphasize that the tension between these modalities offers an opportunity for creativity and self-invention. In the case of Erinle, this ability to hold tensions is gendered and sexualized in Cuban mythology, iconography, and ritual. As historic speculation through residual transcripts, the brilliant ritual Cabrera describes also acts as a defiant reaffirmation of Erinle's promise to be many things, in this case fire and water all at once.

Santería, transformista, and diva performances can heal by speaking and singing through different voices. As we see with La Valentina's performance, which saves Sirena Selena's life, it is not only the notion of truth but also existence that is relative. The figures of Erinle, Sirena Selena, and La Valentina recreate multiple editions of themselves in order to heal and negotiate the hostilities and violence shown them and their kin. Santos-Febres draws heavily on modes of personhood that reconstruct the self in flux through constant rehearsal in building her characters (Santos-Febres 2000b:60; Castillo 2001:17). And, as I have been exploring in this chapter, the refashioning of a shared embodiment is a central mode of being and becoming in both Santería and in transformista folk cultures that rely on conjuring their own archives of memory.

Literature that quotes religious and folk vernacular performance, and ritual performances that quote mythological narrative, are relational components of the texture of Caribbean transphysical poetics that also shape archives of conjure.[103] In the novel *Sirena Selena vestida de pena*, and in patakís about

Erinle, embodiment, desire, trauma, and healing result from complicated performances of sexuality and gender that do not conform to dyadic categories. Rather, like the tensions that frame ritual play,[104] these performances reimagine new kinds of kin, bodies, and emotive realities through storytelling and song. They also speak to histories and experiences that resist both universalizing and transcendence because specificity and complexity are constitutive of their enactment. Afrolatinx ritual and drag performances promote ways of listening, feeling, and participation that are uniquely pliable, slippery, and resistant to homogenization. Likewise, Glissant's words that open this chapter remind us that reality, materiality, and the imagination are constructed through each other. Literary work, ritual, and song are important kinds of participation in imagining that asks us to use different senses and modes of interaction. Yet these different modes of expression can take their textures, themes, aesthetics, and semiotics from a recognized cultural palette. Afrolatinx queer and feminist cultures of performing diva spiritualities reflect Ochumaré,[105] the rainbow deity that traces the affective geography of emotion and desire through an archive of conjure that regenerates, remembers, and recreates.

CONCLUSION
Espuma del Mar, Sea-Foam

Mi amante el mar pulsa una canción sonora y amante,
tiende una alfombra de espumas amantes,
abre su inmenso pecho de amante, mueve sus labios tibios
de amante: —*ven de noche, ven al oscurecer, parte rápido.*
No piensas que te vigilan, y corre; no oigas los disparos y
huye. Sigue huyendo, huyendo siempre, huye.

> —Reinaldo Arenas, excerpt from "Mi amante el mar," *Inferno*

My lover the sea pulsates a sonorous and loving song,
unfurls a carpet of loving sea-foam,
opens its immense lover's chest, moves its warm lips
of a lover: —*come at night, come at dusk, leave quickly.*
Don't think that they watch you, and run; don't listen to the shots,
and flee. Keep fleeing, always fleeing, flee.

Arenas's ode to the sea is marked by a feverish sense of flight. The *espuma del mar*, the sea-foam in the poem, creates a sensation of respite and love for an otherwise persecuted subject. The sea's song is one of life, love, warning. Like a vigilant lover, it asks Arenas's speaker to flee, keep moving in the night, at dusk. The ocean's amorous voice and resplendent blue presence starkly contrasts with the backdrop of surveillance and violence that follows Arenas's subject. It is a safe space for what is otherwise hell, *inferno*, the title of the trilogy containing this poem. It seems no coincidence that Arenas's last name means "sand" and that much of his work heralds the ocean. Both he and his dear friend Lydia Cabrera adored Yemayá because of her unwavering ability to witness, wash, and remain.

The stanza selected to open the conclusion of this volume rightly highlights the pain, rejection, and sense of persecution that many LGBTQ+ practitioners of Afrolatinx spiritual practices have encountered. Sea-foam acts as an important site of conjure in the poem and in this book because of its effervescence. Sea-foam evokes memory because of the many ways we hear, feel, smell, or see it. As a rhythmic aftermath of a wave, it acts as a residual transcript. The fleeting nature of sea-foam is a testimony to nature, to action, and to experience. The archives of conjure explored in this book work like sea-foam in their multivalent ability to signal the surfacing of ritual histories from the depths of writing, divination, and cohabitation with the dead. The patterns, legacies, and trajectories for each narrative of discovery is unique, yet connected to the larger whole, a sea of traditions. These traditions form a vernacular way of remembering and enacting life histories through ritual and conjure. The conjuring of sea-foam, as a talisman or an embodied sensation, offers a kind of persistence. It asks us to stay with the ephemeral, to be in the moment, to believe in and activate the passing of things.

This approach has ramifications for work with Afrolatinx communities, texts, and material culture. Spiritual work that commemorates and vivifies the dead in the African and Latinx

Americas illustrates the way in which creative expression operates as a weapon. For example, the layering of *armamentos*, weapons, in objects like ngangas illustrate an understanding of the power of this work.[1] The objective is not only to provide a line of spiritual resistance but also to create a chimera that confuses enemies, sends them off track. Thus coding is inherent in how spiritual warfare effectively operates in Afrolatinx conjure of protection. In conducting ethical ethnographic, critical, and/or historical research with communities that keep such guardian dead, we must take into account the reasons for this first line of defense. Often manifesting as African or Amerindian warriors, these spiritual fighters are conjured from the justified rage simmering from centuries of white supremacy, slavery, sexual violence, economic and territorial disenfranchisement. The knowledge that creates their power acts as mirrors of conjure, *mpakas*,[2] that reflect and deflect strangers' intentions. This conjure arms and protects, actively interfering with harmful work and thoughts.

How do *guerrero* (warrior) spirits and sea-foam come together as frameworks for doing research in Afrolatinx religions, then? The answer lies in the power of the imagination and the senses to pay attention to the unbelievable, uncomfortable, and the forgotten. Taking the dialogic thrust of reciprocal ethnography seriously means facing our own roles in perpetuating some of the forms of power that the mpaka and the sea's mist reflects back. Race, national citizenship, gender, institutional affiliation, and economic position all are a portion of this refracted picture.[3] Moreover, Afrolatinx spiritual communities assess the risks and benefits of working with outsiders for scholarship, resources, and the religious proliferation of traditions. Thus the relationships I describe and analyze in the chapters of this volume are already based on various kinds of negotiations.

Acknowledging that the dead and orichas serve as vital actors influencing events, encounters, and collaborations between believers and outsiders centers an Afrolatinx spiritual worldview.[4] The work of rituals and their residual transcriptions are action oriented. Change is a central motivating factor in the creation of spells, cleansing, and talismans. Conjure is thus a set of practices that invites innovation through often unexpected means. One must be open to risk and uncertainty in order to enact metaphysical outcomes. This book has been an exploration of points of contact facilitated by the embodied acts of writing, ritual, and the creation of material culture as conjure. Interlocutors like Yemayá, Oxúm, and Ta José push us toward points of interest that connect unlikely ancestors and practitioners together in scholarly and spiritual pursuits.

Residual transcripts allow for there to be a record that is also a call to action based on points of connection drawn in communication with spiritual interlocutors. The notes scribbled on a calling card in the archive, instructions on a piece of paper for a cleansing from a misa, or a beaded necklace inherited from a loved one are calls for enacted practices. What I am suggesting is that there are coded practices of continuity within Afrolatinx cultural and religious expression that provide models for how to engage more equitably and respectfully in research with and about these traditions. By following the leads left by spirits and imperfect ancestors, important narratives about the past and present are uncovered to reveal entanglements and relationships that complicate the construction of an ethnographic present or the description of an authentic tradition. Who we ask, what outcomes are considered plausible, and how cause/effect is understood in the analysis of culture must be reexamined in light of the ritual imagination I am invoking in this work. Taking in the whole picture means taking in the importance of egun, Oxúm, and divination to Landes's development as a scholar of the spirit, for example. This also means we take Madre de Agua's song at the séance, Cabrera's gossip about the gods,[5] and the oríkì of drag seriously as expressions of the transphysical poetics that govern Afrolatinx and Caribbean means of being and becoming through words of embodiment.

In this study, antiracist, intersectional feminist, and LGBTQ+ epistemologies govern the aesthetics of performing the archives of conjure. The focus on rhizomatic and nonlinear temporalities mirror Afrolatinx religious understandings of the cyclical nature of ritual and ecological time. This book has argued that the transmigration of souls in misas create the template for understanding the movement of race and culture in the idea of transculturation, especially in Cuba, Puerto Rico, and Brazil. Spirit guides are gendered, raced, and religiously aligned with multiple forms of Catholic, African, and Indigenous vernacular practices, including and especially conjure. The crossings of transnational selves and intersubjective accumulation of centuries of violence and revolt are witnessed and told through mediums' bodies. The visceral experience of communication with the dead during a misa is one laden with touch, sound, smell, and taste. It is in the spirit's handshake of mutual exchange and recognition: "¡Sala malekum! ¡Malekum sala!"[6] Or, in the wafting smell of cigar smoke in the air as the candles burn and the rum is sprayed in a benediction of the bodies present. The presence of the dead is felt through bodies and recorded in sensorial memory. Bodies also record spirits' advice on paper with pencil as part of the misa's work. It is understood that the communion between worlds prompts further action, will require personal journeys for each medium and participant enacting the ritual. These scraps of paper move from misa to purses and bags, kitchen tables, and later drawers. They create, in another sense, an archive of conjure that can tell a history of a community's interactive life with spirit guides and the work they do collectively in the world together.

This dialogue across existence is a powerful, creative tool that can serve as a reciprocal model of listening and exchange. More than reflexivity, looking and listening to residual transcripts requires a suspension of disbelief, a letting go of the Eurocentric models of positivism and social Darwinism that can underlie assumptions about spiritual cultural practices and their ability to promote agency. Too often the models for social justice and change that researchers want to see reflected in the cultures they study are their own. This study has focused on the spiritual component to liberation in Afrolatinx religious practices, which conjures multiple forms of materiality that blur the boundaries of race, sexuality, and gender. Liberation here means the continual process of communication with key entities that facilitate flowing through ecologies of being. The work mediums and scholars do in the world with Yemayá's and Ochún's special relationship of flow, for example, illustrate the power of conjure to reproduce itself through tradition and innovation. Cabrera's mosaic history of the LGBTQ+ roads of the orichas and their priestesses constitutes a space for recovery vital to creating spiritual kinship. These stories and ritual details are weapons in combating some of the machista and homophobic practices and ideologies that strive to marginalize some practitioners of Santería and Palo.[7]

Cabrera's coded subversion of cultural authenticity by introducing queer and feminist readings of Yemayá, Ochún, and Erinle are important residual transcripts for folklorists and anthropologists to consider. For too long, the "authentic" has been the currency for validating the traditionality of cultural practices.⁸ Yet traditions of challenging authenticity abound in Afrolatinx spiritual practices that embrace the multiplicity of becoming. Espirtismo's focus on the inhabitation of various subjectivities and points of view in a misa is a perfect example of how seemingly binary modes of materiality and spirituality are deeply intertwined. Whether it is the racially charged movement of doubled spirit guides like El Indio and El Congo or the fluid sexualities of La Gitana and La Monja, a dense yet playful layering of social categories influence the kinds of conjure these entities provoke. Thus the joining of the spiritual and the material is fueled by what mediums, scholars, and the dead see as mutual and lasting interests. In terms of methodology, that means listening to and taking mutable and occasionally material entities like Yemayá and Ta José seriously.

There is a cyclical factor at play when scholar-practitioners like Cabrera and Landes become egun that must also be attended through work inspired by their residual transcriptions. We can see citational practices as a kind of conjure that is located, for example, on the page, in a ritual bath, and around an ileke for Oxúm. My goal in this book has been to locate "cites" of conjure for women and LGBTQ+ practitioners of Afrolatinx religions at the behest of our shared community and dead. Empowerment lies in shifting modes of transmission in scholarly engagements so that ideologies of white supremacy, patriarchy, and heteronormativity are challenged. Poetry, pataki, boleros, and drag performance contain the aesthetics that drive this revolutionary work. These artistic forms of expression illustrate how the page and the stage create a powerful matrix for conjure.

In writing about transgendered sirens, I have investigated narratives of Erinle and the literature of Mayra Santos-Febres. The stories that emerge about fluid gender performance and healing through sensuality work against a Cartesian split between mind and body. The embrace of nonbinary modes of being, especially through sexual becoming, reinforces the flowing cycles of life and death. Again, the sea provides voice and inspiration for expressing multiplicity, dissolution, and regeneration of forms of existence in Santería patakí and Afrolatinx literature. Influencing both kinds of texts is ritual play. Play at the borders of sexuality and gender is an important ritual framework for Yoruba-inspired religious cultures.[9] It produces aché, freedom, and consciousness. Performances that enact female power, traditions like the Gẹlẹdẹ festival, the lip sync, and oríkì praise poetry, rely on embodied transformations that cross ontological boundaries.[10] *Iyami Osoronga* (wise women) who become birds,[11] transformistas, and Cuban polymorphous orichas all represent beings whose conjured forms break patriarchal and homophobic taxonomies. Whether it be eugenics or religion, Erinle's and Sirena Selena's tales wreak havoc on social orders that impose male domination and heteronormativity. More to the point, the cross-pollination of traditions of self-expression and actualization are creating situated examples of diasporic becoming that highlight potent alliances.

Afrolatinx transformistas perform lip syncs as oríkì that tell vernacular histories, invoke sacred sexualities, and generate community empowerment. Their performance traditions borrow from, honor, and divert importantly from Yoruba women's oríkì traditions. Yet both expressive forms share the ability to conjure moments of freedom by embodying strength through artistry.[12] These ritual revolts occur in a deterritorialized Atlantic continuum: alliances are recorded and passed on through residual transcripts that, like sea-foam, are observable but also subtly evasive. The residues of the defiant ritual performances I discuss in this volume indicate vital movements that continue to develop and transform.

As with most kinds of folklore, new expressions among Afrolatinx spiritual practitioners are constantly being created to indicate deep and lasting connections between the sacred and popular culture, especially through social media.[13] Here the circum-Caribbean has a special resonance in locating archives of conjure connected through a transphysical poetics that embraces transnationalism and orality. The generation of vernacular Caribbean and Afrolatinx religious practice occurs in tandem with the enjoyment of music, dance, and video. Caribbean authors like Cabrera and Santos-Febres offer narratives of translocal cultural exchanges based on intertextual and interoral aesthetics. Storytelling based on local Cuban and Puerto Rican oral traditions is a vital factor for the ways in which they allow us to experience vernacular culture through their written forms.[14] As Glissant rightly reminds us, "we should perhaps not forget that we have a role to play in the complex reuniting of writing and speech" (1992:108). I see this comment as pointing out the false dichotomy drawn between the oral and the written, often used as the basis for deciphering levels of "development" and "progress"—two notions clearly generated from a colonial teleology.[15] Thus the Afrolatinx communities studied in this book fight against such flattening of their words and acts. They perform the complex work of uniting the written and the oral through the embodied enactment of rituals that generate residual transcriptions in archives of conjure.

The stories told by mediums and their spirits take on multiple forms. Transcripts, spells, and stitches change the texture of the narratives offered and how we read them. Our receptive repertoires need to expand to include symbols of conjure whose signification recall the material semiotics discussed in the introduction.[16] The long-lasting and regenerative aspects highlighted in spiritual expressive culture include elements from the sea and rivers like sand, shells, and stones. These natural objects hold stories of movement, narratives of ecological journeys that involve us all in geological time. Afrolatinx spiritual traditions allow for the acceptance of such contexts, which are larger than individual selves and lifetimes. The narratives told by mediums and priestesses in this book point repeatedly to the importance of the allegorical pedagogies that natural and supernatural elements offer. Attention to ancestors, deities, and to the natural world creates mutual respect for multiple ways of being.

In terms of the methods that can be adopted from such observations, perhaps thinking through the relationship between authorship and authority may be the most useful. In working through archives of conjure with mediums and spiritual interlocutors, I believe that writing and listening to residual transcriptions are vital points of arrival and departure for folklorists, anthropologists, historians, and literary critics. Adopting the leads given to us by residual transcripts reveals elements central to how Afrolatinx communities survive and thrive. The connections to the people and topics we study reveal the mystery and responsibility in creating our scholarship and relationships. The effects of working conjure in the field, archive, and on the page occur as a trust in the logic of transforming reality in the face of the ongoing adversarial components of hate, ignorance, and intolerance.

I would like to return to Arenas in closing this study. His poem goes on to tell us what the speaker sees as he flees at the sea's insistence. He writes:

> Yo veo
> catedrales y cielos,
> transatlánticos, trenes y

conciertos, playas, neblinas y
auténtica soledad.[17]

    I see
cathedrals and skies,
transatlantics, trains and
concerts, beaches, fog and
authentic solitude.

The sea's lover focuses on movement: across the water,
through the air, via trains. There is the witnessing of life through
music, the shore, fog, and yet also an experience of true loneliness. The mixture of gusto and sorrow is a quality that Arenas
masters to express the persecution he experienced as a gay writer
and Cuban exile.[18] In the stanza, we see that transatlantic movement gives the lover a unique perspective of the world. The sea's
(Yemayá's) advice of flight offers him a language of observation
and experience. His solitude is always a writer's solitude, one
who writes from a space of desire, rage, and sublime curiosity.

The larger work of *Inferno* consists of poetry written between
1963 and 1983—a lifetime of accomplishments and disappoint-
ments for Arenas in and out of Cuba. The ocean's place in this
dark oeuvre is one of lover, mother, and executioner. The sea in
this poem operates as it does in many of his other works: as a
constant setting, an observer, and an inspiration. "Mi amante el
mar" invokes two other works, Arenas's novel, *El color del verano*
(1999) (*The Color of Summer*, 2001), and his autobiography *Antes
que anochezca* (1992) (*Before Night Falls*, 1994).[19] All three reveal
the importance of the ocean as a textual space for negotiating
the deterritorialization from Cuba and in the world that he experiences.[20] His biting and satirical observations of sex, politics,
and art are written with a touching reflexivity. Always obsessed

FIGURE C.1 Left to right, authors Hilda Perera, Enrique Labrador Ruiz, Lydia Cabrera, and Reinaldo Arenas at an homage to Cabrera, Miami, 1982. Courtesy of the Cuban Heritage Collection, University of Miami Libraries, Coral Gables, Florida.

with the ability to express himself freely as an author, Arenas wrote incessantly from prison, on the run, and in exile. His work "continues a tradition of frictional life-writing," in line with many other Cuban authors whose aesthetics consisted of establishing sustained tensions in their texts (Ette 2016:149).[21] It is telling that Arenas's work, like Ortiz's and Cabrera's, balances folk and avant-garde elements of Cuban culture in ways that orient readers toward this complexity.

Arenas ended his life in 1990 in New York City when complications from AIDS made his existence unbearable. It is illuminating that his work continues to be read and analyzed after his passing, as with Cabrera. This indicates to me that there is an audience hungry to hear these voices, their presence as queer Cuban muertos is unwilling to be silenced. Tellingly, on February 3, 1980, Arenas wrote these words to Cabrera in a letter:

> En fin, el tiempo pasa, y nosotros también, pero, al menos nos queda el consuelo de haber enmarañado algunas hojas que de no ser así se hubieran quedado en blanco. Y ahí está nuestra Victoria.[22]

> In the end, time passes, we do as well, but, at least we have the comfort of having hashed out some messy pages that would have been left blank otherwise. And that is our Victory.

Arenas understands that he and Cabrera are unconventional writers, tricksters whose work is written in layers and codes. They both relished an irreverence that could quickly turn to awe in their observation of the world, especially the sea. For Arenas, *el mar* provided solace and a space of freedom in his search for liberation. For Cabrera, Yemayá was a real presence in her spiritual life, acting as her tutelary deity. The passion that both of them felt as writers and for the ocean helped them to situate stories about their sexuality that made up the very texture of their words. The victory Arenas points to is leaving those tangled narratives behind as residual transcriptions for scholars, believers, and LGBTQ+ readers to find and build upon.

Afrolatinx narratives of the sea illustrate how Yemayá can return innocence, promise death, and give liberty.[23] Such imagery of womb and watery tomb aligns with how the ocean is seen as the land of the dead and also a space of renewal in Santería and Vodou beliefs. Thinking through cyclical time and the logic of fluid becoming makes sense in writing this book from within the cultural perspectives that create the worlds of conjure I explore. Arenas puts the sea's embrace in this way: "Libre al fin, muerto al fin, cabalgando en tus brazos" (Free at last, dead at last, riding in your arms) (246). His final freedom is wrapped into a transformation, one of water. These words and other residual transcriptions point to powerful feelings of liberation left by the dead reflexively as tools for further acts. In conjuring these archives, where ancestors speak freely and often, Afrolatinx spirituality provides strategies of living, dying, and working that are timeless.

NOTES

INTRODUCTION: ARCHIVES OF CONJURE

1. A neighborhood on the outskirts of Havana, Cuba.
2. Spengler Suárez, interview and participant observation, Cuba, October 5, 2008. Translation from Spanish to English mine.
3. Palo is an Afro-Cuban religious practice centered on communication with the dead; see Ochoa 2010b.
4. Goodison 2017:215.
5. *Residual* here refers to clues for activating the coded epistemologies found in multitemporal Afrolatinx religious cultures. It is distinct from Raymond Williams's teleological yet enmeshed conception of the residual, dominant, and emergent aspects of culture (1977).
6. See Otero and Martínez-Rivera's use of Latinx and Afrolatinx in their introduction to the ideas of *poder y cultura* in the folkloristics of resistance to U.S. xenophobia (2017); as well as Mayer-García's definition of Latinx in relation to theater, performance, and ethnicity (2018).
7. For more on Cuban misas as a common and popular practice see Otero 2015 and Wirtz 2014b.
8. See Kardec 2011 [1857]; Otero 2016a; Espírito-Santo 2015; Ochoa 2010a; and Román 2007b.
9. La Gitana (the gypsy) is a variation on Rom spirits that are common guides in Afrolatinx spiritual work with the dead. For a full discussion, see Otero 2016a.
10. See Strongman for how Black Atlantic queer transcorporeality may also be understood in the Cuban film *Fresa y Chocolate* (2019:103–52).

11. A full discussion of Ortiz's transculturation can be found in chapter 2 of this volume. The concept's origins lie in early Cuban cultural anthropology of colonialism and grapples with racial, social, and cultural mixing and appropriation. For more on receptions of the term from a Queer Latinx perspective, see Arrizón 2006. For a look on how the concept works in a hemispheric view, see Taylor 2003. For a perspective from transarea studies, see Ette 2016:136–40.

12. See Lakoff and Johnson 1980 and Ricoeur 2004 for more on the importance of metonymy in the development of cognition and linguistic expression.

13. For examples of conjure as *trabajo* in Afro-Cuban religion, see Cabrera 1980:290–341.

14. For more on the initiated reader and/or observer of Afro-Cuban religious texts and culture, see Otero 2007b.

15. I use this inclusive terminology in order to recognize the range of gendered and sexual subjects that do not conform to binary categories.

16. For a theory of health and affliction and the conjured dead in Cuban Palo, see Ochoa 2010a:11–12.

17. Here I am invoking James Scott's term, which describes how forms of culture can subvert the social script in a clandestine fashion that can also be used as a tool of resistance (1985, 1990).

18. See also Beliso-De Jesús 2015:92–93.

19. For studies of the folklore, ethnomusicology, and material culture of African-inspired religions, see Ortiz 2001 [1950]; Hagedorn 2001; Cosentino 1998; Flores-Peña 2001; Mason 2002. For anthropological analysis, see Wirtz 2014a; Matory 2005; Beliso-De Jesús 2015; Ochoa 2010a; Pérez 2016; Palmié 2002.

20. For early examples of how racism and the fields of physical and cultural anthropology worked in tandem to create violence through methods of "scientific" and "philosophical" representation of nonwhite bodies, individuals, cultures, and beliefs, see Hrdlička 1918; Lévy-Bruhl 1922.

21. Silvia Federici studies how contemporary women in India and Africa are being tried for being "witches" (2010).

22. See Palmié 2014.

23. The CHC is located at the University of Miami Libraries.

24. See also Cuesta 2016; Piña 2016.

25. See chapter 4 of this volume for more on Caribbean sexual exiles and Latinx queer cultures. See also Cuesta 2016; Pérez Rosario 2014; Guzmán 2008; Quiroga 2000; Arenas 2013 [1992].

26. See Piña 2016; Cuesta 2015.

27. Lydia Cabrera Papers (LCP), Cuban Heritage Collection (CHC) 0339, series 3, box 26, Orichas, folder 1, Ochún.

28. See Abiodun 2001.

29. For more on Agwe and the dead's home in the sea, consult Deren 1983; for Olókùn, see Ferrer Castro and Alegre 2007.

30. For discussions of homophobia and patriarchy in African diaspora religious cultures, see for example Beliso-De Jesús 2013a; Riggs 1995:17; Conner and Sparks 2004; Strongman 2019; Pérez 2016; and Alexander 2005.

31. Oxúm is the Brazilian manifestation of Ọ̀ṣun, the Yoruba river deity from Osogbo.

32. For a detailed analysis of Ruth Landes as an imperfect ancestor in the archives of conjure, see Otero 2018a and chapter 1 of this volume.

33. See, for example, her description of rituals she participated in from the Ruth Landes Papers (RLP), National Anthropological Archives (NAA), series 2, research materials, subseries: notebooks, box 9, folder Bahia Texts V, notebook V, 1938:18–19.

34. See Matory 2005; Faria 2016; Otero 2016a; Beliso-De Jesús 2015.

35. For a wonderful analysis of *Contrapunteo*'s frictions, see Ette 2016:137, 139.

36. For more on Espiritismo and the development of Cuban national culture in the Republican era, see Román 2007a.

37. See Lindsay 2013; Ayorinde 2004; Otero 2015.

38. Here I take to heart the ways of studying transareas through literature that Ottmar Ette explores (2016).

39. See Broyles-González 2002.

40. For more on trans* nomenclature, see Halberstam 2018. It is an all-inclusive term that supports gender variance, especially in its regards to histories of transfeminism.

41. I am building upon Deborah Vargas's notion of divascapes here, especially in her reorientation of Chicana feminist and queer understandings of the history of border music and the bolero (2012:xx, 225).

42. I prefer to use the term *transformistas* when referring to Afrolatinx drag queens because of the term's relationship to transformation, magic, and world-making through performance.

43. For a good example of women's vernacular material culture as altars, see Turner 1993; and in Chicana church art, see Lucero 2002. For an example of vernacular belief from a gay Catholic perspective, see Primiano 1993.

I. RESIDUAL TRANSCRIPTIONS

Epigraph: Landes's Oxúm necklace and other beaded items were once held at the Smithsonian's National Museum of Natural History. A 1986 memorandum from the museum's curator, William Sturtevant, describes the Oxúm necklace as "gold-colored beads sewn in circular patterns." However, they are no longer in the Landes collection and their whereabouts are unknown. *Despacho* is a kind of sorcery. RLP, NAA, series 2, research materials, subseries: notebooks, Brazil, box 9, folder Brazil VII, notebook VII, 1938, 22. Landes is describing a conversation with Candomblé priestess Eulalia here.

1. Eulalia is referring to both the Christian high god and also to Olúdumare, the Yoruba high god. Candomblé, like Santería, has elements of syncretism with Catholicism.

2. See chapter 3, this volume, for more on Lydia Cabrera's archive.

3. See chapter 2, "Crossings," this volume, for more on nineteenth-century spiritist doctrine.

4. Beliso-De Jesús sees Santería's ontologies working through energy as electric currents (2015:40–78).

5. See Romberg 2009; Lewgoy 2001; Román 2007a; Perez Mena 1998; Vega 1999; Olmos and Paravisini-Gebert 2003.

6. For two interesting consideration of spirits arriving at unexpected and inappropriate moments in Cuban rituals see Palmié 2014 and Viarnés 2007.

7. Belief in spirits' mischievous nature is found in many different cultures. From poltergeists to friendly ghosts, popular culture and folklore abounds with legends and personal experience narratives about spirits' benevolent and malevolent contacts with humans. For more on the belief in spirits, see Hufford 1995. For material culture surrounding Cuban Palo traditions with the dead see Ochoa 2010a.

8. Two examples here include the work of Zora Neale Hurston and Lydia Cabrera.

9. For more on the analysis of linguistic registers performed during ritual in Afro-Cuban religion, see Wirtz 2007.

10. José Días Casada, misa espritual, Havana, Cuba, December 2015.

11. Indeed, spirits of the dead can interfere with rituals dedicated to oricha cohabitation in unsettling ways if not appeased appropriately.

12. Here, I am reminded of James C. Scott's "hidden transcripts" (1990) in relation to material cultures of the African diaspora.

13. See, for example, the way sewing and weaving work in literature exploring women's memory and self-sufficiency in Goodison 2009; Cisneros 2003; and Danticat 1998.

14. This is not unlike the experience of "technorituals" that Beliso-De Jesús explores in *Electric Santería* (2015:52, 61–62).

15. See Pérez 2016.

16. See also altars for *el día de los muertos* in Latin America and the United States; with regard to issues of commemoration and cultural appropriation, see Marchi 2013.

17. The Ruth Landes Papers are housed at the National Anthropological Archives, Smithsonian Institution.

18. See also Cuesta 2016 and Piña 2016.

19. See Beliso-De Jesús on Cabrera and *mundele* (2015:33–35).

20. Cabrera and Verger exchange commentary about and using Yemayá as a symbol of affection throughout their lengthy and warm correspondence. Both scholars held very private intimate lives with same-sex partners. For example, Cabrera signs off to Verger in a letter dated August 16, 1983: "Recibe un fuerte abracote de Yemayá/Receive a strong embrace from Yemayá." Lydia Cabrera Papers, Cuban Heritage Collection 0339, series 1, box 1, folder 10.

21. RLP, NAA, series 2, research materials, subseries: notebooks, Brazil, box 9, folder II A Bahia texts, notebook II, 1938, 1–5; folder Brazil IV, notebook IV, 1938, 62–68; folder Brazil V, notebook V, 1938, 4–7, 18.

22. For an example of Ruth Landes's notes on homosexuality, see RLP, series 2, research materials, subseries: notebooks, Bahian texts, folder Brazil IV, notebook IV; and for Carneiro, see RLP, NAA, series 2, research materials, subseries: Brazil, box 19, folder materials by Edison Carneiro, 1936–1950.

23. RLP, NAA, series 2, research materials, subseries: Brazil, box 19, folder materials by Edison Carneiro, 1936–1950. These notes do not paint the priests in a sympathetic light.

24. See Abimbola 1994 and Otero 2010.

25. See chapters 3 and 4, this volume, for other considerations of the routes initiated by the water divinities Yemayá, Ochún, and Erinle.

26. See chapters 3 and 4, this volume, with regard to chisme and divascapes.

27. RLP, NAA, series 2, research materials, subseries: notebooks, Bahia texts, box 9, folder Brazil V, notebook V, 1938, 31.

28. Slope. All translations from Portuguese to English are mine unless otherwise indicated.

RLP, NAA, series 2, research materials, subseries: notebooks, Bahia texts, box 9, folder Brazil V, notebook V, 1938, 31.

29. RLP, NAA, series 2, research materials, subseries: notebooks, Bahia texts, box 9, folder Brazil V, notebook V, 1938, 31.

30. For example, Landes describes going to a *santo* celebration, an initiation, for Oxúm from September 12–15, 1938. She also witnessed a cleansing, a *despacho* ceremony, during these dates. RLP, NAA, series 2, research materials, subseries: notebooks, Bahia texts, box 9, folder Brazil V, notebook V, 1938, 18–19.

31. RLP, NAA, series 2, subseries: notebooks, Bahía texts, box 9, folder II A, Bahia texts, notebook II, 1938.

32. In Cuba a similar dish for Ochún is called *ochinchin*.

33. RLP, NAA, series 2, subseries: notebooks, Bahía texts, box 9, folder II A, Bahia texts, 1938.

34. RLP, NAA, series 2, subseries: notebooks, Bahía texts, box 9, folder II A, Bahia texts, 1938.

35. RLP, NAA, series 2, subseries: notebooks, Brazil V, box 9, folder Brazil V, notebook V, 1938, 74.

36. RLP, NAA, series 2, subseries: notebooks, Brazil V, box 9, folder Brazil V, notebook V, 1938, 74.

37. See Vega 2001.

38. Vega 2001

39. I am developing this idea of Oxúm's mirror logics from personal conversations with practitioners like Efun Bile in Cuba, Cabrera's depiction of Ochún's personality (1980), and Ribeiro dos Santos 2001.

40. The most obvious example of the negative effects of visibility is the Indo-European and Mediterranean belief in the evil eye. See Dundes 1992.

41. The incorporation of outsiders as kin is a well-accounted social strategy for constructing a cosmopolitan sense of power and influence in West African contexts. For transatlantic examples pertinent to the ways that Nigerian, Cuban, and Brazilian religious affiliations do so, see Otero 2010; Matory 2005; and Miller 2009.

42. RLP, NAA, series 2, subseries: research materials, Brazil, box 19, folder "Notes."

43. RLP, NAA, series 2, subseries: research materials, Brazil, box 19, folder "Notes."

44. Verger 1969; Otero 2007b.

45. See "Honoring Lydia Cabrera's Story" 2016.

46. RLP, NAA, series 2, subseries: research materials, Brazil, box 19, folder "Notes."

47. For a good discussion of how slavery and race are reinscribed into Cuban notions of African ancestors, see Routon 2008.

48. I include the illegible question as a reminder that recreating a situation from residual transcripts is always incomplete and an exercise in decoding.

49. RLP, NAA, series 2, research materials, subseries: notebooks, Brazil V, box 9, folder Brazil V, notebook V, 1938, 8.

50. RLP, NAA, series 2, research materials, subseries: notebooks, Brazil V, box 9, folder Brazil V, notebook V, 1938, 4–5.

51. RLP, NAA, series 2, research materials, subseries: notebooks, Brazil V, box 9, folder Brazil V, notebook V, 1938,10–11.

52. RLP, NAA, series 2, research materials, subseries: notebooks, box 9, folder Brazil V, notebook V, 1938, 53.

53. RLP, NAA, series 2, subseries: notebooks, Bahía texts, box 9, folder Brazil V, notebook V, 1938.

54. See Hammad 2004; Moraga 1983 [1981]; Piña 2016; Cantú and Nájera-Ramírez 2002.

55. See Tsang 2017; Lindsay 1996, 2013; Brown 2003; Flores-Peña and Evanchuck 1994; Ochoa 2010b:72, 246, 261; Hayes 2011; Long 2001.

56. Here, I think of the work that Cvetkovich's "archive of feeling" (2003) does in resituating the public and private, and the nature of trauma, in lesbian vernacular history and activism.

57. Matory's exhibit *Spirit Things: Sacred Arts of the Black Atlantics* was displayed at the Fleming Museum of Art, University of Vermont in 2017.

58. Of course, artists in visual, performing, and literary genres also take inspiration from Afrolatinx religiosity. See, for example, the work of Alan West-Durán on María Magdalena Campos Pons (2013); Alexandra Vazquez on Graciela Pérez (2013); and Nancy Morejón and David Frye (2005).

59. From the Smithsonian Museum of Natural History, Department of Anthropology catalog: https://collections.nmnh.si.edu/search/anth /(last accessed May 15, 2019).

60. The dolls are housed in the Department of Anthropology's Ethnology Collection at the Smithsonian Museum of Natural History.

61. RLP, NAA, series 2, research materials: Brazil, notes, box 19, folder notes.

62. In one journal entry, Landes excitedly notes that Zeze promised to teach her and other women how to embroider using a sewing machine. RLP, NAA, series 2, research materials: Brazil, notebooks, box 9, folder Brazil XVIII, 41.

63. RLP, NAA, series 2, research materials: Brazil, notebooks, box 9, folder Brazil XVIII, 41–42.

64. Oxala is an elderly deity of purity who created the human form and is associated with white cloth. The set of ceremonies Landes attends in December of 1939 is called the making of Agua de Oxala ("water of Oxala"). The activities consisted of a complex series of rituals that included the community bathing in blessed water and offering songs and foods for the orixas. RLP, series 2, research materials: Brazil, notebooks, box 9, folder Brazil XVIII, 3–25.

65. RLP, NAA, series 2, research materials: Brazil, notebooks, box 9, folder Brazil XVIII, 4.

66. RLP, NAA, series 2, research materials: Brazil, notebooks, box 9, folder Brazil XX, texts Bahia Río, 47–49.

67. See Hayes 2011:38.

68. Ruth Landes commented the importance of beading, sewing, and embroidery in conducting Candomblé and spiritist work in Bahia. In particular, she remarks that the making of initiation regalia and orixa vestments is a communal enterprise undertaken primarily between women. RLP, NAA, series 2, research materials, subseries: notebooks, box 9, folder Brazil VII, notebook V, 1938, 11.

69. On October 22, 2016, a special program hosted by the American Folklore Society, the Cuban Heritage Collection, housed at the HistoryMiami Museum, celebrated Lydia Cabrera's life and legacy through an altar created from objects in her archive and a dance performance inspired by one of her short stories, "Suandende." The exhibit was curated by Kay Turner, Martin Tsang, Eric Mayer-García, and Solimar Otero.

70. Magical temporalities in Afrolatinx religiosity take into account queer temporalities found in multiple kinds of narrative (Dinshaw 2012) as well as experiences of African-inspired senses of time (Curtis and Johnson 2014).

2. CROSSINGS

Epigraph: "I am not a Spiritist." All translations from Spanish to English in this chapter are the author's unless indicated. Ortiz 2012 [1924]:11.

1. I am using the term *performative* following Judith Butler, Jacques Derrida, and J. L. Austin in terms of there being "events of speech" that create a method of citation for the construction of subjectivity within cultural, social, and legal contexts; see Butler 1993 and 1997. Espiritismo is the religious culture that directly emerges from spiritism in Latin America and the Hispanic Caribbean.

2. For Kardec, it was important to distinguish Spiritism from other popular esoteric religious practices like mesmerism and spiritualism. In the introduction to *Le livre des Esprits*, he clarifies that spiritism is mainly concerned with the movement of spirits in between spiritual and material worlds without posing a contradiction between the two, which he believed some spiritualist writings and practices produced. See Kardec 2011 [1857]:19; Oberhausen 2009; Chapin 2004; and Tromp 2003.

3. See Kardec 2011 [1857]; Palmié 2013; Román 2007a; Romberg 2007; Otero 2015; Pérez 2011; Flores-Peña 2004; Perez Mena 1998; Espírito Santo 2015.

4. See Kardec 2011 [1857]:164–67; Espírito Santo 2015:49–51.

5. All translations of Kardec and the spirits from French and Portuguese into English are mine.

6. Díaz-Quiñonez 1999.

7. In *The Social Life of Spirits*, Diana Espírito Santo and Ruy Blanes suggest that a socially phenomenological analysis of spirits allows for a broadening of methodological questions (2014:5).

8. Similar work on energy and sensation as a way of communicating with the supernatural world has been done by Todd Ramón Ochoa (2010) and *Electric Santería* by Aisha Beliso-De Jesús (2015).

9. This translation is by Harriet De Onís (1995 [1947]:98).

10. Díaz-Quiñones 1999.

11. Díaz-Quiñonez 1999:28.

12. See Deleuze and Guattari 1987; Glissant 1981:327, 336–40. See also Maryse Condé's brilliant deployment of the rhizomatic metaphor of the mangrove in her novel *Traversée de la Mangrove* (1989). As Ruthmarie Mitsch has noted (1997), Condé's mangroves reveal the deeply intertwined histories shared between seemingly separate islands and societies in the Caribbean.

13. José Estaban Muñoz conceptualizes a "performed manifestation of consciousness" to relate how signification happens through relational connections (2000:71).

14. Otero 2015; Espírito Santo 2015; Wirtz 2014b; Pérez 2011.

15. Glissant 1992:96–102; Benítez-Rojo 1992 [1989]:xvi–xxiii; Palmié 2014:221–22.

16. Important work on spirituality and race is done outside of Havana. Wirtz's book on Santiago, *Performing Afro-Cuba*, is an excellent case in point (2014a). The misas I am referring to occurred in May of 2013 and December of 2014.

17. For the purposes of consistency, I am using the mediums' first names only here. Espiritismo *cruzado* incorporates elements of other Afro-Cuban religious practice, like Santería and Palo, in its understanding of spiritual worlds; see Ochoa 2010b; Espírito Santo 2015; Romberg 2007.

18. Kardec and contemporary mediums recognize a class of spirits, guardian spirits, that have specific missions on earth (Kardec 2011 [1857]: 309–11). Mediums have multiple protector spirits that make-up a spiritual "court" (Kardec 2011 [1857]:311; Espírito Santo 2015).

19. See Romberg 2003, 2007; Viarnés 2007:140–41; Perez Mena 1998; Pérez 2011; Espírito Santo 2015, 125; Wirtz 2014b; Beliso De-Jesús 2015:69.

20. The "seven nations" are spirits of different races, ethnicities, nationalities, and religious backgrounds that can appear in Latinx and Caribbean misas (see Román 2007b:123). Seven is a significant ritual number in Palo, Santería, and Espiritismo. For Palo, see Routon 2008:642–43; for Santería, see Cabrera 1980:276, 302, 316; for Espiritismo examples, including the *Siete Potencias Africanas* (Seven African Powers), see Romberg 2003:134; 245, 267.

21. Vazquez 2013:19–22; Quiroga 2005.

22. Crawley investigates Black Pentecostal religiosity through sound (2016).

23. Stephan Palmié remarks on "temporal hybridization" in his work on historicity and an ethnographic account of a Cuban *cajón pa' muerto*, celebration for the dead (2014:220).

24. The songs and prayers that accompany a misa provide a unique perspective, as they can be sung in the voices of the spirit guides (see Pérez 2011:342). The song "Los Clavelitos" (The little carnations) prompted *la gitana* (gypsy) to appear in a crucial moment at a *misa de coronación* (coronation ceremony).

25. The deity Oya, known for her association with the river Niger, hurricanes, and the rainbow, is crossed with the Palo entity Centella in Espiritismo cruzado. Centella has her own fierce and protective characteristics in Cuban vernacular religious crossings (see Ochoa 2010a:88, 140, 145, 220–21).

26. Soñia Bustamonte and José Días Casada, misa de coronación, May 22, 2013, Havana, Cuba.

27. See Wirtz 2014a:131–33.

28. See Aparicio and Chávez-Silverman 1997:5–7, 11–14.

29. Otero 2016a; Quiroga 2005.

30. R. L. Román explores the depiction of two espiritistas—Hilario Mustelier, who was Afro-Cuban, and Juan Manso Estevéz, who was Spanish, in periodicals and legal documents (2007b).

31. See Espírito Santos's ethnographic discussion of gitana spirits (2015:229–30).

32. Instances where these traditions cross, or are cruzados, occur frequently in the negotiation of religious praxis based on individual contexts and situations (Ochoa 2010a:193).

33. Both Oya and Centella are associated with the cemetery and the dead in specific ways that render them especially potent spiritual beings.

34. See, for example, Benítez Rojo 1992 [1989]:xxxv–xxxviii; Glave 2003:614, 616, 620; Hernández Cruz 2001:66–67; Suárez 2011;Vasquez 2013; and Glissant 1992:100–2.

35. Kahn has argued for an understanding of celibacy as a kind of sexuality with its own parameters of experience (2013:14–16).

36. Palmié 2014; Pérez 2011, 337; Wirtz 2007, 2014a; Taylor 2003.

37. For the importance of sensual acuity for practitioners in Afro-Cuban religions, see Beliso-De Jesús 2015; Wirtz 2014b; Espírito Santo 2015; Otero 2015; and Ochoa 2010a.

38. Wirtz has commented on Espiritismo's connected spiritual collectives as "commissions" that can be called upon in doing ritual work (2014b:138).

39. This participant wants to remain anonymous.

40. Verger 1969; Deren 1983; Viarnés 2007.

41. See also Flores-Peña 2004.

42. Palmié 2014.

43. Ontological questions about historicity and Afro-Cuban rituals of cohabitation have been adequately addressed: Palmié 2014; Wirtz 2007, 2014b; Beliso-De Jesús 2014, 2015; Otero 2015; Ochoa 2010b; and Espírito Santo 2015.

44. Ette sees Ortiz's notion of transculturation as embodying the cultural frictions of Cuban history, literature, and society (2016:138–39).

45. Anzaldúa also discusses linguistic silences, code-switching, and combined frames of Spanish, English, and Spanglish in borderland language. She includes Chicana, Cuban, and Puerto Rican examples of solidarity in her analysis (1999 [1987]:76–77).

46. See Ochoa for more on the presence of physical afflictions on the bodies of practitioners who work with the dead (2010a).
47. See Beliso-De Jesús's discussion of spiritual transcendence in Afro-Cuban religious cultures (2015).
48. This is from Michael Dash's English translation of *Caribbean Discourse* (Glissant 1992:100–1).
49. Buck-Morss 2009.
50. Palmié considers looking at historiography as a kind of ritual work (2014:238).
51. Taylor explores a similar tension in looking at hemispheric performatives' relationships with the archive (2003).
52. Palmié refers to how "North Atlantic" universalism obscures what Afro-Cuban ritual can do to help us understand the construction of historicity (2014:221–24).
53. Dundes invokes texture as a specific quality of folklore, the verbal substance (words) expressions are made of, that cannot easily be translated and is dependent on specific cultural contexts (1980:22–24). I am expanding this usage of texture to refer to registers of cultural admixture that are specific to Cuban transculturation and Ortiz's articulation of the concept.
54. See Fabian's classic *Time and the Other* (1983).
55. Alina Troyano is a Cuban-American performance artist whose work as Carmelita Tropicana is representative of queer *latinidad* in the United States since the 1980s (Muñoz 1999:119–41).
56. See Williams 1978.
57. See Taylor 2003; Esparza 2000:70–89; Troyano 2000:173–78; Fusco 1995:159–68.
58. Dávila engages in similar critical work that investigates the transnational production of Latinx and Latin American localities and identities (2012).
59. For a good analysis of blackface in early Cuban and Cuban American theater, see Mayer-García 2016.

3. FLOWS

Epigraph: "With water from the river, with water from the sea, with the water from the river, I take away all the bad [energy]."

The original from Verger reads: "Con *Yemayá y Ochún* nos abre un mundo encantado, el de las aguas primordiales, las saladas y dulces, puestas por los lucumís bajo la potestad de estos dos divinidades."

This English translation is from the LCP, CHC, series 3, box 20, folder 10, dated 1974. It appears as an advertisement typeset on onion paper with the cover displayed in black and white. The Spanish version of the quote attributing it to Pierre Fatumbi Verger appears on the back cover, and in Rosario Hiriart's "Prologue," of *Yemayá y Ochún* (Cabrera 1980:iv).

1. The ritual, mythological, and discursive boundary crossing found between Yemayá and Ochún in Cuba have parallel expressions in Africa and Brazil; see Sanford 2001:240; Abraham 1958:528; Matory 2005:247–48.

2. For a good contextual definition of *ìmọ̀ jinlẹ̀* see Abraham 1958:306.

3. Within this designation, devotees of Ochún and Yemayá faithfully attend to other water divinities and spirits. This and other religious designations are revealed through divination, dream interpretation, and rituals of communication with the spirit world like the misa espiritual (Cabrera 1980:115; Brown 2003:152–57).

4. Otero and Falola 2013; Murphy and Sanford 2001.

5. For example, "masculine" orichas like Elegua, Ogún, and Ochossi often cooperate ritually, especially with regard to spiritual work done in the *igbo/maniguá*, or forest. Natural and supernatural boundaries emphasizing gendered ritual thresholds are found consistently in the African diaspora in multiple urban sites, like New Orleans; see Wehmeyer 2007; Brown 2003:20, 134.

6. For a sampling of the discussion regarding women's roles in Yoruba and Yoruba-inspired religions, see Olajubu 2003: Olademo 2009; Olupona 2001:47–67; Lawal 1996:42–43, 49, 256; Harding 2001:171–73; Matory 2005:151, 247–48; Cabrera 1980:43–46; and Conner and Sparks 2004: 108–9, 235–37.

7. Otero 2010.

8. Here I am reminded of the seascape epistemology born from Indigenous Hawaiian beliefs explored by Karin Animoto Ingersoll (2016).

9. All excerpts on Claudina Abreo González, "Tita," in this chapter are taken from interviews that took place in her home in Havana on November 10, 2009. Tita also practices the spiritual traditions of Palo and Espiritismo.

10. An earlier version of this research focuses specifically on interorality as a dimension for studying performatives in folk narrative (Otero 2015).

11. See also Bolívar 1990; Brown 2003.

12. Bakhtin 1981:324–25; Ngugi wa Thiong'o 1993:18–19; Nuttal 2007:12–14; Briggs 1996:26–28.

13. The religious cultures of Santería, Palo, and Espiritismo have their distinct realms of ritual knowledge, but are interconnected in daily practice; see Cabrera 1980; Ochoa 2010b; Pérez 2011; Romberg 2003, 2007. Note that Palo has many subgenres and regional differences in practice and religious history in Cuba; see Ochoa 2010b.

14. This is similar to how Yoruba traditional orature has an oral literary criticism and accepted aesthetic based on quotation; see Barber 1999.

15. For a good working definition of metafolklore, see Dundes 2007.

16. Abreo González, interview 2009, Havana, Cuba.

17. A mixed-race woman, usually Black and white, but in Cuba can also include the mixing of Asian and Native American backgrounds. See Kutzinski 1993; Arrizón 2006:83–117; Otero 2012:154–56.

18. Yemayá is associated with mermaids, and her long hair in the tale may be related to the folk literature motif B81.9.1, Mermaid's hair reaches her waist; see Thompson 1955–58:370–71.

19. All translations from Spanish to English are my own. Some quotations not drawn from storytelling performances are presented directly in translation.

20. Briggs 1996:26–27; Wirtz 2007:251–56, 269; and Wirtz 2014a.

21. There is an alternate version of this story told in Ifa divination verse, in the *odu* (sign) of Baba Oshe Meyi, where Yemayá conversely steals Ochún's hair out of envy. There are multiple readings and interpretations of this *odu* that contain different patakí. A version is published online by Ernesto Valdés Jane, Proyecto-Orunmila, under the title "Los caminos de los amores de Oshún." https://www.academia.edu/29796003 /Compilado_por_Ernesto_Vald%C3%A9s_Jane_Caminos_de _If%C3%A1_Documentos_para_la_Historia_y_la_Cultura_de_Osha -If%C3%A1_en_Cuba (last accessed June 5, 2019).

22. See Cabrera 1980:118.

23. Butler 1993, 1997.

24. Ruth Landes asserts, in her unpublished notes on Bahian Candomblé, that the well-known babalawo Martiniano Eliseu do Bonfim believed that "Yemanja, with two big breasts, also lives in waters in Nigeria, in the sea," RLP, NAA series 2, research materials, subseries: notebooks, Brazil, box 9, folder V, notebook V, 1938, 10.

25. Yoruba children born with soft curly hair are called *momolokun*, children of the sea. Their hair is worn long, compared to seashells, and it is

believed that they have an affinity with sea sprits (Drewal, Pemberton, and Abiodun 1989:27).

26. Drewal 2008:1–18.
27. *Mulatez* is the act and/or quality of embodying being of mixed race heritage.
28. For more on interorality in the Caribbean, see Veté-Congolo 2016 and Otero 2016a.
29. Derrida's discussion of archives and the inherent aspects of forgetting that archives as sites engender are relevant here (1995:2).
30. See, for example, Alarcón 1984; López 1997; and Otero 2016b.
31. I am reframing José Estaban Muñoz's theory of disidentification which unsettles stereotypical performances and representations of race, gender, and sexuality through irony, satire, and intense reflexivity (1999).
32. Tita's story is related to oral traditions of secrecy and hidden female power inspired by Yoruba religious discourses. Scholarship on Yoruba traditions of secrecy and gender also take into account personal creativity and colonialism (Barber 1990, 1991; Olajubu 2003; Olademo 2009). For discussions on how supernatural power is historically gendered through the orichas Iya Nla (the great mother), Yemayá, and Ochún in the Ifa divination verses of the Osa Odu Meji and the Ose Ode Tura, and the Àjẹ́ magical traditions of the Gẹlẹdẹ masquerade, see Olajubu (2003:27–28); Olademo (2009:105–9); Lawal (1996:71–74); Ferrer Castro and Acosta Alegre (2007:58). Cabrera also cites Pierre Verger's work on the religious sect of Iyamí Osoronga in Nigeria (1980:72). Cabrera adds to this citation her own analysis of how the Cuban road of Ochún Ibu Kolé has similar powerful attributes related to sorcery.
33. This sharing between the two orichas also works in terms of symbolic attributes like the peacock. As Cabrera writes in her notes on the oricha Ochún: "Yemayá le cedió a Oshún el pavo real. A quien verdaderamente le corresponde es a Yemayá," LCP, CHC 0339, series 3, box 26, folder 1, n.d.
34. Abreo González, interview November 10, 2009, Havana, Cuba.
35. Flores-Peña 2001:113–27; Brown 2003:218–19, 224; Cabrera 1980:114–5.
36. This kind of transportability of ritual art and practices also occurs in Palo and Espiritismo. See Ochoa 2010b:114–5; Flores-Peña 2004:88–90, 92; Brown 2003:187–8, 244, 326, 359; Pérez 2011:350–52.
37. See note 33 for an example of sharing of symbols and generosity from Yemayá to Ochún from Cabrera's handwritten notes.

38. An intertextual/interoral note about the relationship between Ochún and Yemayá in Cabrera's papers reads: "Tanta riqueza se la debe a su hermana Yemayá que hizo los ríos y se los dio. ('La hizo dueña de omí dudú, del agua dulce')," LCP, CHC 0339, series 3, box 26, folder 1, 2, n.d. The voice in parentheses is the reported speech of Calazán, one of Cabrera's main interlocutors in the field. This is example shows how Cabrera textualizes moments where authority shifts during the ethnographic interview process.

39. LCP, CHC 0339, series 3, box 26, folder 1, 2, n.d.

40. Orichas have different *caminos* (roads) or avatars that reflect a different manifestation of their existence in narrative and ritual.

41. Lucumí refers both to the religious practices and linguistic dialect inspired by Yoruba cultures found in Cuba (see Wirtz 2007, 2014a). I use the term *Lucumí* in this chapter for the purposes of distinguishing between ethnic registers marked during ritual work.

42. LCP, CHC 0339, series 3, box 26: Orichas, folder 1, Ochún.

43. Lucumí word for "orange."

44. This long rendition also included a statement about Yemayá's generosity: "da dos manos de riqueza y con una la quita" (she gives two handfuls of riches and with one [hand] removes it). CHC 0339, Lydia Cabrera Papers, series 3, box 26: Orichas: folder 1, Ochún.

45. See Beliso-De Jesús on cohabitation in Santería (2013a, 2015).

46. See Espírito Santo 2015; Otero 2015; Pérez 2011; Romberg 2003, 2005; Román 2007b; Díaz-Quiñones 1999; Hess 1987.

47. Pérez 2011.

48. See Ortiz 1963 [1940]; Benítez Rojo 1992 [1989]; Arrizón 2006; Palmié 2013:78–79; Lowe 2016.

49. See Palmié 2014; Wirtz 2014b.

50. Names and terms of endearment used with exclusive permission. I use agreed-on pseudonyms in cases where collaborators do not want to be identified directly.

51. See Espírito Santo 2015; Otero 2015, 2016a.

52. Though there has been a significant shift in attitudes toward LGBTQ communities on the island, with an emphasis on the "fight against homophobia" led by Mariela Castro Espín, the director of CENE-SEX (Centro Nacional de Educación Sexual), attitudes of sexual discrimination still exist in some traditional spiritual communities. For more on the changing views of sexuality on the island, see Beliso-De Jesús (2013b); Allen (2012b:329); and the online post and audio feed

"Director Jon Albert Talks Mariela Castro's March" by Charlotte Robinson from the *Huffington Post* (2017): https://www.huffpost.com /entry/director-jon-alpert-talks_b_12896788 (last accessed June 5, 2019).

53. See Romberg 2003, 2005; Pérez 2011; Ochoa 2010b; Viarnés 2007:140–44; Espírito Santo 2015.

54. For more on religious cross-referencing in Cuban altars and Santería practices, see Brown 2003:xiii, 72, 116. For more on the complex performance of race based specifically on this example, see Otero's blog (2014), "Dreaming in Cuban: Affect in the Performance of *Misa Espirituales*," HowlRound Theatre Commons, https://howlround.com /dreaming-cuban-0 (last accessed June 5, 2019).

55. Ruth Landes noted the connection between Yemanja/Iemanjá and the idea of the *madre de agua* (mother of water) in Brazil in her field notes. She wrote about Candomblé priestesses' belief in Yemanja/Iemanjá as a "mãe d' agua" (mother of the waters) and that the orixa (oricha) has aspects that are "prateado" (silver), a color associated with the moon, the sea, and Yemanja/Iemanjá in Brazil. RLP, NAA, series 2, research materials, subseries: notebooks, box 9, folder Brazil V, notebook V, 1938, 38.

56. José Días Casada and Mercedes Albuquerque, misa de coronación, May 22, 2013, Havana, Cuba. Emphasis added to *la corriente*.

57. A prenda and a nganga are spiritual receptacles made by practitioners of the Congo-inspired religions of Palo in Cuba for work with the dead (Ochoa 2010a, 2010b:12, 131–39).

58. *Brujería* refers to strong spiritual work that includes elements of divination, conjure, and sorcery; sometimes translated as "witchcraft." Brujería in this context refers to the level of intensity, as well as the rapid nature of the magical efficacy of the spirit guide's work (see Romberg 2003:xi–xii, 18–22, 206–8).

59. Briggs 1996:27; Ochoa 2010a:392; Ochoa 2010b:145; Pérez 2011:346, 348; Cabrera 1986a. Palo Cruzado is religious work that combines elements of Palo with Santería and Espiritismo (Ochoa 2010b:145). Aisha Beliso-De Jesús also notes the crossing of Palo, Espiritismo, and Santería in the practice of Afro-Cuban religious culture on a transnational scale, as well as in Matanzas, Cuba, in the practices of Santo Parado (2013a:707; personal communication, July 2013). Cabrera likewise creates an intertextual image that crosses religious registers based on oral associations when she describes La Virgen de Regla, Yemayá, and Madre de Agua as one (Cabrera 1980:16; Otero 2013:101–2).

60. Otero and Falola 2013; Cabrera 1980:115–16.
61. Ochoa 2010a:389; Ochoa 2010b:10; Viarnés 2007:131, 140; Romberg 2007:75, 97.
62. Black woman, or figuratively, black womanhood.
63. Otero 2013; Piña 2016.
64. Conner and Sparks 2004; Otero and Falola 2013:xvii–xxxii; Ayorinde 2004.
65. Beliso De-Jesús 2015; Otero 2015.
66. Espírito Santo 2015.
67. See Ochoa 2010a:90; Ochoa 2010b:13.
68. Romberg takes her lead from Roger Abrahams's view of creolization whereby the conflicts that arise from the perceived "contagion" of cultural mixing and miscegenation recast Caribbean history and folklore against other perceived kinds of authentic, pure elements of culture (Abrahams 2003). Folklorists have looked at the creativity of creolization as a means to understanding past and present complexities of globalization and transnational encounters (Baron and Cara 2011).
69. Viarnés 2007 and Palmié 2014.
70. Wirtz 2007:266; Palmié 2013:4–5, 46, 115–16; Romberg 2007.
71. Flores-Peña 2004:97; Taylor 2003:142–44.
72. See Beliso-De Jesús 2014; Taylor 2003:116–21; Arrizón 2006:66, 87; Quiroga 2000:101–13; Santos-Febres 2000b.
73. See Allen 2011; Beliso-De Jesús 2015; Thorne 2013; Cabezas 2009:137; Sheller 2003:164.
74. For more on Cuban longing and aesthetics, see Quiroga 2005, 2000; Behar 1996; Otero 2012, Otero 2007b.
75. For "texture," see Dundes 1980:20.
76. For example, theater scholar Eric Mayer-García's work on the Teresa María Rojas theatrical adaptation of Cabrera's short story "Suandende" by Teatro Prometeo in Miami argues that Cabrera's writings exude a theatricality based on a Cuban queer aesthetics that is also spiritual (2016b).
77. For "speakerly," see Gates 1989:170–216; for African diaspora aural texts, see Turner 1993.
78. See also, for an example containing Yemayá, Cabrera 2006 [1954]):41–42.
79. Cabrera's own connection to Yemayá is deeply related to her lesbian sexuality. The coding of her connection to the ocean deity resembles the kinds of hidden conversations that exist about sexual preference in the religion (Otero 2013:98–100; Quiroga 2000:76–77; Rodríguez-Mangual 2004:13).

80. Ruth Landes depicts and comments upon the existence of prominent *adé*, homosexual Candomblé priests in 1930s–1940s Brazil (RLP, NAA, series 2, research materials, subseries: notebooks, Brazil, box 9, folder [Brazil] Bahia texts IV, notebook IV, 1938). In revisiting Landes, Matory adds fresh ethnographic and historical material that resituates the adé priest as a vital component of the religious culture of Candomblé (Matory 2005:188–223).

81. Clark 2005:99, 151, 166; Beliso-De Jesús 2013b; Matory 2005:218; Rubiera Castillo 2011:107–49.

82. Cabrera also uses the term *adodí*, a Lucumí designation related to *adó*, to refer to openly gay men in her narratives; see Cabrera 1980:44–45; Rodríguez-Mangual 2004:91–92; Matory 2005:189, 196, 206, 212; Landes 1940:394–95). Cabrera's textualized talk about the gendering and sexing of the orichas takes on the form of hearsay: as unofficial knowledge that is neither confirmed nor denied by her or her interlocutors for the reader. For more on hearsay, and especially rumor, in African American and African diasporic contexts, see Turner 1993.

83. See Conner and Sparks 2004; Beliso-De Jesús 2015; Otero and Falola 2013; Matory 2005; Landes 1940.

84. Mañach 1969 [1928]; Muñoz 1999:119–20; Pérez Firmat 1984; Mayer-García 2016a.

85. Vargas 2012; Samper 2002:1–32; Beauregard 2000:135–51; Dabove 2000:269–87; Anzaldúa 1999 [1987]:76; Turner 1993:xv, 4, 212–13.

86. Vargas 2012; Harris 1996:3–30; Turner 1993.

87. Edna Rodríguez-Mangual provides an example of chisme about Cabrera. She relates an instance of hearing that Cabrera actually left Cuba because of death threats issued by *Abakuá* priests, known as *Ñañigos*, for the revelation of their secrets in her book on their all-male secret society (2004:13; see also Cabrera 1998 [1959]; Miller 2009:102, 224). As Rodríguez-Mangual concludes, "I am fascinated by these sorts of stories and interpretations, for one cannot find them in any book and nobody dares to talk about them" (2004:5).

88. See Otero 2007a; Quiroga 2000; Johnson 2005.

89. Deborah Vargas has a distinctly Chicana understanding of how chisme can provide an alternative discourse to patriarchal modes of knowing and historiography (2012).

90. Friend of a friend (FOAF) sources are commented upon in folklore studies of legend and rumor in particular.

91. Cabrera 1980:44–45, Rodríguez-Mangual 2004:90–92.

92. Landes also identifies mythology, ritual, and gossip that comment on bisexuality, lesbianism, and gender crossing with regard to the gods in Brazilian Candomblé. In her work, the orixa Yansan, goddess of thunder and wife of the orixa Xangó, is described as a "masculine woman, or even a man" and also as "the man-woman" (1940:395).

93. LCP, CHC 0339, series 3, box 26, Orichas, folder 11, n.d.

94. LCP, CHC 0339, series 3, box 26, Orichas, folder 1, Ochún.

95. In Ruth Landes's unpublished papers, we also find instances in Brazilian Candomblé where devotees possessed with "Yemanjá [dance] com espada e abebe" (dance with a sword and a fan). Landes also remarks in her field notes that this manifestation of Yemanjá represents "a fighting woman" for the religious community. Note that the sword and fan are instruments attributed to male and female deities, respectively, and in this instance Yemanjá wields both as a sign of her emergent qualities. RLP, NAA, series 2, research materials, subseries: notebooks, Brazil box 9, folder Brazil VII, notebook VII, 1938, 47.

96. Muñoz 1999:21–22.

97. See Haraway 2016.

98. For example, Cabrera and Pierre Fatumbi Verger were good friends who referred to Yemayá as a symbol of their affection throughout their correspondence. Cabrera signs off to Verger in a letter dated August 16, 1983: "Reciba un fuerte abracote [sic] de Yemayá" (Receive a strong embrace from Yemayá) (LCP, CHC 0339, series 1, box 1, folder 10). And Verger dedicates his opus, *Orixás: Deuses Iorubás na África E No Novo Mundo,* to Lydia Cabrera in this manner: "A Lydia Cabrera hija predilecta de Yemaya con el cariño y amor de Fatumbi" (To Lydia Cabrera, Yemaya's favorite daughter, with affection and love from Fatumbi) (1981:7).

99. CHC 0339, series 1, box 3, folder 7, Arenas to Cabrera 1980–1988, "Carta a Lydia Cabrera de Reinaldo Arenas, Nueva York, julio 15 de 1982" (typed).

100. LCP, CHC 0339, series 1, box 3, folder 7, Arenas to Cabrera 1980–1988, "Carta a Lydia Cabrera de Reinaldo Arenas, Nueva York, julio 15, 1982" (typed).

101. See Arenas 2013 [1992], 1999; Cabrera 1980.

102. Otero and Falola 2013:2–4; Quiroga 2000:76–77; Rodríguez-Mangual 2004:13; Matory 2005:209. In their unpublished notes, both Ruth Landes and Edison Carneiro remark upon the layered forms of gender and sexuality among Candomblé's deities and practitioners in a manner also resembling chisme, as well as the potential for gossip to create avenues

for queer histories of Afro-Atlantic religions. For example, I found a set of notes on gay priests composed by Carneiro that suggested that one priest, Manuelzinho de Oxossi, was the "tipo do homem que não se incomoda por nada" (type of man who does not let anything bother him). RLP, NAA, series 2, research materials, Brazil, box 19, folder 2, materials by Edison Carneiro.

103. See Rivera-Servera 2012:21; Anzaldúa 1999 [1987]:76–79; Arrizón 2006:160–175; Samper 2002:1–32; Yarbro-Bejarano 2000:202, 204–5; Rodríguez-Mangual 2004:13; 60–99.

104. Beliso De-Jesús sees videoscapes as a kind of ethnoscape in the context of Afro-Cuban religious cosmopolitanism (2015).

105. The original 1974 pamphlet advertising the book *Yemayá y Ochún* states about Cabrera's ethnography: "Her books are not a cold pedantic display of her investigations but reflect a deep and spiritual identification with the immense and poetic world of African mythology" (LCP, CHC 0339, series 1, box 20, folder 10, one-sided page, 1974).

106. See Ochoa 2010b; Beliso-De Jesús 2015; Pérez 2016; Wirtz 2014a; Palmié 2014.

107. For more on the importance of the kitchen in Santería's religious micropractices, see Pérez 2016.

4. SIRENS

Epigraph: "Total existence is always relative," trans. Michael Dash (Glissant 1992:109).

1. In Brazil, a female *Exú* by the name of Padilha also occupies a transgendered space. As iron artist Samuel Rodrigues explains it, "Padilha is flighty and wild, a beautiful woman who can be fat or thin, tall or short. She can have both a penis and a vagina. She can be elegantly dressed, with flowers. The original Padilha was white and maybe transsexual" (Glassie and Shukla 2018:400).

2. Pérez speaks of the Atlantic world as a historically "queer Atlantic" (2016:177).

3. I use the term *transformista* to refer to Latinx and Afrolatinx drag queens.

4. Elephants are associated with royalty and divination.

5. Cabrera says that Abata is sometimes seen as Erinle's brother, and both are "inseparable" from Ochún (1980:88).

6. During a cholera epidemic in the Spanish colonial era, Cuban folklore credits Erinle for healing children with a remedy of river water, almond

oil, soothing balsam oil, and by putting a chain marking them as devotees on the arm (Cabrera 1980:88).

7. Glissant 1992:142; Conner and Sparks 2004:79.

8. Glissant writes that the "transphysique de la Relation" of creolization found in the Caribbean helps to resist a kind of transcendental metaphysics associated with the West and colonialism (1992:141–44).

9. Antonio Vilches, interview by Solimar Otero, May 11, 2013, Havana, Cuba.

10. See Cabrera 1980:45.

11. Otin is also considered to be a "helper" oricha of Yemayá in Afro-Cuban religion (Ramos 1996:63).

12. Ramos 1996; Conner and Sparks 2004:78; Tsang 2013:171.

13. Glissant 1992:142; Cuesta 2016.

14. In Standard Yoruba, the verb *dó* refers to copulation in a vulgar way, equivalent to the English "to fuck" or the Spanish vernacular *chingar* (Abraham 1958:140).

15. See the usage of the term in Matory 2005:216–19; Conner and Sparks 2004:108; Pérez 2016.

16. See Clark 2005:99, 148; Brown 2003:347*n*141; Conner and Sparks 2004:135–40, 182–84; Matory 2005:205, 209, 211–13; Miller 2009:178. In the Puerto Rican documentary *Mala Mala* (2014), an Ifa devotee, whose identity is not so subtly revealed by a pan shot to his *ide* (initiatory bracelet) hugging the hips of his transsexual girlfriend, is said to not be interested in her "front parts" (penis). The interesting component is that it is the girlfriend who asserts this disavowal of her boyfriend's desire due to her job as a "top" in her trade as a sex worker. For a good analysis of the film, see La Fontain-Stokes 2016.

17. See Clark 2005:151, 166; Beliso-De Jesús 2013b, 2015; Rubiera Castillo 2011:107–49.

18. Otero 2013.

19. Baumann 1955; Conner and Sparks 2004.

20. *Our Lady of the Night* is about the influential and wealthy Afro-Puerto Rican madame Isabel "La Negra" Luberza Oppenheimer whose political influence was felt in Ponce from the 1930s through the 1960s.

21. "Mayra Santos-Fébres Conversatorio," https://www.youtube.com/watch?v=oNJJnEKU7B4 (last accessed June 14, 2019).

22. This close relationship between folklore and literature has been explored in a wide array of contexts; see de Caro and Jordon 2004; for Cuba, see Otero 2012.

23. I am aware that both the bolero and the topic of transformistas have been treated extensively by other Caribbean authors. For example, Severo Sarduy's *Cobra* (1972); Luis Rafael Sánchez's *La importancia de llamarse Daniel Santos* (1988); and Cabrera Infante's *Ella cantaba boleros* (1996) all feature the genre as a kind of motif.

24. See Castillo 2001; Rodríguez 2009; Garcés 2007; González-Allende 2005.

25. Here cohabitation refers to the shared embodiment and consciousness of divinities and spirits in Afrolatinx ritual work. See Otero 2015, 2013; Beliso De-Jesús 2015; Palmié 2014; Wirtz 2014a, 2014b; Pérez 2011; Ochoa 2010.

26. Mayra Santos-Fébres speaks about her own mother's love of music in the home: "La sandugería de mi madre que era una mujer espectacular, guapísima, que le encantaba bailar mientras limpiaba," from an interview in the show *Conversan Dos*, produced by the Centro Virtual Isaacs, 2013, https://www.youtube.com/watch?v=43y-rJPgLao (last accessed June 14, 2019).

27. Translation from Spanish to English mine.

28. See Broyles-González 2002; Vargas 2008:178, 185; and, in Santería, Beliso-De Jesús 2015:13.

29. See Moraga 1983 [1981]:xvi–xvii; Anzaldúa 1999 [1987]:107, 216–17; Quiroga 2000:145–68; Rivera-Servera 2012:6–8; Muñoz 1999:162–64; Arrizón 2006:38–46, 100; Troyano 2000; Vargas 2008.

30. See Severiche 2013.

31. From the English translation of *Sirena Serena* by Stephen Lytle (2000a:164–65).

32. See Vazquez 2013; Quiroga 2000:145–68; Monsváis 2004; Glasser 1995; Broyles-González 2002; Aparicio 1998; Vargas 2008:173–97; Campos 1991.

33. See, for example, the important emotive framing that the bolero plays in the novels *Te di la vida entera* (1996) by Zoé Valdés and *Caramelo* by Sandra Cisneros (2002).

34. Vargas also sees the bolero as a "powerfully emotional means of invoking communal memory" (2008:178).

35. See Rivera-Servera 2012:148–50; Broyles-González 2002; Vargas 2008:181; Campos 1991:637; Monsiváis 1997.

36. See Monsiváis 1997:166–97; Aparicio 1998:137; Campos 1991:638; Vargas 2008; Pedelty 1999:43–44.

37. Vargas 2008:178.

38. To listen to a rendition of Ema Elena Valdelamar's *Cheque en blanco* (Blank check) by Chelo Silva, see https://www.youtube.com/watch ?v=vhhDmVcKBDQ (last accessed June 14, 2019).

39. See Monsiváis 1997:167; Campos 1991; Vargas 2008.

40. René Campos (1991) argues that the bolero creates the poetics in Puig's *Kiss of the Spider Woman* that allow for an "affective and sexual relationship" between Molina and Valentín (639). Campos is suspicious of the ventriloquism of sentimentality the patriarchal voice may perform through the bolero.

41. For example, listen to a hybrid bolero/ranchero song like "Al ver que te vas" by Chayito Valdéz, interpreted by Chelo Silva, https://www .youtube.com/watch?v=me-AYZtrKeo. (last accessed June 14, 2019).

42. Carlos Monsiváis speaks of how the bolero, originally from Havana, cures the isolation felt in Yucatán during the early twentieth century by injecting a "bit of spiritual excess" into popular culture (1997:178).

43. Beliso De-Jesús 2015:94–95, 103–4, 117; Wirtz 2014a:62–63, 68–69, 126–27.

44. For a good discussion of the importance of interpreting the bolero from a feminist perspective, see Vargas 2008:185.

45. See, for example, the documentary series, made for Mexican television, *Las que viven en Ciudad Bolero* (1994), which investigates, through oral history interviews and performances, female *boleristas* and composers.

46. Based upon Martin Tsang's description of Erinle's "refined elegance" in his work on the oricha (2013:121).

47. See Palmié 2014; Wirtz 2014a; Beliso-De-Jesús 2015; Otero 2018a.

48. This consideration of time and anthropology is not new, especially with regard to African cultures and the creation of an "Other" based on non-linear temporalities, see Fabian 1983 for a classic example.

49. Though not within the scope of this chapter, it is necessary to mention the aesthetic and performative work of spiritual leaders in African American Creole traditions like Big Chief Allison "Tootie" Montana, from the New Orleans' Mardi Gras Indian tribe of the Yellow Pocahontas. See *All on a Mardi Gras Day* (2003), directed by Royce Osborn.

50. See Palmié 2014:232; Beliso-De Jesús 2015:216–20.

51. Vargas attributes the idea of divascapes to Licia Fiol-Matta's paper, "Body, Space, Sexuality," given at the New Directions in Queer Latino Studies Conference, University of Southern California and University of California, Los Angeles, November 2005.

52. Augustín Lara wrote the bolero "Mujer" in 1930; see Wood 2014:47.

53. Vargas asks us to consider the bolero as another kind of "border ballad" that tells the histories of morally ambivalent gendered and sexualized subjects who do not conform to *machista* notions of *mexicanidad* (2012:63–66).

54. Here one can also relate this projected danger of women to theories of feminine abjection reflected in mythology, literature, and popular culture. For a classic discussion, see Kristeva 1980.

55. For examples, see Halberstam 1998 and Butler 2004.

56. Elizabeth Pérez thinks through the synesthetics, the emotive and somatic aspects of gendered and sexualized micropractices in Afro-Cuban religion (2016). Perhaps the kitchen and the stage share the potential for creating "memoryscapes" that become resources for sensual and spiritual nourishment.

57. Lucy Fabery was an Afro-Puerto Rican Jazz singer known for her elegant singing style. Sylvia Rexach was an influential Puerto Rican composer, music critic, and singer of boleros. One of her most famous compositions is "Alma Adentro." See Rodríguez Santaliz 2009. La Lupe, Guadalupe Victoria Yolí, was an Afro-Cuban singer and performer who influenced multiple genres of music, including bolero, salsa, and bugaloo. For more on La Lupe, see the film by Ela Troyano, *La Lupe: Queen of Latin Soul* (2007).

58. The 2008 edition of the *Sirena Selena* contains a footnote to this opening passage that correlates Sirena with the deity Ochún and the coconut shells to divination (2).

59. Translation by Stephen Lytle (2000a:1).

60. This kind of ritual opening often occurs in Caribbean literature and performance because of the deep influence of African, especially Yoruba, cultures in creating the arts in Atlantic societies. For more on literary reading practices that create an "initiated reader," see Otero 2007b.

61. See Otero and Falola 2013.

62. XEW from Mexico City was a major radio station broadcasting the bolero internationally to cities like New York, Havana, and Buenos Aires (Pedelty 1999:39–41).

63. This song was made popular by the great jazz vocalist Ella Fitzgerald and the prolific composer Cole Porter.

64. See Drewal 1992; Otero 2007b. Recall that Santos-Febres is inspired by these very connections in developing her work.

65. See chapters 2 and 3, this volume.

66. See also Haitian Vodou and the role that the *lwa* Erzulie plays in framing women's and transgendered priests' expressive culture and history. See Dayan 1994 and the documentary film *Des hommes et Dieux* (*Of Men and Gods*, 2002).

67. De Burgos 1997; Pérez 2014; Guzmán 2008.

68. Woman centered.

69. Martin Tsang offers another version of the story where Erinle leaves Yemayá for Ochún and that is why Yemayá renders him mute (2013:121).

70. Another version of the narrative suggests a love triangle between Yemayá, Erinle, and Ochún as the source of Yemayá's rage and retributive silencing (Tsang 2013).

71. See *Mala Mala* (2015) by Santini and Sickles; La Fontain-Stokes 2016.

72. Dundes 2007.

73. Thorne 2013; Conner and Sparks 2004; Otero 2013; Beliso-De Jesús 2013; Strongman 2019.

74. Tsang 2013:118; Conner and Sparks 2004.

75. Cabrera 1980; Beliso De-Jesús 2013; Tsang 2013:121.

76. For *el pato* and Yemayá, see Beliso-De Jesús 2013.

77. This art form is taken very seriously in the hit reality television series *RuPaul's Drag Race*, where contestants are commanded to "lip-synch for your life!" or face elimination from the show.

78. Here I am thinking of the rhizomatic as performative assemblages that disrupt notions of an "authentic" original source of history or cultural production (Deleuze and Guattari 1987:1–28).

79. Nina Flowers is the drag persona of Puerto Rican transformista and DJ Jorge Luis Flores Sanchez. For a riveting performance of Nina Flowers as La Lupe see https://www.youtube.com/watch?v=y9_xCbzurmo (last accessed June 14, 2019).

80. For more on copresences, see Beliso De-Jesús 2015.

81. This is also not unlike the ways the body and consciousness enact with the dead in Palo (Ochoa 2010a; Cabrera 1986b).

82. See Valdez 2016 for *queer* maternity in *Sirena Selena*. For more on kinship and drag in Afrolatinx, Latinx, and African diasporic popular culture, see *Paris Is Burning* (1991); *Pose* (2018–2019); Butler 1993:121–42; and Muñoz 1999:162–63.

83. See Muñoz 2000; Quiroga 2000; Moraga 1983 [1981]; Anzaldúa 1999 [1987]; Arrizón 2006.

84. In Conner and Sparks 2004:112.

85. In Conner and Sparks 2004:112.

86. Appadurai 1996:176–77; Ranger 1983.
87. Turner 1977 [1969]; Turner 1999.
88. Thorne 2013.
89. For more on queer speech and performativity, see Livia and Hall 1997.
90. See, for example, the ongoing section "Reading Is Fundamental" in *RuPaul's Drag Race*. A personal favorite is Juju Bee's excellent execution of the "read." See https://www.youtube.com/watch?v=KBqrBnvnlLU (last accessed June 14, 2019).
91. Beliso-De Jesús has an excellent discussion of copresences and media in transnational Santería (2015).
92. Rodríguez 2009.
93. Conner and Sparks 2004:78; Cabrera 1975 [1954]:58–59, Tsang, personal communication, 2016.
94. Sundermann 2008:156.
95. Smoked fish is an important healing and cleansing ingredient in Afro-Cuban ritual work and traditional medicine.
96. Sundermann 2008:156.
97. Otero 2010, 2013, 2016a.
98. Both Otero 2016a and Beliso-De Jesús 2015 have discussed how different kinds of nation-building projects in Afro-Cuban religion speak to race, sexuality, and gender.
99. A well-known pilgrimage site and Catholic church in Havana where oricha worship and commerce is openly displayed alongside "official" Catholic practices.
100. For more on the importance of chisme in Afro-Cuban religious communication and vernacular history-making, see chapter 3, this volume.
101. Cabrera 1975 [1954]:58–59.
102. As discussed in the previous chapter, Cabrera creates a layered and queer religious history for Santería with her chisme about the gods and practitioners. She thus constructs an orally inspired archechisme (Vargas 2012:56).
103. For "texture," see Dundes 1980:20–32. Rinaldo Walcott has articulated a "homopoetics" that places Blackness and queerness at the center of Glissant's transphysical poetics (2007).
104. Drewal 1992.
105. Ochumaré is the oricha of the rainbow and is associated with regeneration, renewal, and the celestial serpent. Ochumaré's symbolism and pataki have been adopted and reimagined by environmental activists

to resist pollution and the erosion of Indigenous land rights in the United States (Williams and Anguiano 2018).

CONCLUSION: ESPUMA DEL MAR, SEA-FOAM

Epigraph: Reinaldo Arenas, excerpt from "Mi amante el mar" (2001:244). All translations to English in this chapter are mine. "Mi amante el mar" was originally written in 1973 in Havana.

1. For more ngangas and Palo objects of protection see Ochoa 2010a. For Ogun's power over iron, including weapons, see Barnes 1997. For the placement of warrior spirits in a larger African diaspora context, see Wehmeyer 2007.

2. A mpaka is a Palo divinatory device using a mirror, a bull's horn, beads, and other materials. See Cabrera 1986b.

3. Here I am reminded of the important work Kristina Wirtz does with race, especially Blackness, in Cuba in terms of its multiple valences socially and religiously (2014a).

4. For a Yoruba example of the oricha Olókùn inviting outsiders into Lagos, Nigeria, through ritual, see Otero 2010:80–83.

5. For more on the importance of gossip as a rhetorical mode in the Yoruba-inspired religions of Brazil, see Johnson 2005. For chisme as a feminist reclaiming of narrative see chapter 3, this volume, and Vargas 2012. For the importance of rumor in African American folk traditions as a related subversive public discourse see Turner 1993.

6. A common greeting for the dead in Espiritismo.

7. See Conner and Sparks 2004; Beliso De-Jesús 2013a; Pérez 2016; Strongman 2019; and Otero 2018a.

8. See Bendix 1997.

9. See Matory 1994; Drewal 1992; Hayes 2011; Cabrera 1980; *Des hommes et Dieux* 2002.TK

10. See Lawal 1996; Drewal and Drewal 1983; Barber 1990.

11. Drewal and Drewal 1983:74; Cabrera 1980:72–73.

12. For "moments of freedom" with regard to Shaba religious and popular culture, see Fabian 1998.

13. See, for example, the Cuban transformista El Chupitazo Kiriam Caridad del Cobre Oshun performing her own version of the oricha and La Lupe: https://www.youtube.com/watch?v=n6nhIqjkbGw (last accessed June 15, 2019).

14. A most recent example is Santos-Febres's story collection *Cuentos de Huracán* (Hurricane stories, 2018), inspired by the tales people told in the aftermath of Hurricane María. She presented some of the stories on April 8, 2018, at the Festival de la Palabra in San Juan, Puerto Rico.

15. See Glissant 1981:333–36 for more on trans-Caribbean colonialism, national literatures, and orality.

16. Haraway 2016:4.

17. Arenas 2001:244.

18. See Quiroga 2000:19, 121, 130, 150; Manrique 2001; and Kaebnick 1997.

19. Julian Schnabel directed a film version of *Before Night Falls* in 2000 staring Javier Bardem as Arenas.

20. See Ette 2016:151.

21. Fernando Ortiz's *Contrapunteo cubano* (1940); Lydia Cabrera's *El Monte* (1975 [1954]); Virgilio Piñera's *Electra Garrigó* 2014 [1948]; Guillermo Cabrera Infante's *Tres tristes tigres* (1981 [1967]); and Zoé Valdés's *Te di la vida entera* (1996) represent various genres of work that use friction to balance the avant-garde and the quotidian in their depiction of Cuban culture.

22. LCP, CHC 0339, series 1, box 3, folder 7, Arenas to Cabrera, 1980–1988.

23. For more on tales of Yemayá's power to heal and kill, see Cabrera 1980:23–27.

REFERENCES

Abelove, Henry. 2003. *Deep Gossip*. Minneapolis: University of Minnesota Press.

Abimbola, Wande. 1994. "Lagbayi: The Itinerant Wood Carver of Ojowon." In *The Yoruba Artist: New Theoretical Perspectives on African Arts*, ed. Rowland Abiodun, Henry Drewal, and John Pemberton III, 137–42. Washington, DC: Smithsonian Institution Press.

Abiodun, Rowland. 2001. "Hidden Power: `Oṣun, the Seventeenth Odu." In `*Oṣun Across the Waters: A Yoruba Goddess in Africa and the Americas*, ed. Joseph Murphy and Mei Mei Sandford, 10–33. Bloomington: Indiana University Press.

Abraham, Roy Clive. 1958. *Dictionary of Modern Yoruba*. London: University of London Press.

Abrahams, Roger D. 2003. "Questions of Criolian Contagion." *Journal of American Folklore* 116, no. 59: 73–87.

——. 1984 [1977]. "The Training of the Man of Words in Talking Sweet." In *Verbal Art as Performance*, ed. Richard Bauman, 117–32. Long Grove, IL: Waveland.

Acosta, Liza Ann, and Alexandra Mena. 2015. "Teatro Luna Manifesto: Ensemble Collective Work and Our Place in the Twenty-first-Century Latin@ Theater." *Gestos* 60 (November): 151–60.

Adepegba, Cornelius O. 2001. "Osun and Brass: An Insight Into Yoruba Religious Symbology." In `*Oṣun Across the Waters: A Yoruba Goddess in Africa and the Americas*, ed. Joseph Murphy and Mei Mei Sandford, 102–12. Bloomington: Indiana University Press.

Alarcón, Norma. 1984. "Chicana Feminist Literature: A Re-Vision Through Malintzin/or Malintzin: Putting the Flesh Back on the Object." *In This*

Bridge Called My Back: Writings by Radical Women of Color, ed. Cherríe Moraga and Gloria Anzaldúa, 182–89. New York: Kitchen Table/Women of Color.

Alexander, Jacqui M. 2005. *Pedagogies of Crossing: Meditations on Feminism, Sexual Politics, Memory, and the Sacred*. Durham, NC: Duke University Press.

All on a Mardi Gras Day. 2003. Dir. Royce Osborn. English, 60 minutes, color, USA. New Orleans, LA: Spy Boy Pictures.

Allen, Jafari S. 2012a. "Black/Queer/Diaspora at the Current Conjuncture." *GLQ: A Journal of Lesbian and Gay Studies* 18, no. 2–3: 211–48.

——. 2012b. "One Way or Another: Erotic Subjectivity in Cuba." *American Ethnologist*. 39, no. 2: 325–38.

——. 2011. *¡Venceremos?: The Erotics of Black Self-Mneaking in Cuba*. Durham, NC: Duke University Press.

Anderson, Benedict. 1983. *Imagined Communities: Reflections on the Origins and Spread of Nationalism*. London: Verso.

Anzaldúa, Gloria. 1999 [1987]. *Borderlands/La Frontera: The New Mestiza*. San Francisco: Aunt Lute.

Aparicio, Frances. R. 1997. *Listening to Salsa: Gender, Latin Popular Music, and Puerto Rican Cultures*. Middletown, CT: Wesleyan University Press.

Aparicio, Frances R., and Susana Chávez-Silverman, eds. 1997. *Tropicalizations: Transcultural Representations of Latinidad*. Hanover, NH: Dartmouth College Press.

Appadurai, Arjun. 1996. *Modernity at Large: Cultural Dimensions of Globalization*. Ann Arbor: University of Michigan Press.

Arenas, Reinaldo. 2013 [1992]. *Antes que anochezca*. Barcelona: Planeta.

——. 2001. *Inferno (poesía completa)*. Barcelona: Lumen.

——. 1999. *El color del verano*. Barcelona: TusQuets.

Argyriadis, Kali. 1999. *La religion à la Havane: Actualités des représentations et des pratiques cultuelles havanaises*. Amsterdam: Archives Contemporaines.

Arrizón, Alicia. 2006. *Queering Mestizaje: Transculturation and Performance*. Ann Arbor: University of Michigan Press.

Ayorinde, Christina. 2004. *Afro-Cuban Religiosity, Revolution and National Identity*. Gainesville: University Press of Florida.

Bakhtin, M. M. 1981. *The Dialogic Imagination: Four Essays*. Ed and trans. Michael Holquist and Carl Emerson. Austin: University of Texas Press.

Barber, Karin. 1999. "Quotation and the Constitution of Yoruba Oral Texts." *Research in African Literatures* 30, no. 2: 1–17.

——. 1991. *I Could Speak Until Tomorrow: Oríkì, Women and the Past in a Yoruba Town*. Washington, DC: Smithsonian Institution Press.

———. 1990. "Oríkì, Women, and the Proliferation and Merging of Orisa." *Africa* 60, no. 3: 313–337.

Barnes, Sandra, ed. 1997. *Africa's Ogun: Old World and New*. Bloomington: Indiana University Press.

Baron, Robert A., and Ana C. Cara, eds. 2011. *Creolization as Cultural Creativity*. Jackson: University Press of Mississippi.

Bascom, William. 1991 [1969]. *Ifa Divination: Communication Between Gods and Men in West Africa*. Bloomington: Indiana University Press.

Baumann, Hermann. 1955. *Das Doppelte Geschlecht: Ethnologische Studien zur Bisexualität in Ritus und Mythos*. Berlin: Deitrich Reimer.

Beauregard, Paulette Silva. 2000. "La feminización del héroe moderno y la novela en 'Lucía Jerez' y 'El hombre de hierro.'" *Revista de Crítica Literaria Latinoamericana* 26, no. 52: 135–51.

Behar, Ruth. 1996. *The Vulnerable Observer: Anthropology That Breaks Your Heart*. Boston: Beacon.

Beliso-De Jesús, Aisha M. 2015. *Electric Santería: Racial and Sexual Assemblages of Transnational Religion*. New York: Columbia University Press.

———. 2013a. "Religious Cosmopolitanisms: Media, Transnational Santería, and Travel Between the United States and Cuba." *American Ethnologist* 40, no. 4: 704–20.

———. 2013b. "Yemaya's Duck: Irony, Ambivalence, and the Effeminate Male Subject in Cuban Santería." In *Yemoja: Gender, Sexuality, and Creativity in the Latina/o and Afro-Atlantic Diasporas*, ed. Solimar Otero and Toyin Falola, 43–84. Albany: State University of New York Press.

Bendix, Regina. 1997. *In Search of Authenticity: The Formation of Folklore Studies*. Madison: University of Wisconsin Press.

Benítez Rojo, Antonio. 1992 [1989]. *La isla que se repite: El Caribe y la perspectiva posmoderna*. Hanover, NH: del Norte.

Blanes, Ruy, and Diana Espíritu Santo, eds. 2014. *The Social Life of Spirits*. Chicago: University of Chicago Press.

Bolívar Aróstegui, Natalia. 1990. *Los Orishas en Cuba*. Havana: Unión.

Braude, Ann. 1989. *Radical Spirits: Spiritualism and Women's Rights in Nineteenth-Century America*. Boston: Beacon.

Briggs, Charles L., ed. 1996. *Disorderly Discourse: Narrative Conflict and Inequality*. Oxford: Oxford University Press.

Brown, David Hilary. 2003. *Santería Enthroned: Art, Ritual, and Innovation in Afro-Cuban Religion*. Chicago: University of Chicago Press.

Broyles-González, Yolanda. 2002. "Ranchera Music(s) and the Legendary Lydia Mendoza: Performing Social Locations and Relation." In *Chicana*

Traditions: Continuity and Change, ed. Norma E. Cantú and Olga Nájera-Ramírez, 183–206. Urbana: University of Illinois Press,

Buck-Morss, Susan. 2009. *Hegel, Haiti, and Universal History*. Pittsburgh: University of Pittsburgh Press.

Butler, Judith. 2004. *Undoing Gender*. New York: Routledge.

———. 1997. *Excitable Speech: A Politics of the Performative*. New York: Routledge.

———. 1993. *Bodies That Matter: Feminism and the Subversion of Identity*. New York: Routledge.

Cabezas, Amelia. 2009. *Economies of Desire: Sex and Tourism in Cuba and the Dominican Republic*. Philadelphia: Temple University Press.

Cabrera, Lydia. 2006 [1954]. *El Monte: Igbo, finda, ewe orisha, vititi nfinda*, 9th ed. Miami: Universal.

———. 1998 [1959]. *La sociedad secreta Abakuá: narrada por viejos adeptos*. Miami: Universal.

———. 1986a. *Anagó, vocabulario Lucumi*. Miami: Universal.

———. 1986b. *Reglas de Congo: Palo Monte, Mayombe*. Miami: Universal.

———. 1980. *Yemayá y Ochún: Kariocha, Iyalorichas, y Olorichas*. Miami: Universal.

———. 1975 [1954]. *El Monte: Igbo, finda, ewe orisha, vititi nfinda*, 4th ed. Miami: Universal.

Cabrera Infante, Guillermo. 1996. *Ella cantaba boleros*. New York: Vintage.

———. 1981 [1967]. *Tres tristes tigres*. Barcelona: Seix Barral.

Callaci, Emily. 2017. *Street Archives and City Life: Popular Intellectuals in Postcolonial Tanzania*. Durham, NC: Duke University Press.

Campos, René A. 1991. "The Poetics of the Bolero in the Novels of Manuel Puig." *World Literature Today* 65, no. 4: 637–42.

Cantú, Norma E., and Olga Nájera-Ramírez, eds. 2002. *Chicana Traditions: Continuity and Change*. Urbana: University of Illinois Press.

Castellanos, Isabel. 2001. "A River of Many Turns: The Polysemy of Ochún in Afro-Cuban Tradition." ` *Ọsun Across the Waters: A Yoruba Goddess in Africa and the Americas*, ed. Joseph Murphy and Mei Mei Sanford, 34–45. Bloomington: Indiana University Press.

Castillo, Debra A. 2001. "She Sings Boleros: Santos-Febres' *Sirena Selena*." *Latin American Literary Review* 29, no. 57: 13–25.

Chapin, David. 2004. *Exploring Other Worlds: Margaret Fox, Elisha Kent Kane, and the Antebellum Culture of Curiosity*. Amherst, MA: University of Massachusetts Press.

A Cidade das Mulheres. 2016. Dir. Lázaro Faria. 72 minutes, color, Portuguese, Brazil. Porto Alegre: Casa de Cinema.

Cisneros, Sandra. 2003. *Caramelo*. New York: Vintage.

Clark, Mary Ann. 2005. *Where Men Are Wives and Mothers Rule: Santería Ritual Practices and Their Gender Implications*. Gainesville, FL: University of Florida Press.

Cole, Sally. 2003. *Ruth Landes: A Life in Anthropology*. Lincoln: University of Nebraska Press.

Condé, Maryse. 1989. *Traversée de la Mangrove*. Skokie, IL: Distribooks.

Conner, Randy P., and David Hatfield Sparks. 2004. *Queering Creole Spiritual Traditions: Lesbian, Gay, Bisexual, and Transgender Participation in African-Inspired Tradituions in the Americas*. New York: Harrington Park.

Cosentino, Donald. 1998. *Vodou Things: The Art of Pierrot Barra and Marie Cassaise*. Jackson: University Press of Mississippi.

Crawley, Ashon T. 2016. *Blackpentecostal Breath: The Aesthetics of Possibility*. New York: Fordham University Press.

Csordas, Thomas J. 2008. "Intersubjectivity and Intercorporeality." *Subjectivity* 22, no. 1: 110–21.

Cuesta, Mabel. 2016. "Nuestro Caribe: Poder, raza y postnacionalismos desde los límites del Mapa LGBTQ." In *Nuestro Caribe: Poder, raza y postnacionalismos desde los límites del Mapa LGBTQ*, ed. Mabel Cuesta, 9–20. San Juan: Isla Negra.

———. 2015. "Lydia Cabrera entre amigas: Un tren de sores para una ciénaga cementada." *Cuadernos Hispanoamericanos* 779 (May): 12–23.

Curtis, Edward E., and Sylvester A. Johnson. 2014. "Theorizing Africana Religions: A Journal of Africana Religions Inaugural Symposium." *Journal of Africana Religions* 2, no. 1: 125–28.

Cvetkovich, Ann. 2003. *An Archive of Feelings: Trauma, Sexuality, and Lesbian Public Cultures*. Durham, NC: Duke University Press.

Dabove, Juan Pablo. 2000. "Los pasquines como alegoría de la disolución de la ciudadanía en *La mala hora* de Gabriel García Márquez." *Revista de Crítica Literaria Latinoamericana* 26, no. 52: 269–87.

Danticat, Edwidge. 2013. *Claire of the Sea Light*. New York: Vintage.

———. 1998. *The Farming of Bones*. New York: Soho.

Dávila, Arlene. 2012. *Culture Works: Space, Value, and Mobility Across the Neoliberal Americas*. New York: New York University Press.

Dayan, Joan. 1994. "Erzulie: A Women's History of Haiti." *Research in African Literatures* 25, no. 2: 5–31.

De Burgos, Julia. 1997. *Song of the Simple Truth*, trans. Jack Agüeros. Bilingual ed. Willimantic, CT: Curbstone.

De Caro, Frank, and Rosan Augusta Jordon. 2004. *Re-Situating Folklore: Folk Contexts and Twentieth-Century Literature and Art*. Knoxville: University of Tennessee Press.

Deleuze, Gilles, and Felix Guattari. 1987. *A Thousand Plateaus: Capitalism and Schizophrenia*, trans. Brian Massumi. Minneapolis: University of Minnesota Press.

Deren, Maya. 1983. *Divine Horsemen: The Living Gods of Haiti*. New York: McPherson.

Derrida, Jacques. 1995. *Archive Fever: A Freudian Impression*, trans. Eric Prenowitz. Chicago, IL: University of Chicago Press.

Des hommes et Dieux (Of Men and Gods). 2002. Dir. Ann Lescot and Laurence Magloire. Creole, English subtitles, 52 minutes, Haiti. Watertown, MA: Documentary Educational Resources (DER).

Díaz-Quiñones, Arcadio. 1999. "Fernando Ortiz y Allan Kardec: Espiritismo y transculturación." *Catauro: Revista Cubana de Antropología* 1, no. 0: 14–31.

Díaz-Sánchez, Micaela 2013. "'Yemayá Blew That Wire Fence Down.' Invoking African Spiritualities in Gloria Anzaldúa's *Borderlands/La Frontera*: The New Mestiza and the Mural Art of Juana Alicia." In *Yemoja: Gender, Sexuality, and Creativity in the Latina/o and Afro-Atlantic Diasporas*, ed. Solimar Otero and Toyin Falola, 153–86. Albany: State University of New York Press.

Dinshaw, Carolyn. 2012. *How Soon Is Now? Medieval Texts, Amateur Readers, and the Queerness of Time*. Durham, NC: Duke University Press.

Drewal, Henry John. 2008. "Introduction: Charting the Voyage." In *Sacred Waters: Arts for Mami Wata and Other Divinities in Africa and the Diaspora*, ed. Henry Drewal, 1–18. Bloomington: Indiana University Press.

Drewal, Henry John, and Margaret Thompson Drewal. 1983. *Gẹlẹdẹ: Art and Female Power Among the Yoruba*. Bloomington: Indiana University Press.

Drewal, Henry John, John Pemberton III, and Rowland Abiodun. 1989. *Yoruba: Nine Centuries of Art and Thought*. New York: Center for African Art and Abrams.

Drewal, Margaret Thompson. 1992. *Yoruba Ritual: Performers, Play, Agency*. Bloomington: Indiana University Press.

Dundes, Alan. 2007. "Metafolklore and Oral Literary Criticism." In *The Meaning of Folklore: The Analytical Essays of Alan Dundes*, ed. Simon J. Bronner, 80–87. Logan, UT: Utah State University Press.

——, ed. 1992. *The Evil Eye: A Casebook by Alan Dundes*. Madison: University of Wisconsin Press.

——. 1980. *Interpreting Folklore*. Bloomington: Indiana University Press.

Esparza, Laura. 2000. "I DisMember the Alamo: A Long Poem for Performance." *Latinas on Stage: Practice and Theory*, ed. Alicia Arrizón and Lillian Manzor, 70–89. Berkeley: Third Woman.

Espírito Santo, Diana. 2015. *Developing the Dead: Mediumship and Selfhood in Cuban Espiritismo*. Gainesville: University Press of Florida.

Ette, Omar. 2016. *Writing-Between-Worlds: TransArea Studies and the Literatures-Without-a-Fixed-Abode*. Berlin: De Gruyter.

Fabian, Johannes. 1998. *Moments of Freedom: Anthropology and Popular Culture*. Charlottesville: University Press of Virginia.

——. 1983. *Time and the Other: How Anthropology Makes Its Object*. New York: Columbia University Press.

Federici, Silvia. 2010. "Women, Witch-Hunting and Enclosures in Africa Today." *Sozial Geschichte Online* 3:10–27. Last accessed June 17, 2019.

Fernández, Alexander. 2017. "Odú in Motion: Embodiment, Autoethnography, and the [Un]Texting of a Living Religious Practice." *Chiricú: Latina/o Literatures, Arts, and Cultures* 2, no. 1: 101–17.

Ferrer Castro, Armando, and Mayda Acosta Alegre. 2007. *Fermina Gómez y la casa olvidada de Olókun*. La Habana: José Martí.

Flores-Peña, Ysamur. 2004. "'Candles, Flowers, and Perfume': Puerto Rican Spiritism on the Move." In *Botánica Los Angeles: Latino Popular Religious Arts in the City of Angels*, ed. Patrick Arthur Polk, 88–97. Los Angeles: UCLA Fowler Museum.

——. 2001. "Overflowing with Beauty: The Ochún Altar in *Lucumí* Aesthetic Tradition." In `Ọsun Across the Waters: A Yoruba Goddess in Africa and the Americas*, ed. Joseph Murphy and Mei Mei Sandford, 113–27. Bloomington: Indiana University Press.

Flores-Peña, Ysamur, and Roberta J. Evanchuck. 1994. *Santería Garments and Altars: Speaking Without a Voice*. Jackson: University Press of Mississippi.

Fusco, Coco. 1995. *English Is Broken Here: Notes on the Cultural Fusion in the Americas*. New York: New Press.

Garcés, Elizabeth Montes. 2007. "Cuerpo, deseo y lenguaje en *La Celestina* y *Sirena Selena vestida de pena*." *Revista Canadiense de Estudios Hispánicos* 32, no. 1: 189–202.

Gates Jr., Henry Louis. 1989. *The Signifying Monkey: A Theory of African-American Literary Criticism*. Oxford: Oxford University Press.

Glasser, Ruth. 1995. *My Music Is My Flag: Puerto Rican Musicians and Their New York Communities, 1917–1940*. Berkeley: University of California Press.

Glassie, Henry. 2010. *Prince Twins Seven-Seven: His Art, His Life in Nigeria, His Exile in America*. Bloomington: Indiana University Press.

Glassie, Henry, and Pravina Shukla. 2018. *Sacred Art: Catholic Saints and Candomblé Gods in Modern Brazil*. Bloomington: Indiana University Press

Glave, Thomas. 2003. "Fire and Ink: Toward a Quest for Language, History, and a Moral Imagination." *Callaloo* 26, no. 3: 614–21.

Gilroy, Paul. 1993. *The Black Atlantic: Modernity and Double Consciousness.* Cambridge, MA: Harvard University Press.

Glissant, Édouard. 1997 [1981]. *Le discours antillais.* Paris: Gallimard.

——. 1992. *Caribbean Discourse: Selected Essays,* ed. and trans. Michael Dash. Charlottesville: University of Virginia Press.

——. 1981. *Le discours antillais.* Ann Arbor: University of Michigan Press.

Goldstein, Diane E., ed. 2017. *The Stigmatized Vernacular: Where Reflexivity Meets Untellability.* Bloomington: Indiana University Press.

González, Flora M. 2005. "Cultural Mestizaje in the Essays and Poetry of Nancy Morejón." *Callaloo* 28, no. 4: 990–1011.

González-Allende, Iker. 2005. "De la pasividad al poder sexual y economico: El sujeto activo en *Sirena Selena.*" *Chasqui* 34, no. 1: 51–64.

Goodison, Lorna. 2017. *Collected Poems.* Manchester: Carcanet.

——. 2009. *From Harvey River: A Memoir of My Mother and Her Island.* New York: Amistad.

Guzmán, Mañuel. 2008. "'Pa' La Escuelita con Mucho Cuida'o y por la Orillita': A Journey Through the Contested Terrains of the Nation and Sexual Orientation." In *Puerto Rican Jam: Essays on Culture and Politics,* ed. Frances Negrón-Muntaner and Ramón Grosfoguel, 209–28. Minneapolis: University of Minnesota Press.

Hagedorn, Katherine J. 2001. *Divine Utterances: The Performance of Afro-Cuban Santeria.* Washington, DC: Smithsonian Institution Press.

Halberstam, Jack. 2018. *Trans*: A Quick and Quirky Account of Gender Variability.* Berkeley: University of California Press.

——. 1998. *Female Masculinity.* Durham, NC: Duke University Press.

Hale, Lindsay. 2009. *"Hearing the Mermaid's Song: The Umbanda Religion in Rio de Janeiro.* Albuquerque: University of New Mexico Press.

Haraway, Donna. 2016. *Staying with the Trouble: Making Kin in the Chthulucene.* Durham, NC: Duke University Press.

Harding, Rachel Elizabeth. 2001. "What Part of the River You're In." In `*O̩sun Across the Waters: A Yoruba Goddess in Africa and the Americas,* ed. Joseph Murphy and Mei Mei Sanford, 165–88. Bloomington: Indiana University Press.

Harris, Laura Alexandra. 1996. "Queer Black Feminism: The Pleasure Principle." *Feminist Review* 54, no. 1: 3–30.

Hayes, Kelley. 2011. *Holy Harlots: Femininity, Sexuality, and Black Magic in Brazil.* Berkeley: University of California Press.

Hammad, Suheir. 2004. "Forward: From Margin to Center." In *Word: On Being a [Woman] Writer,* ed. Jocelyn Burrell, xi–xiv. New York: Feminist Press at CUNY.

Hernández Cruz, Victor. 2001. "Geography of the Trinity Corona." In *Maraca: New and Selected Poems 1965–2000*, 66–67. Minneapolis: Coffee House Press.

Hess, David. 1987. "The Many Rooms of Spiritism in Brazil." *Luso-Brazilian Review* 24, no. 2: 15–34.

"Honoring Lydia Cabrera's Story: Altar, Performance, and the Living Archive." 2016. Exhibit and performance at the HistoryMiami Museum, October 18–31, curated by Solimar Otero, Kay Turner, Martin Tsang, and Eric Mayer-García, Miami, Florida.

Hrdlička, Aleš. 1918. "Physical Anthropology: Its Scopes and Aims; Its History and Present Status in America." *Journal of Physical Anthropology* 1, no. 1: 3–23.

Hufford, David. 1995. "Beings Without Bodies: An Experience-Centered Theory of the Belief in Spirits." In *Out of the Ordinary: Folklore and the Supernatural*, ed. Barbara Walker, 11–45. Logan: Utah State University Press.

Hurston, Zora Neale. 1990 [1935]. *Mules and Men*. New York: Harper Perennial.

Ingersoll, Karen Amimoto. 2016. *Waves of Knowing: A Seascape Epistemology*. Durham, NC: Duke University Press.

Johnson, Patrick E., and Ramón Rivera-Servera, eds. 2016. *Blacktino Queer Performance*. Durham, NC: Duke University Press.

Johnson, Paul C. 2005. *Secrets, Gossip, and Gods: The Transformation of Brazilian Candomblé*. Oxford: Oxford University Press.

——, ed. 2014. *Spirited Things: The Work of "Possession" in Afro-Atlantic Religions*. Chicago: University of Chicago Press.

Kaebnick, Suzanne. 1997. "The 'Loca' Freedom Fighter in 'Antes Que Anochezca' and 'El Color del Verano.'" *Chasqui* 26, no. 1: 102–14.

Kahn, Benjamin. 2013. *Celibacies: American Modernism and Sexual Life*. Durham, NC: Duke University Press.

Kardec, Allan. 2011 [1857]. *El libro de los espíritus* [*Le livre des Esprits*], 2d ed., trans by Gustavo N. Martínez. Brasilia: Consejo Espírita Internacional.

Kristeva, Julia. 1980. *Pouvoirs de l'horreur*. Paris: Seuil.

Kutzinski, Vera M. 1993. *Sugar's Secrets: Race and the Erotics of Cuban Nationalism*. Charlottesville: University of Virginia Press.

La Fontain-Stokes, Lawrence. 2016. "*Mala Mala* y la representación transgénero y transformista en el cine puertorriqueño." In *Nuestro Caribe: Poder, raza, postnacionalismos desde los límites del Mapa LGBTQ*, ed. Mabel Cuesta, 167–84. San Juan: Isla Negra.

Lakoff, George, and Mark Johnson. 1980. *Metaphors We Live By*. Chicago: University of Chicago Press.

La Lupe: Queen of Latin Soul. 2007. Dir. Ela Troyano. English and Spanish, 60 minutes, USA. Arlington, VA: PBS Independent Lens.

Landes, Ruth. 1994 [1947]. *The City of Women*. Albuquerque: University of New Mexico Press.

——. 1940. "A Cult Matriarchate and Male Homosexuality." *Journal of Abnormal Psychology* 35, no. 3: 386–397.

Lara, Ana Maurine. 2017. "I Wanted to Be More of a Person: Conjuring [Afro] [Latinx] [Queer] Futures." *Bilingual Review/La Revista Belingüe* 33, no. 4: 1–14.

Las que viven en Ciudad Bolero. 1994. Dir. Leopold Best. Spanish, 136 minutes, Mexico. Mexico City: Consejo nacional para la cultura y las artes.

Lau, Kimberly. 2010. "The Political Lives of Avatars: Play and Democracy in Virtual Worlds." *Western Folklore* 69, nos. 3/4: 369–94.

Lawal, Babatunde. 1996. *The Gẹlẹdẹ Spectacle: Art, Gender, and Social Harmony in African Culture*. Seattle: University of Washington Press.

Lawless, Elaine. 2000. "'Reciprocal' Ethnography: No One Said It Was Easy." *Journal of Folklore Research* 37, nos. 2/3: 197–205.

——. 1991. "Women's Life Stories and Reciprocal Ethnography as Feminist and Emergent." *Journal of Folklore Research* 28, no. 1: 35–60.

Lévy-Bruhl, Lucien. 1922. *La mentalité primitive*. Paris: Presses universitaires de France.

Lewgoy, Bernardo. 2001. "Chico Xavier e a cultura brasileira." *Revista de Antropologia* 44, no. 1: 53–116.

Lindsay, Arturo. 2013. "Dancing with *Aché* with Yemayá in My Life and in My Art: An Artist Statement." In *Yemoja: Gender, Sexuality, and Creativity in the Latina/o and Afro-Atlantic Diasporas*, ed. Solimar Otero and Toyin Falola, 187–96. Albany: State University of New York Press.

——. 1996. *Santería Aesthetics in Contemporary Latin American Art*. Washington, DC: Smithsonian Institution Press.

Linebaugh, Peter, and Marcus Rediker. 2001. *The Many-Headed Hydra: Sailors, Slaves, Commoners, and the Hidden History of the Revolutionary Atlantic*. Boston: Beacon.

Livia, Anna, and Kira Hall, eds. 1997. *Queerly Phrased: Language, Gender, and Sexuality*. Oxford: Oxford University Press.

Long, Carolyn M. 2001. *Spiritual Merchants: Religion, Magic, and Commerce*. Berkeley: University of California Press.

López, Josefina. 1997. *Unconquered Spirits*. Woodstock, IL: Dramatic.

Lorde, Audre. 1978. *The Black Unicorn: Poems*. New York: Norton.

Lowe, John W. 2016. *Calypso Magnolia: The Crosscurrents of Caribbean and Southern Literature*. Chapel Hill: University of North Carolina Press.

Lucero, Helen. 2002. "The Art of the Santera." *Chicana Traditions: Continuity and Change*, ed. Norma Cantú and Olga Nájera-Ramírez, 35–54. Urbana: University of Illinois Press.

Lydia Cabrera Papers (LCP), Cuban Heritage Collection (CHC), 0339, series 1, boxes 1, 2, 3, and 10; and LCP, CHC 0339, series 3, box 26.

Magliocco, Sabina. 2004. *Witching Culture: Folklore and Neo-Paganism in America*. Philadelphia: University of Pennsylvania Press.

Mala Mala. 2015. Dir. Antonio Santini and Dan Sickles. Spanish and English, 87 minutes, Puerto Rico, USA. New York: El Peligro, Killer Films, and Moxie Pictures.

Manrique, Jaime. 2001. *Eminent Maricones: Arenas, Lorca, Puig, and Me*. Madison: University of Wisconsin Press.

Mañach, Jorge. 1969 [1928]. *Indagación del choteo*. Miami: Mnemosyne.

Marchi, Regina. 2013. "Hybridity and Authenticity in US Day of the Dead Celebrations." *Journal of American Folklore* 126, no. 501: 272–301.

Mason, Michael Atwood. 2002. *Living Santería: Rituals and Experiences in Afro-Cuban Religion*. Washington, DC: Smithsonian Institution Press.

——. 1994. "'I Bow My Head to the Ground': The Creation of Bodily Experience in a Cuban American Santeria Initiation." *Journal of American Folklore* 107, no. 423: 23–39.

Matory, J. Lorand. 2018. *The Fetish Revisited: Marx, Freud, and the Gods Black People Make*. Durham, NC: Duke University Press.

——. 2005. *Black Atlantic Religion: Tradition, Transnationalism, and Matriarchy in Afro-Brazilian Candomblé*. Princeton: Princeton University Press.

——. 1994. *Sex and the Empire That Is No More: Gender and the Politics of Metaphor in Oyo Yoruba Religion*. Minneapolis: University of Minnesota Press.

Mayer-García, Eric. 2018. "Feeling Brown Like You: Creación Colectiva and Latinx Affect in Fornés' *Cap-a-Pie*." *Chiricú Journal: Latina/o Literatures, Arts, and Cultures* 3, no. 1: 23–48.

——. 2016a. "Reconfiguring Race and Citizenship: The *Teatro Vernáculo* of La Unión Martí-Maceo." In *Experiments in Democracy: Interracial and Cross-Cultural Exchange in American Theatre*, 1912–1945, ed. Cheryl Black and Jonathon Shandell, 49—66. Carbondale: Southern Illinois University Press.

——. 2016b. "Theatricalizing the Queer Aesthetics of Lydia Cabrera's *Suandende*." Talk delivered at the New Directions in Cuban Studies conference,

November 20, Cuban Heritage Collection, University of Miami, Coral Gables.

Miller, Ivor. 2009. *Voice of the Leopard: African Secret Societies and Cuba*. Jackson: University Press of Mississippi.

Mitsch, Ruthmarie H. 1997. "Maryse Condé's Mangroves." *Research in African Literatures* 28, no. 4: 54–70.

Monsiváis, Carlos. 2004. "Introducción." In *Bolero: Clave del corazón*, ed. Federico Krafft Vera and Elena Tamargo Cordero, 9–22. México, DF: Alejo Peralta Fundación.

——. 1997. *Mexican Postcards*, trans. John Kraniauskas. New York: Verso.

Moraga, Cherríe. 1983 [1981]. "Preface." In *This Bridge Called My Back: Writings by Radical Women of Color*, ed. Cherríe Moraga and Gloria Anzaldúa, xiii–xix. New York: Kitchen Table/Women of Color.

Morejón, Nancy. 2001. *Black Woman and Other Poems*, trans. Jean Andrews. London: Mango.

Morejón, Nancy, and David Frye. 2005. "Cuba and Its Deep Africanity." *Callaloo* 28, no. 4: 933–51.

Muñoz, José Estaban. 2009. *Cruising Utopia: The Then and There of Queer Futurity*. New York: New York University Press.

——. 2000. "Feeling Brown: Ethnicity and Affect in Ricardo Bracho's *The Sweetest Hangover (and Other STDs)*." *Theatre Journal* 52, no. 1: 67–79.

——. 1999. *Disidentifications: Queers of Color and the Performance of Politics*. Minneapolis: University of Minnesota Press.

Murphy, Joseph M. 2001. "Yéyé Cachita: Ochún in a Cuban Mirror." In `Oṣun Across the Waters: A Yoruba Goddess in Africa and the Americas*, ed. Joseph Murphy and Mei Mei Sanford, 87–101. Bloomington: Indiana University Press.

Murphy, Joseph, and Mei Mei Sandford, eds. 2001. `Oṣun Across the Waters: A Yoruba Goddess in Africa and the Americas*. Bloomington: Indiana University Press.

Ngugi wa Thiong'o. 1993. *Moving the Centre: The Struggle for Cultural Freedoms*. Woodbridge, UK: James Currey.

Nuttal, Sarah, ed. 2007. *Beautiful/Ugly: African and Diaspora Aesthetics*. Durham, NC: Duke University Press.

Oberhausen, Judy. 2009. "Sisters in Spirit: Alice Kipling Fleming, Evelyn Pickering de Morgan and Nineteenth-Century Spiritualism." *British Art Journal* 9, no. 3: 38–42.

Ochoa, Todd Ramón. 2010a. "Prendas-Ngangas-Enquisos: Turbulence and the Influence of the Dead in Cuban-Kongo Material Culture." *Cultural Anthropology* 25, no. 3: 387–420.

——. 2010b. *Society of the Dead: Quita Manaquita and Palo Praise in Cuba.* Berkeley: University of California Press.

Olademo, Oyeronke. 2009. *Gender in Yoruba Oral Traditions.* Lagos: Centre for Black and Africa Arts and Civilizations (CBAAC).

Olajubu, Oyeronke. 2003. *Women in the Yoruba Religious Sphere.* Albany: State University of New York Press.

Olmos, Margarite Fernandez, and Lizabeth Paravisini-Gebert. 2003. *Creole Religions of the Caribbean: An Introduction from Vodou and Santeria to Obeah and Espiritismo.* New York: New York University Press.

Olupona, Jacob K. 2001. "Òrìṣà ` Ọṣun: Sacred Kingship and Civil Religion in Osogbo, Nigeria." In ` Ọṣun Across the Waters: A Yoruba Goddess in Africa and the Americas, ed. Joseph Murphy and Mei Mei Sanford, 47–67. Bloomington: Indiana University Press.

Ortiz, Fernando. 2012 [1924]. *La filosofía penal de los espiritistas.* San Juan: Nuevo Mundo.

——. 2001 [1950]. *La africanía de la música folklórica cubana.* La Habana: Letras Cubanas.

——. 1963 [1940]. *Contrapunteo cubano del tabaco y azúcar.* Madrid: Cátedra.

Otero, Solimar. 2018a. "In the Water with Erinle: Siren Songs and Performance in Caribbean Southern Ports." *Southern Quarterly* 55, no. 4: 144–62.

——. 2018b. "Residual Transcriptions: Ruth Landes and the Archive of Conjure." *Transforming Anthropology* 26, no. 1 (April 2018): 3–17.

——. 2016a "Crossing Spirits, Negotiating Cultures: Transmigration, Transculturation, and Interorality in Cuban Espiritismo." In *Tradition: Literature, Performance, and Practice*, ed. Hanetha Veté-Congolo, 85–107. New York: Palgrave MacMillan.

——. 2016b. "La Llorona." In *Ghosts in Popular Culture and Legend*, ed. June Pulliam and Anthony Fonseca, 196–98. Santa Barbara: ABC-CLIO Greenwood.

——. 2015."Entre las aguas/Between Waters: Interorality in Cuban Vernacular Religious Storytelling," *Journal of American Folklore* 128, no. 508: 195–221.

——. 2013. "Yemayá y Ochún: Queering the Vernacular Logics of the Waters." In *Yemoja: Gender, Sexuality, and Creativity in the Latina/o and Afro-Atlantic Diasporas*, ed. Solimar Otero and Toyin Falola, 85–112. Albany: State University of New York Press.

——. 2012. "The Ruins of Havana: Representations of Memory, Religion, and Gender." *Atlantic Studies* 9, no. 2: 143–63.

——. 2010. *Afro-Cuban Diasporas in the Atlantic World*. Rochester, NY: University of Rochester Press.

——. 2007a. "Barrio, Bodega, and Botanica Aesthetics: The Layered Traditions of the Latino Imaginary." *Atlantic Studies* 4, no. 2: 173–94.

——. 2007b. "Spirit Possession, Havana, and the Night: Listening and Ritual in Cuban Fiction. *Western Folklore* 66, nos. 1/2: 45–74.

——. 1996. "Fearing Our Mothers: An Overview of the Psychoanalytic Theories Concerning the Vagina Dentata Motif, F547.1.1." *American Journal of Psychoanalysis* 56, no. 3: 269–88.

Otero, Solimar, and Toyin Falola, eds. 2013. *Yemoja: Gender, Sexuality, and Creativity in the Latina/o and Afro-Atlantic Diasporas*. Albany: State University of New York Press.

Otero, Solimar, and Mintzi Auanda Martínez-Rivera. 2017. "Introduction. *Poder y cultura*: Latinx Folklore and Popular Culture." *Chiricú Journal: Latina/o Literatures, Arts, and Cultures* 2, no. 1: 6–15.

Palmié, Stephan. 2014. "Historicist Knowledge and Its Conditions of Impossibility." In *The Social Life of Spirits*, ed. Ruy Blanes and Diana Espírito Santo, 218–40. Chicago: University of Chicago Press.

——. 2013. *The Cooking of History: How Not to Study Afro-Cuban Religion*. Chicago: University of Chicago Press.

——. 2002. *Wizards and Scientists: Explorations in Afro-Cuban Modernity and Tradition*. Durham, NC: Duke University Press.

Paris Is Burning. 1991. Dir. Jennie Livingston. English, 71 min., USA. New York: Art Matters.

Pedelty, Mark. 1999. "The Bolero: The Birth, Life, and Decline of Mexican Modernity." *Latin American Music Review/Revista de Música Latinoamericana* 20, no. 1: 30–58.

Pérez, Elizabeth. 2016. *Religion in the Kitchen: Cooking, Talking, and the Making of Black Atlantic Traditions*. New York: New York University Press.

——. 2013. "Nobody's Mammy: Yemayá as aFierce Foremother in Afro-Cuban Religions." In *Yemoja: Gender, Sexuality, and Creativity in the Latina/o and Afro-Atlantic Diasporas*, ed. Solimar Otero and Toyin Falola, 9–42. Albany: State University of New York Press.

——. 2011. "Spiritist Mediumship as Historical Mediation: African-American Pasts, Black Ancestral Presence, and Afro-Cuban Religions." *Journal of Religion in Africa* 41, no. 4: 330–65.

Pérez Firmat, Gustavo. 1984. "Riddles of the Sphincter: Another Look at the Cuban Choteo." *Diacritics* 14, no. 4: 67–77.

Perez Mena, Andres I. 1998. "Cuban Santeria, Haitian Vodun, Puerto Rican Spiritualism: A Multiculturalist Inquiry Into Syncretism." *Journal for the Scientific Study of Religion* 37 no. 1: 15–28.

Pérez Rosario, Vanessa. 2014. *Becoming Julia de Burgos: The Making of a Puerto Rican Icon.* Urbana: University of Illinois Press.

Piña, Sarah E. 2016. "Habla Yemayá: El archivo y la ethnografía feminist-queer de Lydia Cabrera." In *Nuestro Caribe: Poder, raza, postnacionalismos desde los límites del Mapa LGBTQ*, ed. Mabel Cuesta, 45–64. San Juan: Isla Negra.

Piñera, Virgilio. 2014 [1948]. *Electra Garrigó.* Mexico City: Universidad Nacional Autonoma de Mexico.

Pose. 2018–2019. Created by Ryan Murphy, Brad Falchuck, and Steven Canals. Los Angeles: FX.

Primiano, Leonard. 1993. "Intrinsically Catholic: Vernacular Religion and Philadelphia's 'Dignity.'" PhD Thesis, Philadelphia: University of Pennsylvania.

Quiroga, José. 2005. *Cuban Palimpsests.* Minneapolis: University of Minnesota Press.

——. 2000. *Tropics of Desire: Interventions from Queer Latino America.* New York: New York University Press.

Ramos, Miguel Willie. 1996. "Afro-Cuban Orisha Worship." In *Santería Aesthetics in Contemporary Latin American Art*, ed. Arturo Lindsay, 51–76. Washington, DC: Smithsonian Institution Press.

Ranger, Terence. 1983. "The Invention of Tradition in Colonial Africa." In *The Invention of Tradition*, ed. Terence Ranger and Eric Hobsbawm, 211–62. Cambridge: Cambridge University Press.

Ribeiro dos Santos, Ieda Machado. 2001. "Nesta cidade todo mundo é d'Oxum. In this city everybody is Oxum's." In `Ọṣun Across the Waters: A Yoruba Goddess in Africa and the Americas*, ed. Joseph Murphy and Mei Mei Sanford, 68–83. Bloomington: Indiana University Press.

Ricoeur, Paul. 2004. *Memory, History, Forgetting*, trans. David Pellauer. Chicago: University of Chicago Press.

Riggs, Marlon. 1995. *Black Is . . . Black Ain't* (transcript). Berkeley: Signifyin' Works.

Rivera-Servera, Ramón H. 2012. *Performing Queer Latinidad: Dance, Sexuality, Politics.* Ann Arbor: University of Michigan Press.

Rodríguez, Juana María. 2009. "Translating Queer Caribbean Localities in *Sirena Selena vestida de pena.*" *MELUS* 34, no. 3: 205–23.

Rodríguez-Mangual, Edna M. 2004. *Lydia Cabrera and the Construction of an Afro-Cuban Cultural Identity.* Chapel Hill: University of North Carolina Press.

Rodríguez Santaliz, Virianai. 2009. *Sylvia Rexach: Passion Adentro/Inner Passion*. San Juan: Callejón.

Román, Reinaldo M. 2007a. "Governing Man-Gods: Spiritism and the Struggle for Progress in Republican Cuba." *Journal of Religion in Africa* 37 no. 2: 212–41.

——. 2007b. *Governing Spirits: Religion, Miracles, and Spectacles in Cuba and Puerto Rico, 1898–1956*. Chapel Hill, NC: University of North Carolina Press.

Romberg, Raquel. 2009. *Healing Dramas: Divination and Magic in Modern Puerto Rico*. Austin: University of Texas Press.

——. 2007. "'Today, Changó Is Changó': How Africanness Becomes a Ritual Commodity in Puerto Rico." *Western Folklore* 66, no. 1/2: 75–106.

——. 2005. "Ritual Piracy of Creolization with an Attitude." *New West Indian Guide* 79, no. 3/4: 175–218.

——. 2003. *Witchcraft and Welfare: Spiritual Capital and the Business of Magic in Modern Puerto Rico*. Austin: University of Texas Press.

Routon, Kenneth. 2008. "Conjuring the Past: Slavery and the Historical Imagination in Cuba." *American Ethnologist* 35, no. 4: 632–49.

Rubiera Castillo, Daisy. 2011."La mujer en la santería o La Regla de Ocha: Género, mitos, y realidad." In *Afrocubanas*, ed. Daisy Rubiera Castillo and Ines Maria Martitatu, 107–49. Havana: Editorial de Ciencias Sociales.

Ruth Landes Papers (RLP), National Anthropological Archives (NAA), series 2 research materials, subseries: Brazil, boxes 9 and 19.

Samper, David. 2002. "Cannibalizing Kids: Rumor and Resistance in Latin America." *Journal of Folklore Research* 39, no. 1: 1–32.

Sánchez, Luis Rafael. 2000 [1988]. *La importancia de llamarse Daniel Santos*. San Juan: Editorial de la Universidad de Puerto Rico.

Sanford, Mei Mei. 2001. "Living Water: `Ọṣun, Mami Wata, and Olókùn in the Lives of Four Contemporary Nigerian Christian Women." In `Ọṣun Across the Waters: A Yoruba Goddess Africa and the Americas, ed. Joseph Murphy and Mei Mei Sanford, 237–50. Bloomington: Indiana University Press.

Santos-Febres, Mayra. 2009 [2000]. *Sirena Selena vestida de pena*. New York: Penguin Random House.

——. 2008. *Nuestra señora de la noche*. New York: Rayo.

——. 2000a. *Sirena Selena*, trans. Steven Lytle. London: Picador.

——. 2000b. *Sirena Selena vestida de pena*. New York: Penguin Random House.

Sarduy, Severo. 1986 [1972]. *Cobra*. Buenos Aires: Sudamericana.

Scott, James C. 1990. *Domination and the Arts of Resistance: Hidden Transcripts.* New Haven: Yale University Press.

———. 1985. *Weapons of the Weak: Everyday Forms of Peasant Resistance.* New Haven: Yale University Press.

Sedgwick, Eve Kosofsky. 2003. *Touching Feeling: Affect, Pedagogy, Performativity.* Durham, NC: Duke University Press.

Severiche, Guillermo. 2013. "El Hombre/Mujer, el Ángel/Demonio: Cuerpo, misterio e inquietud en *Sirena Selena vestida de pena.*" *Revista de Estudios Hispánicos* 4 no. 1: 1–12.

Sheller, Mimi. 2003. *Consuming the Caribbean: From Arawaks to Zombies.* New York: Routledge.

Shukla, Pravina. 2015. *Costume: Performing Identities Through Dress.* Bloomington: Indiana University Press.

Silverman, Carol. 2012. *Romani Routes: Cultural Politics and Balkan Music in Diaspora.* Oxford: Oxford University Press.

Strongman, Roberto. 2019. *Queering Black Atlantic Religions: Transcorporeality in Candomblé, Santería, and Vodou.* Durham, NC: Duke University Press.

Suárez, Lucía M. 2011. "Consuming Cubanas: ¿Quién diablos es Juliette?" *Cuban Studies* 42: 155–71.

Sundermann, Werner. 2008. "Zoroastrian Motifs in Non-Zoroastrian Traditions." *Journal of the Royal Asiatic Society* 18, no. 2: 155–65.

Taylor, Diana. 2003. *The Archive and the Repertoire: Performing Cultural Memory in the Americas.* Durham, NC: Duke University Press.

Thompson, Stith. 1955–58. *Motif-Index of Folk-Literature.* Bloomington: Indiana University Press.

Thorne, Cory. 2013. "Saluting the Orishas in a Havana Gay Bar: Queering the Sacred and Secular in a New Gay-Positive Cuba." Talk delivered at the *American Folklore Society Annual Meeting*, October 17, Providence, Rhode Island.

Tromp, Marlene. 2003. "Spirited Sexuality: Sex, Marriage, and Victorian Spiritualism." *Victorian Literature and Culture* 31, no. 1: 67–81.

Troyano, Alina. 2000. *I, Carmelita Tropicana: Performing Between Cultures.* Boston: Beacon.

Tsang, Martin. 2019. "On Becoming the Archive." In *Lydia Cabrera Between the Sum and the Parts*, ed. Karen Marta and Gabriela Rangel, 61–66. London: Americas Society, Koenig.

———. 2017. "The Power of Containing and the Containing of Power: Creating, Collecting, and Documenting an Afro-Cuban Lukumí Beaded Vessel." *Journal of Museum Ethnography* no. 30: 125–47.

———. 2013. "A Different Kind of Sweetness: Yemayá in Afro-Cuban Religion." In *Yemoja: Gender, Sexuality, and Creativity in the Latina/o and Afro-Atlantic Diasporas*, ed. Solimar Otero and Toyin Falola, 113–30. Albany: State University of New York Press.

Turner, Kay. 1999. *Beautiful Necessity: The Art and Meaning of Women's Altars*. New York: Thames and Hudson.

Turner, Patricia A. 1993. *I Heard It Through the Grapevine: Rumor in African-American Culture*. Berkeley: University of California Press.

Turner, Victor W. 1977 [1969]. *The Ritual Process: Structure and Anti-Structure*. Ithaca, NY: Cornell University Press.

Valdés, Ernesto. 2012. "Los Caminos de los Amores de Oshún." *Documentos para la historia y la cultura de Osha-Ifá en Cuba*. Compiled by Ernesto Valdés Jane and Proyecto Orunmila. http://proyecto-orunmila.org/libros-osha -ifa-santeria. Last accessed June 4, 2019.

Valdés, Merceditas. 2013. "Cantos Espirituales Cubanos." In *Merceditas Valdés: La Reina de la Música Afrocubana*. Havana: EGREM Sony Music.

Valdés, Zoé. 1996. *Te di la vida entera*. Barcelona: Planeta.

Valdez, Elena. 2016. "Las maternidades *queer* en *Sirena selena vestida de pena* de Mayra Santos-Febres." *Nuestro Caribe: poder, raza, postnacionalismos desde los límites del Mapa LGBTQ*, ed. Mabel Cuesta, 201–20. San Juan: Isla Negra.

Vargas, Deborah R. 2012. *Dissonant Divas in Chicana Music: The Limits of La Onda*. Minneapolis: University of Minnesota Press.

———. 2008. "Borderland Bolerista: The Licentious Lyricism of Chelo Silva." *Feminist Studies* 34, nos. 1/2: 173–97.

Vazquez, Alexandra T. 2014. "Learning to Live in Miami." *American Quarterly* 66, no. 3: 853–73.

———. 2013. *Listening in Detail: Performances of Cuban Music*. Durham, NC: Duke University Press.

Vega, Manuel. 2001. "Mãe Menininha." In `Ọṣun Across the Waters: A Yoruba Goddess Africa and the Americas*, ed. Joseph Murphy and Mei Mei Sanford, 84–86. Bloomington: Indiana University Press.

Vega, Marta Moreno. 1999. "Espiritismo in the Puerto Rican Community: A New World Recreation with the Elements of Kongo Ancestor Worship." *Journal of Black Studies* 29, no. 3: 325–53.

Verger, Pierre Fatumbi. 1969. "Trance and Convention in Nago-Yoruba Spirit Mediumship." In *Spirit Mediumship and Society in Africa*, ed. John Beattie, 50–66. New York: Africana.

Veté-Congolo, Hanetha, ed. 2016. *The Caribbean Oral Tradition: Literature, Performance, and Practice*. New York: Palgrave MacMillan.

Viarnés, Carrie. 2007. "Cultural Memory in Afro-Cuban Possession: Problematizing Spiritual Categories, Resurfacing 'Other' Histories." *Western Folklore* 66, nos. 1/2: 127–60.

Walcott, Rinaldo. 2007. "*Homopoetics*: Queer Space and the Black Queer Diaspora." In *Black Geographies and the Politics of Place*, ed. Katherine McKittrick and Clyde Woods, 233–46. Cambridge: South End.

Walker, David. 2013. "The Humbug in American Religion: Ritual Theories of Nineteenth-Century Spiritualism." *Religion and American Culture: A Journal of Interpretation* 23, no. 1: 30–74.

Wehmeyer, Stephen C. 2007. "'Indians at the Door:' Power and Placement on New Orleans Spiritual Church Altars." *Western Folklore* 66, nos. 1/2: 15–44.

West-Durán, Alan. 2013. "What the Water Brings and Takes Away: The Work of María Magdalena Campos Pons." In *Yemoja: Gender, Sexuality, and Creativity in the Latina/o and Afro-Atlantic Diasporas*, ed. Solimar Otero and Toyin Falola, 197–214. Albany: State University of New York Press.

Wexler, Anna. 2001. "Dolls and Healing in a Santería House." In *Healing Cultures: Art and Religion as Curative Practices in the Caribbean and Its Diaspora*, ed. Margarite Fernández Olmos and Lizabeth Paravisini-Gebert, 89–114. New York: Palgrave MacMillan.

Williams, Kat, and José Anguiano. 2018. *Ochumaré Takes On the Black Snake*. Lawrence, KS: Thunderbird Brings 3 Fish, IngramSpark.

Williams, Raymond. 1977. *Marxism and Literature*. Oxford: Oxford University Press.

Wirtz, Kristina. 2014a. *Performing Afro-Cuba: Image, Voice, Spectacle in the Making of Race and History*. Chicago: University of Chicago Press.

——. 2014b. "Spirit Materialities in Cuban Folk Religion: Realms of Imaginative Possibility." In *The Social Life of Spirits*, ed. Ruy Blanes and Diana Espírito Santo, 126–56. Chicago: University of Chicago Press.

——. 2007. *Ritual, Discourse, and Community in Cuban Santería: Speaking a Sacred World*. Gainesville: University Press of Florida.

Wood, Andrew Grant. 2014. *Augustín Lara: A Cultural Biography*. Oxford: Oxford University Press.

Yarbro-Bejarano, Yvonne. 2000. "Traveling Transgressions: *Cubanidad* in Performances of Carmelita Tropicana and Marga Gomez." In *Reading and Writing the Ambiente: Queer Sexualities in Latino, Latin American, and Spanish Culture*, ed. Susana Chávez-Silverman and Librada Hernández, 200–17. Madison: University of Wisconsin Press.

INDEX

CPSIA information can be obtained
at www.ICGtesting.com
Printed in the USA
JSHW021650220523
42075JS00002B/373